Christopher dysinger @ yahoo. com

Oh cowboy preacher - youtube

This book is lovingly dedicated to my faithful wife of over 30 years. Tina I love you. Thank you for putting up with the most broken person you know for so long.

CONTENTS

INTRODUCTION

The word "broken" is used to describe something that has been violated, as in a broken promise. The word also describes something that is weak or failing. Something broken is not in its best condition. Being broken can describe someone who is brought into submission by his or her feelings, as in, he is a broken man. Broken is used to describe people who are overcome and crippled by emotions and people who are paralyzed by fear. To be broke is to be bankrupt financially and morally; the meaning here is the same. When you are broke you may be without money or morals. When something is broken it is being described as interrupted and faltering, as in, she told her story in a broken manner. Overall the word broken describes something that is imperfect; something that is not in its best condition; something that is less than pristine. All of humanity is broken in one way or another. Mankind is not what God created us to be. We are broken.

"As it is written, There is none righteous, no, not one: There is none that seeketh after God. They are all gone out of the way, they are together become unprofitable; <u>there is none that doeth good, no, not one.</u> Their throat is an open sepulcher; with their tongues they have used deceit; the poison of asps is under their lips: Whose mouth is full of cursing and bitterness: Their feet are swift to shed blood: Destruction and misery are in their ways: And the way of peace they have not known: There is no fear of God before their eyes." Romans 3:10-18 KJV (Underline Mine)

Humanity is not what God intended us to be. In one way or another everyone falls short of perfection and we are this way because we have been born broken. Every person born into this world, except for the Lord Jesus, has been born into sin. Humanity was created in the image of God, but we are born into the image of Adam. This means we have been born with the inclination toward sin and rebellion.

"All have sinned, and come short of the glory of God." Romans 3:23 KJV.

In the world today there are two kinds of people. There are men and women who know and understand that they are sinners and who recognize what sin does to them and their lives, and there are men and women who do not recognize their sin nor do they understand what their sin nature does to their lives. Many who recognize their sinfulness repent and turn to Jesus where they find forgiveness, salvation, and re-creation.

"Therefore if any man be in Christ, he is a new creature: old things are passed away; behold all things become new." 2 Corinthians 5:17 KJV

At the point of saving faith being placed in the Lord Jesus we go from being born into the image of Adam to being born-again into the image and likeness of Christ.

"Know ye not, that so many of us as were baptized into Christ Jesus were baptized into His death? Therefore we are buried with Him by baptism into death: that like as Christ was raised up from the dead by the glory of the Father, even so we also should walk in newness of life. For if we have been planted together in the likeness of His death, we shall be also in the likeness of His resurrection." Romans 6:3-5 KJV (Underline Mine)

Men and women who refuse to recognize their sinful condition continue in their sin never fully realizing the death and destruction it brings. Thus, there are men and women who know that the struggles people face in this life are not only physical but also spiritual, and who understand that our struggles are in reality a struggle against sin. There are men and women who understand that sin leaves us fallen and broken while others are struggling along in life in their sin unaware of what it is doing to them. The point is, in one way or another all people are broken and our imperfection has come about because of sin.

Most everyone can see the toll sin takes on humanity, physically. If something is taken from us we feel the loss. Encountering alcoholics or drug addicts can leave people with emotional and physical wreckage and those who are involved not only see what is happening, but feel it too. Any person who is a slave to sin, be it an addiction of any kind, will always feel the effects. Immorality and unrighteousness is also seen and felt. How many lives have been affected, ruined, and even cut short due to some sexually transmitted disease? Many people how-ever do not understand the toll sin takes on us spiritually and mentally.

Sin affects our physical presence. Sin affects our health and our material state, and it also affects us mentally and spir-itually. Sin affects our overall mental health and well-being. The evidence is seen in the fact that depression is now epidemic world-wide. The evidence is seen in the fact that many do not know how to handle their own emotions. Many people today are overcome by their emotions and subdued by their feelings, and because of this many people today have been brought to a place where they cannot function in society. Many young people today cannot handle the least adversity and this is a conse-quence of a humanity that is broken by sin. In short, sin leaves people physically, emotionally, and spiritually crippled.

Consider carefully what sin does to men and women when it comes to self-perception and self-esteem? Sin will ei-ther inflate a person's ego or destroy it. Sin manipulates how we see ourselves, which then manifests itself in how we interact with others. Which is to say, because of sin you will either have low self-esteem and consider yourself to be worthless, or you will have an over-exaggerated sense of self-worth which leads to holding all others in contempt. Sin makes some incapable of seeing the value in being human, which is the leading cause of many not knowing how to treat others on a level which affirms our basic human dignity. Many people do not understand the difference between what is dignified and undignified when it comes to humanity. Because sin inhabits the heart and influences the spirit, humanity created in the image of God doesn't know who he or she truly is. Because sin inhabits the heart and influences the spirit, humanity doesn't recognize who we belong to. Humanity has lost its way. Humanity has lost focus on God. Humanity now fails to understand the meaning of life and we do not know the reason we have been created. Humanity has no concept of why we are here which is what leaves so many in a crippled emotional state and unable to function on a basic level. We are broken people.

I challenge you to examine closely any person's life, whether this person is unkown, famous, or infamous, and see if there is not one or two things about him or her that does not reveal that he or she was dealing with brokenness in some way. Everybody has something he or she struggles with. It may be some besetting sin, or self-esteem issues, or issues of determining self-worth. Everyone has something that is working against them mentally, spiritually, and sometimes physically due to the fact that we are all broken people. Consider Moses, the man God called to deliver Israel from the bondage of Egypt. Did Moses have any issues? Aside from having a temper and murdering an Egyptian, he had to contend with a speech impediment and confidence problems.

"And Moses said unto the LORD, I am not eloquent, neither heretofore, nor since Thou hast spoken unto Thy servant: but I am slow of speech, and of a slow tongue." Exodus 4:10 KJV

Consider Gideon, a judge God called on to deliver Israel from the Midianites. Did this man have any issues? Yes, he was at one time cowardly. When the Lord called on him He found Gideon in hiding. Consider John the Baptist. The fearless herald of the coming Messiah. The man who proclaimed, "Behold the Lamb of God who takes away the sins of the world!" When he was thrown into a prison cell he began to have doubts about whether or not Jesus truly was the Messiah. Consider Peter the apostle of our Lord. He was brave, brash, and bold. This outspoken disciple denied Christ and cowered before a servant girl. Every person who has ever lived, except for the Lord Jesus, has struggled with sin and has been left battered, bruised, and broken in some way. Everybody has struggles in life. Every person, except the Lord Jesus, is broken in some way. What we need to know and understand is that the Lord loves to fix broken people.

"The word which came to Jeremiah from the LORD, saying, Arise, and go down to the potter's house, and there I will cause thee to hear My words. Then I went down to the potter's house, and, behold, he wrought a work on the wheels. And the vessel that he made of clay was marred in the hand of the potter: (The vessel was imperfect.) So he made it again another vessel, as seemed good to the potter. *Then the word of the LORD came to me, saying, O house of Israel, cannot I do with you as this potter? Saith the LORD. Behold, as the clay is in the potter's hand, so are ye in Mine hand, O house of Israel."* Jeremiah 18:1-6 KJV (Parenthesis Mine. Underline Mine)

To take this word to heart and make it more personal simply substitute your name with that of Israel. My name is Christopher and so to make this word personal to me I simply read it in this way, "O Christopher, cannot I do with you as this potter? Saith the Lord. Behold as the clay is in the potter's hand, so are you in My hand." The Lord Jesus knows what changes are necessary to our lives to repair our brokenness to mold us into fit vessels for His own use. The Lord Jesus knows just how to mold us into His own image. The Lord Jesus loves to fix broken people.

What does this mean? It means being broken does not disqualify anyone from being saved. This means being broken doesn't disqualify a person from being called, equipped, and put into the Lord's good service. It means the Lord Jesus is able to restore a broken person and He is able to fix a broken life. This means the Lord is able to take a meaningless existence and give it meaning and purpose. Being broken by sin means we need to be repaired and restored and this is where living by faith in the Lord Jesus leads.

Too many people cling to their brokenness and use it as an excuse to allow their lives to simply fade away. Too many people use brokenness as an excuse to keep them from accomplishing anything significant. Too many people would rather be a victim than to live in victory, but when someone lives by faith in the Lord Jesus his or her desire ought to be to live a victorious life to the glory of God. What has being a victim ever done for anybody? Many people will claim "victim" status to illicit sympathy from others. In today's culture being a victim elevates and promotes people in the eyes of progressives and liberals, all of which claim "victim" status in some way. This is why people of the left side of the political spectrum are clamoring to be identified as minorities, or people with disabilities, or people with alternate lifestyles. These men and women want to be viewed as social outcasts. These men and women desire to be identified as victims in an attempt to raise their political capital among their peers. The truth is there is nothing impressive about being a victim. What is impressive is an over-comer.

If you desire to impress others, don't wear your defeats as a badge of honor. If you desire to impress others, don't seek to be a victim, be victorious. To be truly impressive is to do something with your life in spite of the struggles you may face. To be impressive, overcome disabilities. To be impressive, overcome obstacles. To be impressive, live a victorious life. Though we are all broken people God can fix our brokenness. Though we are all broken people in some way we do not have to be crippled by our shortcomings and failures. We do not have to continue in our inconsistencies because the Lord Jesus loves to fix broken people. The Holy Spirit can and will lead the poor and downtrodden into the pathway of victory.

"The thief cometh not, but for to steal, and to kill, and to destroy: I am come that they might have life, and that they might have it more abundantly." John 10:10 KJV

We have not been saved and sanctified by the Lord Jesus to endure misery and hardship. We have been saved and called to live the abundant life which means we are called to live life victoriously. The apostle Paul wrote about living the victorious life and overcoming obstacles in his letter to the Philippians.

For I have learned, in whatsoever state I am, therewith to be content. I know both how to be abased, and I know how to abound: everywhere and in all things I am instructed both to be full and to be hungry, both to abound and to suffer need. I can do all things through Christ which strengtheneth me." Philippians 4: 11-13 KJV (Underline Mine)

There are people who sometimes use the phrase, "I can do all things through Christ which strengthens me," as encouragement to endeavor to greatness, and there are some people who will criticize them for it. I don't understand where the critical spirit comes from. If believers cannot draw strength and encouragement from our relationship with the Lord Jesus where can we draw it from? Paul meant exactly what he wrote in Philippians 4:13 because it is true. We can do all things through Christ who strengthens us. Yes you can overcome through Christ Jesus who by His Spirit emboldens your faith. You belong to Christ Jesus, therefore there is no obstacle that can stand in your way. There is no deficit that cannot be overcome. There is no disability, either real or imagined that can keep you from fulfilling God's determined purpose for your life. You simply have to believe it and receive it. We are in Christ and He is in us. We can do all things through Christ who strengthens us.

To know the truth of these things you have to go out and live like it is true, because it is. The Lord Jesus loves to fix broken people. The Lord Jesus loves to fix broken lives. The Lord Jesus loves to take men and women that the world has written off and put them to work in His useful service, thereby making their lives essential, meaningful, and powerful.

This is what this book is about. Examining the lives of the men and women we find in the Bible to see their brokenness and to identify what they may have struggled with, with an eye to how God worked to overcome these things in their lives and bring them to a place of victory. Some of these men and women had self-esteem issues. Some of these men and women struggled with physical limitations. Some of these men and women were plagued with sinfulness, and yet in their stories we will see how God took these men and women, who are in every way the same as you and me, and through their lives glorified Himself and made their lives matter.

God has done this for people like Rahab, a prostitute in the city of Jericho. God has done this for people like Hannah, a barren woman tormented by her family. God has done this for people like Gideon, a coward who put armies to flight. God has done this for people like David, a man who fell prey to temptation and committed adultery and murder, but who also found forgiveness and restoration in the Lord. God has done this for people like Jonah, a racist and reluctant prophet through whom God brought revival to the very people he despised. God has done this for people like Naomi, a bitter woman to whom God restored her joy. The list goes on and on. God has interacted with broken people throughout history changing their lives forever. The Lord Jesus makes people's lives count.

You do not have to read through this book in order to let the Lord Jesus come into your life and make it count. You can call on the Lord Jesus presently and He will save you and transform your broken life. As a matter of fact, it is better not to wait. Why not let the Lord Jesus fix your broken life? If this is your desire simply lift up a prayer of faith and ask the Lord Jesus to save you.

CHAPTER ONE

Abraham

Death immediately changes our perception of people. We may not like someone, even to the point of holding them in contempt, but when they die all we seem to remember about them is their finer attributes. Attend any funeral and you will hear nothing but good things; this is because when someone dies we only want to remember the good things about them. When death comes we tend to ignore all the bad things people have done. When someone dies we choose to highlight their victories. This is especially true of the men and women we count as heroes. This is especially true of the men and women we idolize whether they are leaders, or athletes, or simply famous in some way. After death we only recount the victories and cast off everything else.

Men and women do this when it comes to our heroes of the faith as well. When it comes to Bible heroes we gravitate to their triumphs of faith while overlooking their failures. We remember king David as the man after God's own heart while often overlooking the fact that he was also a man who took another man's wife and then had the man killed over the matter. We like to remember how David slew Goliath, but then we forget that he made mistakes and fell prey to temptation. We think of Noah being lifted up by the flood waters safe in the ark that was built by faith, but forget that he drank himself into a stupor, falling asleep naked and shaming himself in front of his children; and how do we remember Abraham? As a man of great faith, so much so he is known as the father of the faithful.

"By faith Abraham, when he was called to go out into a place which he should after receive for an inheritance, obeyed; and he went out, not knowing whither he went. By faith he sojourned in the land of promise, as in a strange country, dwelling in tabernacles with Isaac and Jacob, the heirs with him of the same promise: For he looked for a city which hath foundations, whose builder and maker is God." Hebrews 11:8-10 KJV

Abraham was the man God called away from his home and family to a land he didn't know and through whom God worked to build a nation of His very own. These are the people known today as the Hebrews. These are the men and women today who are the descendants of Abraham. Abraham's descendants are not limited to the Hebrews however. Abraham's descendants are found in all the nations surrounding Israel as well. Israel are the descendants of Abraham through Isaac, the son of promise. There are other nationalities in the middle-east who are the descendants of Abraham through Ishmael.

Abraham was also the man God called to sacrifice his own promised heir and he obeyed believing that God was able to resurrect him from the dead.

"By faith Abraham, when he was tried, offered up Isaac: and he that had received the promises offered up his only begotten son, Of whom it was said, that in Isaac shall thy seed be called: Accounting God was able to raise him up, even from the dead; from when also he received him in a figure." Hebrews 11:17-19 KJV

This is how Christians like to remember Abraham. Through his triumphs of faith. The church preaches about Abraham's victories and preaches them in such a way that many might believe that Abraham possessed a super-human type of faith. The church presents Abraham as someone near-to-perfect as a man might attain to, and the church also presents that if somehow all other believers do not match Abraham's walk of faith we are failing to live right before God. How often is it the case that you have personally heard a message where a hero of the faith is being praised for his or her faithfulness and when examining your own life in comparison to theirs you feel as if there is really no way that you will ever measure up?

It is for this reason we need to know the whole story when it comes to people's walk of faith. We not only need to be encouraged by our hero's triumphs, but also their tragedies. We need to know the details of their lives in order to see how God was working to bring them to the place of victory. We need to see how God overcame their brokenness so that we will understand how that God can lead us into the pathway of victory as we live by faith in the Lord Jesus. Which means preachers are not doing anyone a service by always casting our heroes in a positive light. Preachers and Bible teachers are not doing the church a service by making it seem as if our heroes of the faith have never had issues or had to deal with sin. The men and women we read about in the Bible were men and women the same as everyone else, and these people were moved by the Holy Spirit and empowered to accomplish God's will with their lives. From Abraham to Moses, to Peter and the apostle Paul, these people were human beings just like everyone else, and they experienced victory and defeat in their lives. God had to overcome their issues in the very same way that He must overcome our issues, which includes Abraham the man who is known as the father of the faithful.

Abraham did not start out in life being the man of faith that we know him as today. Abraham was not the obedient servant we witness offering up Isaac. Abraham had some real trust issues in the beginning. Abraham had some trust issues with God even after he had been walking with the Lord for some time. Abraham's trust issues lingered even after God had given him victory in battle when he rescued his nephew Lot. Abraham lived for one hundred and seventy five years and what is recorded for us in the Bible is not the complete history of those one hundred and seventy-five years. What we have in the Bible are the highlights.

What is revealed in Abraham is the desire to be obedient and to live by faith, but he often allowed his circumstances to get the better of him. There were times when Abraham's doubts short-circuited his trust in God. The Lord would instruct Abraham to move in a certain direction, but something would happen and this would cause Abraham to doubt and these times Abraham would often take matters into his own hands. This, of course, was a recipe for disaster. Abraham was prone to taking over trying to control his circumstances and master his situation and when he did it usually put him and his family in circumstances where it was necessary for God to step in and rescue him.

This is the way it is for many believers. There are men and women who pray and make a pretense of handing their circumstances and situations over to God, but then adversity arises and these men and women want to step up and take control and they try to wrest control from God's hands in an effort to fix everything for God. These are men and women who at first look to the Lord Jesus, but then they quickly look to something or someone else to deliver on the promises of God.

"Now the LORD had said to Abram, Get thee out of thy country, and from thy kindred, and from thy father's house, unto a land that I will shew thee: and I will make of thee a great nation, and I will bless thee, and make thy name great; and thou shalt be a blessing: And I will bless them that bless thee, and curse him that curseth thee: and in thee shall all families of the earth be blessed. So Abram departed as the LORD had spoken unto him." Genesis 12: 1-4 KJV

Initially Abraham obeyed the Lord. When God called, Abraham answered, but when he arrived at the promised land it was not what he expected to find. Instead of a land of plenty Abraham found himself and his family in the middle of a drought.

"And Abram journeyed, going on still toward the south. And there was a famine in the land: and Abram went down to Egypt to sojourn

there; for the famine was grievous in the land (the drought was severe) Genesis 12:9-10 KJV (Parenthesis Mine)

There is more happening in this account than what lies upon the surface. There is a greater understanding of things of a spiritual nature to come to. Egypt in the Bible always pictures the wealth, provision, and help of the world. Egypt in the Bible is often used as a picture or type of the world. Knowing this allows us to understand how God viewed Abraham's journey to Egypt. Abraham answered God's call on his life and in the beginning moved in the direction of obedience, but when he found himself in a difficult situation Abraham didn't trust in God for help, nor did he turn to God for help, Abraham turned to the world. The Lord instructed Abraham to go to the land that would become Israel. He didn't say anything about going to Egypt if things got bad. Abraham desired to be faithful and obedient, but when things became difficult he looked to the world for help and in this Abraham really is no different than anyone else who has ever lived.

Hebrews 11:1 is gospel truth.

"Faith is the substance of things hoped for; the evidence of things unseen." Hebrews 11:1 KJV

Christians know and believe that God is faithful, trustworthy, and true.

"Let your conversation be without covetousness; and be content with such things as ye have: for He hath said, I will never leave thee, nor forsake thee. So that we may boldly say, the Lord is my helper, and I will not fear what man shall do unto me." Hebrews 13:5-6 KJV

And yet, almost the very minute believers face adversity, just like Abraham, we begin looking to the help of the world for our deliverance. We claim to believe in God, but we often look to the world for help in times of need. There is no denying this. If Abraham tended to falter in stress-filled times, it is reasonable to assume most other believers will too. I am not saying this is how it should be. This is how it is. In reading about Abraham going down to Egypt we are not looking at one of his finer moments. The point is, when we make a mistake by failing to trust in the Lord and by trying to fix our circumstances on our own, or by seeking the help of the world, and things get worse, which they always will, when God steps in and rescues us there is no point in kicking ourselves too hard over it. We ought to learn a lesson from all of this so that we do not fail in this way again, and then we ought to set our hearts to pass this test in the future by trusting in God when things look bad; but we ought not to let the mistakes we have made derail our walk with the Lord Jesus.

We are all broken people who have issues we have to deal with which include challenges to our faith, and these challenges come to us from outside of us, and these challenges come from within us, from within our own hearts. On more than one occasion Abraham tried to accomplish God's work for Him. Abraham often moved in the direction of obedience, but then he responded as if fulfilling God's promises was all up to him. When Abraham followed God to the land of Canaan only to find a drought he assumed that Canaan must not be the promised land and kept on going until he found what he believed God was looking for. When Abraham got himself into a jam in Egypt, instead of asking the Lord to deliver him and Sarah, he devised his own scheme which then put his wife in danger. On another occasion God promised Abraham that he would have a child by Sarah but when Sarah failed to conceive year after year Abraham and Sarah decided that they would take matters into their own hands, as if fulfilling the promise God made was up to them. Abraham's life reads like Abraham believes that what God promises to do is up to him to accomplish.

What is witnessed in Abraham is also found in other believers: A belief that it is up to mankind to see that God's will is accomplished on earth. When it comes to God, mankind definitely has trust issues. This attitude is summed up in a proverb which is widely used in the church, but that is not found in scripture and is counter-productive to living by faith, but many Christians hold to it nonetheless. It is: "God helps those who help themselves." There is not one word in the Bible that confirms this in any way. The saying is asinine on its face. Why would God need to help anyone who could help themselves? This is like saying something to the effect of, "It is only when you can do something yourself that God will help you." God does not help those who are able to help themselves. God steps in and helps the helpless. The Lord Jesus steps up to help the poor, the downtrodden, and the oppressed. The Lord Jesus brings victory to the vanquished. The only way to properly understand the help we receive from God is in understanding that no one is righteous before God and we are all helpless while still in our sins. No one can do anything to lift himself or herself up from humanity's lost and fallen state except the Lord Jesus. It is not up to mankind to execute God's will on earth, though many believe it is.

It is this fallacy that leads to people believing they must or even can earn eternal salvation by works. It is this fallacy that leads to people thinking God needs mankind's help building His kingdom. It is the fallacy of believing that God needs our help that leads to men and women believing that God could not exist or operate without humanity and where does this lead? It leads to graceless legalism, cruel hatred, and a multitude of wrong doing. I challenge anyone reading this text to present any works-based religious system in the world that is not cruel and overbearing and that does not leave a trail of victims in its wake. Anytime anyone looks to the world to fulfill the promises of God there will be trouble because the world cannot fulfill the promises of God.

The world will always present that it has all the answers, but the minute a person put his or her faith in the world, the world will take them for everything they have got. When a believer looks within himself or herself to fulfill God's promises, or looks to the world to provide those things the Lord has promised to deliver, this will cause the believer to compromise his or her faith in some degree and in some way. Looking to the world for help always calls for making a compromise. Dealing with the world according to the ways of the world will always cost more than you are willing to pay. The world always takes and never gives. Whatever help a believer receives from the world is not worth the cost.

"And it came to pass, when he was come near to enter into Egypt, that he said unto Sarah his wife, Behold now, I know that thou art a fair woman to look upon: Therefore it shall come to pass, when the Egyptians shall see thee, that they shall say, This is his wife: and they will kill me, but they will save thee alive. Say, I pray thee: that thou art my sister: that it may be well with me for thy sake; and my soul shall live because of thee." Genesis 12:11-13 KJV

Before Abraham steps one foot in the land of Egypt he compromises his marriage vows. Abraham knows that Egypt is a dangerous place and knowing this he is willing to compromise his wife and his marriage in order to protect himself in an attempt to extract a blessing from the world. Abraham, through his actions, reveals this truth: to enjoy the bounty of Egypt (the world) you must lie and make compromises. This is how things are done according to the way of the world. Lies, deception, and compromising convictions is how worldly-minded people accomplish their goals and achieve their desires, but this is not how God fulfills His promises.

Eventually Abraham grew to understand that you cannot achieve God's plans and will through human endeavor. The only way you will ever get to where God wants to take you is to let God take you there. There is only one way to get where the Lord Jesus intends to take you and this is to live by faith.

"What shall we say then, that Abraham our father, as pertaining to the flesh, hath found? For if Abraham were justified by works, he hath whereof to glory; but not before God. For what saith the scripture? <u>Abraham believed God, and it was counted unto him for righteousness</u>." Romans 4:1-3 KJV (Underline Mine)

It wasn't works that placed Abraham in the righteous column. It was faith. The apostle Paul understood that Abraham began by trying to work his way righteous, but then came to understand that the righteous live by faith as he has written so in the book of Romans.

"Now to him that worketh is the reward not reckoned of grace but of debt. But to him that worketh not, but believeth on Him that justifieth the ungodly, his faith is counted for righteousness." Romans 4:4-5 KJV

If righteousness were achieved through works, God would owe mankind something, but God does not owe any person anything. It was only when Abraham realized that his works were getting him nowhere that he decided to live by faith and trust in the Lord for his justification. When Abraham realized that all of his efforts amounted to nothing in the eyes of God he decided the best course of action was to simply believe God and this was added to his account as righteousness.

How did Abraham come to the point in his life where he became the Abraham we know; the father of the faithful? God kept testing Abraham's faith. When Abraham failed, God would test him again. When Abraham passed, God would test him even more. Again and again God brought new challenges into Abraham's life; challenges that not only tested Abraham's faith, but built it as well. God wanted Abraham to trust Him and over time Abraham grew to the point where God could challenge Abraham to sacrifice his son of promise, Isaac, and he did it without hesitation.

If we struggle in our trust of the Lord Jesus He is going to keep testing and challenging our faith, but He will also continue to deliver us to prove His own trustworthiness. The Lord Jesus will continue to challenge all believers because it is to our benefit to completely trust Him. What does it say about Christians if we declare our trust in the Lord and yet from day to day we are always trying to be the answer to our problems? It declares that we do not really believe at all. It says we have trust issues. You cannot keep trusting in yourself and live according to your own will and call it faith. It may be difficult to live by faith at the first but we can do it. The Holy Spirit is continually affirming in our hearts that God is trustworthy.

CHAPTER TWO

Jacob

"They which are the children of the flesh, these are not the children of God: but the children of promise are counted for the seed. For this is the word of promise, At this time will I come, and Sarah shall have a son. And not only this; but when Rebekah had conceived by one, even by our father Isaac; (for the children being not yet born, neither having done any good or evil, that the purpose of God according to election might stand, not of works, but of Him that calleth;) It was said unto her, The elder shall serve the younger. As it is written, Jacob have I loved, but Esau have I hated." Romans 9:8-13 KJV

The calling of God on a person's life is not up to the individual. The calling on a person's life is up to God. God calls whomever He will according to His purposes. Many suppose that a man or woman who has been called and sanctified has been called because God knew something about them or has seen something in them. People often conclude that the called are called because they are special and gifted and this is why God has called them in the first place. The belief, as I understand it, is that in order for someone to be called they must first possess something of a supernatural nature that allows this person to live to a greater degree of faith than all others. Many preachers foster this idea when preaching, wanting people to believe they are something more than an ordinary person. Some preachers, especially many televangelists, want others to believe that they are one step closer to the divine than the rest of the world which is why they deserve to live in the lap of luxury and should have hundreds of thousands of followers. Some unscrupulous people want the church to worship them in the place of worshiping the Lord Jesus. The idea they are hoping people will buy into is that they are a somewhat superior order of Christian as if God plays favorites with His love and blessings.

To understand that God calls and works in and through the lives of whomever He chooses and not due to something being special about them, all a person has to do is examine the life of Jacob. Read through the history of Jacob and you will see there was nothing that made him stand out or made him special other than the fact that God called him for His purposes. Jacob never faced down a giant. Jacob did not lead a nation of people like Moses. In fact, Jacob's life is rather unspectacular when you closely examine it and yet God called Jacob. God sanctified and blessed Jacob and watched over him and his children. God worked through Jacob's life solely because this is what He desired to do.

Jacob was not a good man. Many in the church preach about Jacob's faith, but from the beginning Jacob was not a person you might like to have as a friend. Eventually by the grace and patience of God Jacob became a good man. God transformed Jacob's life and he became a man of God, but early on in Jacob's life and even on into becoming middle-aged, Jacob was crafty and deceitful and exhibited having little to no moral compass. When Jacob saw something that he wanted he would do anything to get it, no low being too low. Before God transformed Jacob he was not a good man. Jacob was in fact everything his name defines him as. He was deceitful. He was a master of trickery. All this means is that when God revealed Himself to Jacob and issued the call on his life Jacob was a broken person just like every one else.

"And after that came his brother out, and his hand took hold on Esau's heel; and his name was called Jacob." Genesis 25:26 KJV

Jacob's crafty and deceitful nature was revealed at birth.

This is why Isaac and Rebekah named him Jacob; a name which literally means, "deceitful." The deceitfulness of Jacob's nature only became more apparent over time.

"And Jacob sod pottage: (Jacob made some stew), *and Esau came from the field, and he was faint: and Esau said to Jacob, Feed me, I pray thee, with that same red pottage; for I am faint: therefore was his name called Edom. <u>And Jacob said, Sell me this day thy birthright</u>. And Esau said, Behold, I am at the point to die: and what profit shall this birthright do to me? And Jacob said, Swear to me this day; and he swear unto him: and he sold his birthright unto Jacob. Then Jacob gave Esau bread and pottage of lentils; and he did eat and drink, and rose up, and went his way: thus Esau despised his birthright."* Genesis 25: 29-34 KJV

A birthright is all the rights afforded to the first born which have to do with headship of the family and any inheritance and property rights. Everything that Esau sold to Jacob for a bowl of stew and some bread was the right to everything that would come to him when his father passed away. Esau should not have despised his birthright because it is something of great value. Esau made a serious mistake. Esau may have been the kind of person who took no thought to the future, simply living for the moment as many people do and Jacob was far wiser than his older brother, but Esau despising his birthright did not give Jacob any right to it. What Jacob did was wrong. What kind of a man will see his brother hungry and thirsty and use this to manipulate the situation to work out a deal for himself?

"But love ye your enemies, and do good, and lend, hoping for nothing again; and your reward shall be great, and ye shall be children of the highest." Luke 6:35 KJV

"Therefore if thine enemy hunger, feed him; if he thirst, give him drink." Romans 12:20 KJV

Jacob would not even give his brother a bowl of stew without charging him something for it. Jacob used his brother's need to manipulate him and gain something valuable for himself and this is wrong. This is not the only occasion in which Jacob put one over on Esau. Jacob swindled Esau out of his birthright and he also stole away Esau's blessing.

"And he said, Thy brother came with subtlety, and hath taken away thy blessing. And he said, Is not he rightly named Jacob? For he hath supplanted me these two times: he took away my birthright; and, behold, now he hath taken away my blessing." Genesis 27: 35-36 KJV

Jacob stole Esau's rights and his blessing. When Isaac believed he was near death he called his son Esau and sent him out to hunt and prepare food. After eating, Isaac intended to pronounce a blessing on Esau. Rebekah, having overheard what was happening sent Jacob to Isaac with food disguised as Esau in order to steal the blessing. Isaac did not recognize Jacob due to his poor eyesight. Jacob at the behest of his mother manipulated the situation and tricked his father into giving him the blessing. Jacob was willing to do anything it took to get everything he wanted out of life. This is not a display of good or godly character and yet, this is exactly how a great many people who claim to be Christian live their lives.

There are men and women who claim to believe in the Lord Jesus who will do whatever it takes to get what they want out of life not caring who it affects or who may be hurt in the process. Almost everybody can identify someone they are familiar with who is this way: manipulative and deceptive. Men and women like this are even deceitful in spiritual matters. In every church I have pastored there has always been one person and sometimes more than one, who is always scheming to get his or her way and he or she will do whatever they feel is necessary to get their way no matter the consequences. These same people often resort to lies, slander, and gossip. These men and women will use flattery and manipulation to cajole others into giving them what they desire. Men and women who display this type of character will even go so far as to attempt to manipulate God.

As Jacob was fleeing the wrath of his brother he stopped for the night in Luz and while there he had a vision. Jacob saw a ladder that reached up to heaven with angels ascending and descending on it. It was here the Lord spoke to Jacob and called him.

"And behold, the LORD stood above it and said, I am the LORD God of Abraham thy father, and the God of Isaac: the land whereon thou liest, to thee will I give it, and to thy seed; and thy seed shall be as the dust of the earth, and thou shalt spread abroad to the west, and to the east, and to the north, and to the south: and in thee and in thy seed shall all the families of the earth be blessed. <u>*And, behold, I am with thee, and will keep thee in all the places whither thou goest, and will bring thee again into this land; for I will not leave thee, until I have done that which I have spoken to thee.*</u>*"* Genesis 28:13-15 KJV (Underline Mine)

Notice Jacob's response:

"And Jacob vowed a vow, saying, If God will be with me, and will keep me in this way that I go, and will give me bread to eat, and raiment to put on, so that I come again to my father's house in peace: <u>*then shall the LORD be my God*</u>*: and this stone, which I have set for a pillar, shall be God's house:*<u>*and all that Thou shalt give me I will surely give the tenth unto Thee*</u>*."* Genesis 28:20-22 KJV (Underlines Mine)

The Lord had already promised Jacob that He would watch over and provide for his needs. The Lord had already promised that He would safely deliver Jacob to his home once again and yet Jacob is trying to make a deal with God. Jacob says, "If you will bless me then you can be my God." Jacob says, "If you will bless me then I will give you a tenth of what is already Yours." What could any man share with the Lord that is not already His? Men and women who are like Jacob believe they are clever, but they are not. People who attempt to manipulate everybody including God, and men and women who attempt to manipulate every circumstance to their benefit are described in one word: reprehensible.

The interesting thing about liars and manipulators is that God very often delivers them into the hands of people are who very much like them. God often delivers the manipulators into the hands of men and women who are much more crafty than themselves and who excel at manipulation and this is so they will grow to the point that they cannot take the craft and deception any more and they simply have to remove themselves from the situation. This is what God did to Jacob.

"And Esau hated Jacob because of the blessing wherewith his father blessed him: and Esau said in his heart, The days of mourning for my father are at hand; then will I slay my brother Jacob. And these words of Esau her elder son were told to Rebekah: and she sent and called Jacob her younger son, and said unto him, Behold, thy brother Esau, as touching thee, doth comfort himself, purposing to kill thee. Now therefore, my son, obey my voice; and arise and flee thou to Laban my brother to Haran; and tarry with him a few days, until thy brother's fury turn away." Genesis 27:41-44 KJV

Rebekah put her son into the hands of her brother Laban who just happened to be a master manipulator himself. The Bible is exposing the way of life which was practiced by Rebekah's family. It was Rebekah who devised the plan to steal Esau's blessing. Rebekah more than likely learned the art of manipulation from her family as Laban is her brother and Laban only deals with his nephew Jacob using lies, deceitfulness, and manipulation.

"Thus have I been twenty years in thy house; I served thee fourteen years for thy two daughters, and six years for thy cattle: <u>and thou hast changed my wages six times</u>. Except the God of my father, the God of Abraham, and the fear of Isaac, had been with me, surely thou hadst sent me away now empty." Genesis 31:41-42 KJV (Underline Mine)

The way of the world is never the way to go. What is the way of the world? To use any means necessary to get what you want. Esau could have very well said the very same thing to Jacob that Jacob said to his uncle Laban. If it had been up to Jacob he would have left his brother with nothing.

"Be not deceived; God is not mocked: for whatsoever a man soweth, that shall he also reap." Galatians 6:7 KJV

In his interaction with Laban, Jacob was only reaping from what he had sown with his own brother Esau, but it took twenty years of Jacob dealing with his deceitful and manipulative uncle before he understood his own lack of character. It was at this point that Jacob was broken and humbled. Jacob realized that he cherished the things of the world over and above the people in his life. Jacob realized that he had cherished his own success in life over and above the relationship he had with his own brother, over the relationship he had with his mother and father, and the relationship he had with his wives and children. Jacob put himself and his desires before everyone, even God. Jacob always came first in his life. He was an inconsiderate and selfish human being. Jacob is no different than anyone else in this world. We are all broken people.

Anyone can display a tendency to be deceitful and manipulative. Anyone at one time or another has placed a selfish desire before friends, family, and even God.

"From whence come wars and fightings among you? Come they not hence, even of your lusts that war in your members? Ye lust, and have not: ye kill, and desire to have, and cannot obtain: ye fight and war, yet ye have not, because ye ask not. Ye ask, and receive not, because ye ask amiss, that ye may consume it upon your lust." James 4:1-3 KJV

Not one person I have ever known has been above putting their personal desires above the needs and desires of others including their own family at one time or another and this is because we all can be selfish and self-centered at times. We are all broken people, but the Lord Jesus loves to fix broken people.

The awesome thing about the story of Jacob is that even though he is thoughtless, careless, manipulative, and selfish, putting his own desires above everything else, God never abandons him not even for one minute. This is what Jacob comes to realize in his confrontation with Laban.

"Except that the God of my father, the God of Abraham, and the fear of Isaac, had been with me, surely thou hadst sent me away empty." Genesis 31:42 KJV

Afterwards Jacob understands that he must now go home and reconcile with his brother, but he is not quite over trying to manipulate the situation. Jacob sent messengers to his brother telling him that he was coming home. Upon hearing the news Esau gathers together an army to go out and meet his brother. Esau still had it in mind to kill his brother. In an attempt to appease his brother Jacob sends him presents in the form of cattle, but Jacob understood there was nothing he could do to protect himself or his family. This is the point Jacob turns to God spending all night in prayer.

"And Jacob was left alone; and there wrestled a man with him until the breaking of day. And when he saw that he prevailed not against him, he touched the hollow of his thigh; and the hollow of Jacob's thigh was out of joint, and he wrestled with him. And he said, Let me go, for the day breaketh. And he said, I will not let thee go, except thou bless me. And he said unto him, What is thy name? And he said, Jacob. And he said, Thy name shall be called no more Jacob, but Israel: for as a prince hast thou power with God and with men, and hast prevailed." Genesis 32:24-28 KJV

Some scholars believe the angel Jacob wrestled with was a pre-incarnate appearance of the Lord Jesus. Jacob's response after this encounter lends weight to this belief. Jacob says, "I have seen God face-to-face, and my life is preserved." It was at this point in his life that Jacob realized he could not do things in his own strength. It was at this point that Jacob realized that trickery and treachery, lies and deceitfulness, and using manipulation will all catch up to you. It may not be today or tomorrow but manipulating others will catch up to you and when it does you will have to face up to the way you have been living. If you have been going through life using and abusing people there will come a point when you will find you have no friends to call on in times of need. When your ticked-off brother is heading your way with an army of 400 men intent on destroying you and everything you have this is when you get serious about prayer and come to terms with how you have been living. This is the point in your life that you will grab hold of Jesus with everything you have got and you will not let go until you have His blessing. This is also the place where God touches the socket of your hip which forever leaves you in a place where you must always lean upon the Lord. This is when God changes the person you are into the person He desires you to be.

"Therefore if any man be in Christ, he is a new creature: old things are passed away; behold, all things are become new." 2 Corinthians 5:17 KJV

From this point the Lord Jesus begins to heal and restore the relationships Jacob had broken.

"And he passed over before them, and bowed himself to the ground seven times, until he came near his brother." Genesis 33:3 KJV

Jacob recognized and restored his brother's birthright by bowing down before him.

"And Esau ran to meet him, and embraced him, and fell on his neck and kissed him: and they wept." Genesis 33:4 KJV

Everything Jacob did after the night he wrestled with God and was forever changed by it was an effort to right the wrongs he had served upon his brother and others. This is the evidence of a life that has been touched by the Lord Jesus. This is the evidence of a man who has had a true encounter with God.

CHAPTER THREE

Joseph

Circumstances Beyond Our Control

Every person has to deal with issues as we live our lives. Sometimes our issues come from our own sinful inclination and actions and sometimes we are left in a bad way due to the sinful actions of others. Sometimes we make terrible decisions that leave us wounded and hurting but there are also times when someone else makes a wrong choice and though we are innocent we suffer the consequences. This is because sin affects everyone.

There are times things will happen that are clearly beyond our control. "Circumstances beyond our control," is the phrase we employ in recognition of this fact: we do not control every area or facet of our lives though at times some people like to imagine that they do. As much as we might like to believe that we are the masters of our fate, the truth is we have no real control over anything but our own selves. Our destiny and our future is not under our control. Humanity's future and destiny is now and has always been in the hands of God.

God has not abandoned humanity to live a life conditioned and controlled by sin. God loves man so much that He sent His only begotten Son to rescue and redeem us from the power of sin. God loves humanity to the point that He is willing and able to fix our brokenness and He does this through salvation which is only found in, and acquired through, a relationship with the Lord Jesus.

In reading through the Bible we find God leading and directing the lives of His faithful children as they respond in faith to His direction. In this way God patterns believer's lives for them leading them to His good end. This is the nature of living by faith as a child of God. We seek His will and direction for our lives. Which identifies that there is only one of two ways a person can live his or her life. We either live according to our own way or according to God's way. My hope is that people will come to understand that God's way is always the best way.

"For I know the thoughts that I think toward you, saith the LORD, *thoughts of peace, and not of evil, to give you an expected end. Then shall ye call upon Me, and ye shall go and pray unto Me, and I will hearken unto you. And ye shall seek Me, and find Me, when ye shall search for Me with all your heart."* Jeremiah 29:11-13 KJV

Moreover, it is the Lord's will that will always be accomplished in the world and in our lives.

"There are many devices in a man's heart nevertheless the counsel of the LORD, *that shall stand."* Proverbs 19:21 KJV

"A man's heart deviseth his way: but the LORD *directs his steps."* Proverbs 16:9 KJV

This truth is made evident in the life of Joseph. Joseph's life is defined by circumstances beyond his control, but Joseph's circumstances were not beyond God's control. Joseph is a man who displays a different attitude toward his circumstances than his great grandfather Abraham or his father Jacob. Whereas Abraham looked to the world to provide when facing trouble, Joseph looked to God. Whereas Jacob attempted to use deception and trickery to make his way through life, Joseph looked to God. Joseph's only hope was in God. His hope had to reside in God alone because his circumstances were beyond his control.

There are two types of people in the world when it comes to circumstances being beyond our control. There are people who always claim that their circumstances are beyond their control in order to avoid taking any responsibility for their lives and the mess they have made of it, and there are men and women who are honestly suffering with difficult circumstances through no fault of their own.

Years ago I preached regularly at a rescue mission in Oklahoma City and there I met many homeless men and women. A clear majority of these people claimed that they were brought to homelessness through no real fault of their own. I didn't t meet very many who claimed to be where they were because of the poor choices they made in their life. I did however meet a great many men and women who denied any culpability in their own situation by claiming that they had been cheated and wronged. A clear majority of people I interacted with in the homeless shelter seemed to be suffering with circumstances beyond their control. I am not uncaring and I don't mean to appear overly critical, but I didn't really believe a lot of the excuses I heard in that place. I believe many people cling to the notion that their circumstances are beyond their control because this allows them to preserve something of their dignity, but if preserving your dignity keeps you from coming to Christ Jesus where you will find help and deliverance from sin, then preserving your dignity is doing you a disservice.

There are men and women who claim that their circumstances are beyond their control, and there are men and women who genuinely suffer with difficult circumstances due to no fault of their own. Joseph was a man of the second type. Joseph was a man who suffered much because of the sinful actions of others. Early on in Joseph's life, as a child in his father's home, he was mistreated by his brothers.

"Now Israel loved Joseph more than all his children, because he was the son of his old age: and he made him a coat of many colors. And when his brethren saw that their father loved him more than all his brethren, they hated him, and could not speak peaceably unto him." Genesis 37:3-4 KJV (Underline Mine)

Joseph's brothers hated him to the degree that they plotted to kill him, and eventually they sold him into slavery.

"And when they saw him afar off, even before he came near unto them, they conspired against him to slay him. And they said one to another, Behold, this dreamer cometh. Come now therefore, and let us slay him, and cast him into some pit, and we will say, Some evil beast hath devoured him: and we shall see what shall become of his dreams." Genesis 37:18-20 KJV

"And Judah said unto his brethren, What profit is it if we slay our brother, and conceal his blood? Come, and let us sell him to the Ishmaelites, and let not our hand be upon him; for he is our brother and our flesh. And his brethren were content." Genesis 37:26-27 KJV

Instead of enjoying his youth Joseph was held as a slave in Egypt. Because of the actions of his brothers Joseph spent his youth engaged in involuntary servitude and if suffering this injustice were not enough, Joseph's master had him thrown into a dungeon for a crime he did not commit.

"And it came to pass after these things, that his master's wife cast her eyes upon Joseph; and she said, Lie with me. But he refused, and said unto his master's wife, Behold, my master wotteth not what is with me in the house, and he hath committed all that he hath to my hand: There is none greater in this house than I; neither hath he kept back anything from me but thee, because thou art his wife: how then can I do this great wickedness, and sin against God? And it came to pass, as she spake to Joseph day by day, that he hearkened not unto her, to lie by her, or to be with her. And it came to pass about this time, that Joseph went into the house to do his business; and there was none of the men of the house there within. And she caught him by his garment, saying, Lie with me: and he left his garment in her hand, and fled, and got him out. And it came to pass, when she saw that he had left his garment in her hand, and was fled forth, that she called unto the men of her house, and spake unto them, saying, See, he hath brought in a Hebrew to mock us; he came in unto me to lie with me, and I cried with a loud voice: and it came to pass, when he heard that

I lifted up my voice and cried, that he left his garment with me, and fled, and got him out. And she laid up his garment by her, until his lord came home. And she spake unto him according to these words, saying, The Hebrew servant, which thou hast brought unto us, came in unto me to mock me. And it came to pass, as I lifted up my voice and cried, that he left his garment with me, and fled out. And it came to pass, when his master heard the words of his wife, which she spake unto him, saying, After this manner did thy servant to me; that his wrath was kindled And Joseph's master took him, and put him into the prison, a place where the king's prisoners were bound: and he was there in prison." Genesis 39: 7-20 KJV

While in prison Joseph languished for over two years having been forgotten.

"And it came to pass the third day, which was Pharaoh's birthday, that he made a feast unto all his servants: and he lifted up the head of the chief butler and of the chief baker among his servants. And he restored the chief butler unto his butlership again; and he gave the cup into pharaoh's hand: but he hanged the chief baker: as Joseph interpreted to them. Yet did not the chief butler remember Joseph, but forgot him. And it came to pass at the end of two full years, that Pharaoh dreamed." Genesis 40:20-23; 41:1 KJV

The only constant in Joseph's life is the fact that he is limited in what he can control. The truth is no person has control of his or her circumstances. Control is an illusion. At any moment in time something may happen that brings chaos into our lives. It doesn't matter if we keep all the rules. It doesn't matter if a person is a saint or a sinner. It doesn't matter if someone is wealthy or poor. We do not control as much of our lives and circumstances as we would like to believe that we do.

In Oklahoma where I live there is one constant threat which is always looming large, especially in the spring, which is a constant reminder of the fact that mankind doesn't have as much control as he or she believes. What is this threat? Tornadoes. Many people I know have had their whole lives turned around in an instant because of a tornado. One young couple who were briefly associated with a church I planted lost their home and much of their livestock to a large storm that devastated their town. This same couple, not wanting to live in an area where they believed themselves to be vulnerable to severe thunder storms moved away, but then they found themselves the victims of wildfires. Nature itself is a constant reminder that circumstances are indeed beyond human control, but there is nothing that is beyond God's control. Nothing extends beyond God's reach.

"And Joseph was brought down to Egypt; and Potiphar, an officer of Pharaoh, captain of the guard, an Egyptian, bought him of the hands of the Ishmaelites, which had brought him down thither. <u>And the LORD was with Joseph</u>, and he was a prosperous man; and he was in the house of his master the Egyptian." Genesis 39:1-2 KJV (underline mine)

"And Joseph's master took him, and put him into the prison, a place where the king's prisoners were bound: and he was in the prison. <u>But the LORD was with Joseph</u>, and shewed him mercy, and gave him favor in the sight of the keeper of the prison." Genesis 39:20-21 KJV (underline mine)

"And Pharaoh said unto Joseph, Forasmuch as God hath shewed thee all this, there is none so discreet and wise as thou art: Thou shalt be over my house and according unto thy word shall all my people be ruled: only in the throne will I be greater than thou. And Pharaoh said unto Joseph, See, I have set thee over all the land of Egypt." Genesis 41:39-41 KJV

God watched over and cared for Joseph when he was a son in his father's house. God watched over and cared for Joseph when he was a slave in his master's house. God watched over and cared for Joseph when he was a prisoner in Pharaoh's dungeon and God moved Joseph from a prison to a palace in one day. This is the manner in which the Lord cares for His faithful.

The Lord Jesus will never abandon us. When facing a difficult circumstance or situation we must continue to trust in Jesus. He will never leave us or desert us.

"Let your conversation be without covetousness; and be content with such things as ye have: for He hath said, I will never leave thee, nor forsake thee. So that we may boldly say, The Lord is my helper, and I will not fear what man shall do unto me." Hebrews 13:5-6 KJV

"Let your character or moral disposition be free from the love of money [including greed, avarice, lust, and craving for earthly possessions] and be satisfied with your present [circumstances and with what you have]; for He [God] Himself has said, I will not in any way fail you, nor give you up, nor leave you without support. [I will] not, [I will] not, [I will] not in any degree leave you helpless nor forsake you, nor let [you] down (relax My hold on you)! [Assuredly not]. So we may take comfort and are encouraged and confidently and boldly say, The Lord is my helper; I will not be seized with alarm [I will not fear or be terrified]. What can man do to me?" Hebrews 13:5-6 Amplified Bible

God did not abandon Joseph. Everything that happened in Joseph's life was all according to God's plan. It was the Lord that was moving Joseph into the place He needed him to be in order to fulfill His will and also so that ultimately Joseph could be used by God as a source of deliverance and great blessings for others. This is what Joseph himself came to realize.

"And when Joseph's brethren saw that their father was dead, they said, Joseph will peradventure hate us, and will certainly requite us all the evil which we did unto him. And they sent a messenger unto Joseph, saying, Thy father did command before he died saying, So shall ye say unto Joseph, Forgive, I pray thee now, the trespass of thy brethren, and their sin; for they did unto thee evil: and now, we pray thee, forgive the trespass of the servants of the God of thy father. And Joseph wept when they spake unto him. And his brethren also went and fell down before his face; and they said, Behold, we be thy

servants. And Joseph said unto them, Fear not: for am I in the place of God? <u>But as for you, ye thought evil against me; but God mean it unto good, to bring to pass, as it is this day, to save much people alive.</u> Now therefore fear ye not: I will nourish you, and your little ones. And he comforted them, and spake kindly unto them." Genesis 50:15-21 KJV (Underline Mine)

A believer must frequently examine his or her life when facing difficulties in order to ascertain whether or not God has them in a place where He will utilize them to save others. Unfortunately many Christians are too caught up in the distractions that are found in the world to recognize when God is working through their lives to be a blessing. In this, many men and women truly lose sight of what is important. What is the most important aspect of our lives? Is it not God's will? What if when Joseph was in the heart of the most trying circumstances he decided to give up? What if Joseph got so caught up in feeling sorry for himself that he could think of nothing else but to end it all? What do you think would have happened to Joseph, and his family, and all of Egypt and Canaan if he decided his circumstances were too much to handle and chose not to use his God given gifts? God was working everything in Joseph's life for the good of those who were called according to God's purpose.

"And we know that all things work together for good to them that love God, to them who are the called according to His purpose." Romans 8:28 KJV

Joseph suffered a great deal because of the sinful actions of others. Joseph suffered because of the brokenness of others, but the good circumstances God brought into Joseph's life were so good it allowed him to forget all the troubles he encountered along the way. This is brought out in the names that Joseph gave to his children.

"And Joseph called the name of his firstborn Manasseh: For God, said he, <u>hath made me forget all my toil, and all my father's house</u>." Gen-

esis 41:51 KJV (Underline Mine)

The name Manasseh literally means, "Forgetful." The good circumstances which lead to the birth of his firstborn son led Joseph to forget all the trouble he suffered in his father's house.

"And the name of the second he called Ephraim: for God hath caused me to be fruitful in the land of my affliction." Genesis 41:52 KJV

The birth of Joseph's second born was such a joy-filled occasion it caused him to forget all the pain he lived through as a slave and as a prisoner in the land of Egypt.

There are no circumstances we may face as we live life that the Lord Jesus cannot overcome. If you are suffering due to circumstances beyond your control, if you are at a place in your life where your friends and family have you feeling like you are on a roller coaster of emotion, and if your circumstances have you at a place where they may be costing you everything, and your circumstances have you feeling as if you are being taken advantage of, and maybe you feel like no one cares if you live or die; God has got you in His hands and because God is watching over you everything will come to a good end. When you are a child of God everything in your life will come to a good conclusion. When you are a child of God everything will always work out for the best just as it did for Joseph and his family, and everyone else touched by his life.

CHAPTER FOUR

Gideon

"A double minded man is unstable in all his ways." James 1:8 KJV

What is a double-minded man? Being double-minded describes someone who vacillates in life moving from one position to another never being sure of himself or herself. A double-minded person is always second guessing every decision and has no confidence in the direction he or she is taking in life. This is brought out in the book of James.

"If any of you lack wisdom, let him ask of God, that gives to all men liberally, and upbraideth not; and it shall be given him. But let him ask in faith, <u>nothing wavering</u>. For he that wavereth (Vacillates) *is like a wave of the sea driven with the wind and tossed. For let not that man think that he shall receive anything of the Lord. A double minded man is unstable in all his ways."* James 1:5-8 KJV (Underline and parenthesis mine)

A double-minded person is moved from one place to another, from one position to another just as the waves of the sea are moved by the wind. James finishes with the statement, *"A double minded man is unstable in all his ways,"* to emphasize that a vacillating person is unstable and undependable. You cannot hold confidence in a person who is vacillating because in always changing their minds they too are always changing their position. You cannot hold confidence in a double-minded person because being double-minded displays a lack of confidence in God. The double-minded person has no confidence in himself or herself. He or she is filled with doubt no matter what reassurances they may have received. A double-minded person trusts no one, not even God. Gideon, the man God called, equipped, and empowered to deliver Israel from the oppression of the Midianites was at first a double-minded man.

Brave Gideon, the man who put an innumerable multitude to flight with just 300 men was plagued with doubt and he continued to have doubts even after the Lord assured him that he would be victorious. Gideon was no superhero. Gideon was no extraordinary human being. He was as human as every other person who ever walked God's good earth. Gideon was as human as every other man or woman who has God's calling on his or her life. Gideon was a broken person whom God had to fix in order for him to fulfill God's will and purpose in and through his life. God loves to fix broken people. Everyone has issues, but God deals with our issues and God brings us to victory. God transformed Gideon from a vacillating coward into a courageous and conquering hero.

The state of being double-minded strikes very close to home for me personally because I have been unstable and double-minded it seems for all of my life. Many times I have wavered between wanting to pastor an existing church or wanting to go out and start a new one. When in the pastorate all I can think about is planting new churches, and when I am planting a church I struggle with doubts and fears about whether I am truly in the will of God, and I often entertain the thought of seeking out a pastorate in an existing church. Back and forth in my head and in my heart I will go again and again. I struggle with doubts. Even today there are times that I am still unsure as to whether or not I am in the will of God. Can you identify with this feeling? Have you personally ever felt this way? Have you ever had doubts about whether or not you are in the will of God?

Maybe you do not have a lack of confidence when it comes to your calling, but maybe you struggle with confidence when it comes to engaging in the work of your calling. Maybe you struggle with using the gifts that the Holy Spirit has given you to fulfill your calling. Maybe you are struggling with public speaking, or teaching the Bible, or being a witness to Jesus. Many people have no confidence in themselves at all when it comes to interacting with others, which then affects there witness and this will hinder the work of the ministry and the church, as all believers are called to be witnesses. All believers are called to serve in some capacity, therefore a lack of confidence in your calling or your gifts will hinder the church's ability to reach out for Jesus. God can, however, overcome a lack of confidence.

Gideon was so courageous when God called him He found him hiding behind a wine-press threshing his wheat.

"And there came an angel of the LORD, and sat under an oak which was in Ophrah, that pertained unto Joash the Abiezrite: and his son Gideon threshed wheat by the wine-press, to hide it from the Midianites." Judges 6:11 KJV

Gideon continued to lack confidence even after the angel of the Lord delivers God's message.

"And the LORD looked upon him and said, Go in this thy might, and thou shalt save Israel from the hand of the Midianites: have not I sent thee? And he said unto Him, Oh my Lord, wherewith shall I save Israel? Behold, my family is poor in Manasseh, and I am the least in my father's house. And the LORD said unto him, Surely I will be with thee, and thou shalt smite the Midianites as one man." Judges 6:14-16 KJV (Underline mine)

Even though Gideon had this interaction with the angel of the Lord he still lacked confidence. Before Gideon will go to war he is still looking for signs. Before Gideon will move he asks for even more assurances beyond God's word.

"And Gideon said unto God, If Thou wilt save Israel by mine hand, as Thou hast said, behold, I will put a fleece of wool in the floor." Judges 6:36 (Underline mine)

Gideon did this not once, but twice, and even after God

had given him greater assurance through the fleece, Gideon continued to be plagued with doubt. On the very night of the battle, God had to once again assure Gideon of his victory.

"And it came to pass the same night, that the LORD said unto him, Arise, get thee down unto the host; for I have delivered it into thine hand. But if thou fear to go down, go thou with Phurah thy servant down to the host: And thou shalt hear what they say; and afterward shall thine hands be strengthened to go down unto the host." Judges 7:9-11 KJV

How many times does God have to assure Gideon of victory before he will have the courage and confidence to act? When the Lord assures you that something is going to happen, it is going to happen. There are no instances in the Bible in which God declared that something was going to come to pass and that thing did not happen.   What is truly interesting in Gideon's interaction with the angel of the Lord is how the angel of the Lord addresses him in the first encounter.

"And the angel of the LORD appeared unto him, and said unto him, The LORD is with thee, thou mighty man of valor." Judges 6:12 KJV (Underline mine)

The angel of the Lord addresses Gideon as a mighty man of valor because God knew something about this man that he did not even know about himself.

"For the LORD seeth not as man seeth; for man looketh on the outward appearance, but the LORD looketh on the heart." 1 Samuel 16:7 KJV

The Lord Jesus sees things in us that we do not see in ourselves because the Lord looks on our heart. The Lord Jesus can look at us and see our potential; all the potential we have as we reside in Christ.

"Blessed be the God and Father of our Lord Jesus Christ, who hath blessed us with all spiritual blessings in heavenly places in Christ."

Ephesians 1:3 KJV

The believer is fully blessed in and through the Lord Jesus by the Holy Spirit. This means all of our potential resides in the Lord Jesus and not in ourselves, but a lack of confidence will certainly keep the believer from moving forward. We must understand that God knows us better than we know ourselves and we must understand that God also knows what He is capable of doing in and through our lives. When the angel of the Lord first called Gideon He did not call a scared boy hiding behind the wine-press. When the angel of the Lord first called Gideon He did not call a double-minded man who was unstable in all his ways, full of doubt, and lacking confidence. God called the man He knew Gideon truly was; a mighty man of valor. This is the very same situation when it comes to every believer in Christ Jesus. All believers have a calling from God and all believers have gifts of the Spirit to put to use in that calling and all believers have the full potential of Christ Jesus through the filling of the Holy Spirit to be what God has ordained us to be.

God does not see what we see when He looks on us. God sees who we are in Christ Jesus and He sees all the potential we have in Jesus, and this is all the potential that resides within the power of God. Still, before any believer will realize his or her full potential he or she must trust in the Lord enough to move in the direction God is leading. Before the believer can realize his or her potential he or she has to exhibit confidence in God's ability to deliver him or her to where God wants him or her to be and to step out in faith. God can steer any ship to wherever He desires it to go but first it must be moving. Even God cannot steer a ship that is sitting still. God can and will direct your life but your life must be moving in a direction for Him to steer it. No one can steer anything that is sitting still; then again, God also knows how to get people moving.

It is often the case, when we have a lack of confidence, wherever that lack of confidence may display itself, that God puts us into a position that challenges our fears and calls upon us to be courageous and to move forward by faith. This is why it often appears as if many men and women who are engaged in ministry are overwhelmed and out of place, and yet they are not because they are operating in the power of the Holy Spirit according to the will of God.

"And lest I should be exalted above measure through the abundance of revelations, there was given to me a thorn in the flesh, the messenger of Satan to buffet me, lest I should be exalted above measure. For this thing I besought the Lord thrice, that it might depart from me. And He said unto me, My grace is sufficient for thee: for My strength is made perfect in weakness. Most gladly therefore will I rather glory in my infirmities, that the power of Christ may rest upon me." 2 Corinthians 12:7-9 KJV

Many times God places us where we think we would rather not be and this is for two reasons. The first reason is so that He may display His power through us and our situation. In our weakness He is made strong. In our inability He shows the world His infinite ability and through these things God receives all the glory due His name. When we are weak in some area of our life and yet even in our weakness we gain a victory, it must be God who has delivered this victory. This is exemplified in God's interaction with Gideon when it came to the size of his army.

"And the LORD said unto Gideon, The people that are with thee are too many for Me to give the Midianites into their hands, lest Israel vaunt themselves against Me, saying, Mine own hand hath saved me." Judges 7:2 KJV

When God acts it is always in a way that no man or woman can claim His glory for his or her own. When God acts it is always in a way that clearly reveals it is God Himself who is at work. For this reason God places His children into situations and circumstances that are beyond their control and beyond their abilities. In this God puts His power and glory on display.

God's strength is made perfect in weakness.

The second reason God puts believers into situations beyond their abilities is so that the believer will learn to fully rely upon God. When God brings victory into the believer's life the believer's confidence in God is boosted. God chose Gideon for the task of delivering Israel from the Midianites expressly because he was double-minded and had confidence problems. Through Gideon's calling and circumstances the Lord was teaching Gideon the extent to which he could trust Him. God was growing Gideon's faith and confidence in Him. God was moving Gideon to a place of genuine faith that would forever allow him to respond in obedience no matter what God called upon him to do. Immediate obedience to God displays real faith and trust as it displays true confidence in God. When you honestly trust in God then you will be immediately obedient to His will. The only way to grow to this place of faith and trust is for God to put you into situations where you have no choice but to trust Him.

If you are struggling with confidence problems you can expect God to put you into circumstances that will challenge your fear and doubts, but in these situations God will bring you through to victory so that your faith and confidence in Him will grow. God will always work in the believer's life to bring him or her to the place where he or she can exclaim, as in the manner of the apostle Paul, *"I can do all things through Christ which strengtheneth me."* God is always moving His children to a place of genuine faith and trust which results in immediate obedience. The Holy Spirit will always move the believer's life in the direction of trust and obedience because, as the song says, "There is no other way, to be happy in Jesus, but to trust and obey."

Honest believers in the Lord Jesus are not victims. Honest and true believers are always victorious. We may not begin this way. In fact, the believer may begin his or her walk of faith much like Gideon: in hiding, full of doubt and lacking confidence, but God will never leave any of His children in this state of mind. God is going to do things that motivate us and move us forward with Him. God will move all believers to the place of exaltation because our exaltation always results in His greater glory. God moves and empowers believers to bless everyone in and around them because in so doing He blesses His children and glorifies Himself and through these things God raises the confidence level of His children to places they may have never thought imaginable.

"And Gideon came to Jordan, and passed over, he, and the three hundred men that were with him, faint, yet pursuing them. And he said to the men of Succoth, Give, I pray you, loaves of bread unto the people that follow me; for they be faint, and I am pursuing after Zebah and Zalmunna, kings of Midian. And the princes of Succoth said, Are the hands of Zebah and Zalmunna now in thine hand, that we should give bread to thine army? And Gideon said, Therefore when the LORD hath delivered Zebah and Zalmunna into mine hand, then I will tear your flesh with thorns of the wilderness and with briers. And he went up thence to Penuel, and spake unto them likewise: and the men of Penuel answered him as the men of Succoth had answered him. And he spake also to the men of Penuel, saying, When I come again in peace, I will break down this tower." Judges 8:4-9 KJV

Gideon is a changed man. He is no longer lacking confidence. This is the same man who had to be reassured by God four times before he would make a move against the Midianites, but now his confidence in the Lord's ability to bring victory is such that when the leaders of the cities of Succoth and Penuel refused to help he promises that when he is done with his pursuit they would answer to him. After God put the Midianite army to flight through Gideon, Gideon now knows in Whom his strength resides. Gideon has no hesitation in promising the leadership of Succoth and Penuel to teach them a lesson because he knew in the strength of the Lord he would succeed in his current mission, and that he could also finish this job as well. This is what having a real confidence in the power of God will do for a true believer. This is the confidence that comes with trusting in the Lord. Knowing God is present in your life will give you great confidence.

What sort of things can honestly challenge the believer's confidence? When you put your faith in the Lord Jesus and allow Him to work in and through your life He will bring you to the place of victory.

"And we know that all things work together for good to them who are called according to His purpose." Romans 8:28 KJV

"Let your conversation be without covetousness; and be content with such things as ye have: <u>For He hath said, I will never leave thee or forsake thee</u>. So that we may boldly say, The Lord is my helper, and I will not fear what man shall do unto me." Hebrews 13:5 KJV (Underline mine)

No matter what situation or what circumstances you may find yourself in, nothing can move you away from the Lord Jesus nor can anyone take the Lord Jesus from you. With these certain promises in mind, how could we who believe in the Lord Jesus exhibit anything less than a bold faith? Let God build you up. Follow where the Lord Jesus is leading through the Holy Spirit. Trust in Him with all your heart and He will lead you all the way to the end of the age. In Jesus you will experience victorious living and it is only in Jesus that you will truly see victory. Trust in Jesus.

CHAPTER FIVE

Samson: Unrealized Potential

What is potential? Potential is what you have the possibility to become, conditioned upon who you are, what you know, and who your life impacts; but none of who you are or what you will become, or who your life will impact has been revealed or come into existence. Potential is the great mystery of where your life will lead you and who you will become. We may even think of potential in this way: an artist sees potential in a blank canvas because the artist doesn't just see a blank canvas. The true artist can envision the painting that will grace the canvas one day.

Every person has potential. Simply being born into this world and having a life to live means that you have potential. When it comes to our potential, the world may only see a blank canvas, but God sees the work of art your life will become. Potential is bound up with vision and aspiration. Potential has to do with where you see your life heading and what you may aspire to be along with what God has envisioned for your life. Every person has potential. However, the sad truth is that most people never realize their potential and the reasons for this are many and varied.

Some people never realize their potential because they have no vision or direction in their life. These men and women are incapable of imagining what they may accomplish and so they never attempt anything. These kinds of people are satisfied with living from day to day, going with the flow, letting life dictate where they will end up. This could easily describe a majority of people living in the world.

Others never realize their potential because they squander every opportunity, never seeing opportunity for what it is. These kinds of men and women often respond with fear and doubt when they are being called upon to act according to faith in the Lord Jesus. People who squander opportunities are men and women who are often cowardly when they ought to be courageous. These men and women cling to excuses when it is time to engage in life. Fear and doubt; failing to move; avoiding responsibility leads to missing out on blessings and reward and not fulfilling our God-given potential. Samson was a man who did not realize his full potential.

All people are born with potential. One of the great things about living in the United States is that our system of government based upon the constitution, which is the safeguard of our rights and liberties, gives its citizens the freedom that allows for just about everyone to realize his or her potential. In the United States you can go as far as you are able to take yourself. Even if the entire world is stacked against you causing you to suffer one defeat after another, the indomitable American spirit keeps many from quitting. When we get knocked down, we Americans will get right back up, dust ourselves off, and get right back to living life on our own terms. At the very least this is the way things used to be and this is the way I was raised to believe. No matter what is before us we must never quit. All people are born with potential. Americans are given a place to realize even greater potential than most, but the Christian is elevated and has potential even beyond this degree. The Christian has potential beyond even human potential by the fact that he or she is positioned in Christ Jesus.

"For I have learned, in whatsoever state I am, therewith to be content. I know both how to be abased, and I know how to abound: every where and in all things I am instructed both to be full and to be hungry, both to abound and to suffer need. I can do all things through Christ which strengtheneth me." Philippians 4:11-13 KJV

(Underline mine)

The believer in Christ Jesus lives according to the power of the indwelling Holy Spirit which empowers us to do all things. In Christ the believer's potential reaches beyond what it may be by virtue of being born and having a life. In Christ the believer's potential is even greater than it may be by virtue of being a citizen of the United States. The Christian is elevated beyond the fullest degree of human potential possible by virtue of being in Christ. In Christ Jesus the believer's potential is off the charts. When it comes to the believer's potential it is entirely correct to state that we have been set apart by God before even being born, to do great things in the name of Jesus, being empowered by the Holy Spirit.

"Having predestinated us unto the adoption as children by Jesus Christ to Himself, according to the good pleasure of His will, to the praise of the glory of His grace, wherein He hath made us accepted in the Beloved." Ephesians 1:5-6 KJV

Being accepted in the beloved does not mean that believers are saved before even being born. What has been predestined is that all who are saved will be saved through the Lord Jesus and all who come to Christ will also gain the potential to do great things in the power of His name. Christian potential is not according to human strength or endeavor. The potential we have in Christ is according to the active presence of the Holy Spirit dwelling within us. The point: the believer's potential is exponentially greater in Christ and being set apart (sanctified) by the Holy Spirit marks the believer as different and special and in a way just like Samson. Samson was set apart by God before he was born.

"And the angel of the LORD appeared unto the woman, and said unto her, Behold now, thou art barren, and barest not: but thou shalt conceive, and bear a son. Now therefore beware, I pray thee, and drink not an unclean thing: for, lo, thou shalt conceive, and bear a son; and

no razor shall come on his head: for the child shall be a Nazarite unto God from the womb: and he shall begin to deliver Israel out of the hand of the Philistines." Judges 13:3-5 KJV

Samson was brought into the world through a miraculous birth and set apart by God for a specific purpose. Samson was sanctified to be a Nazarite which means that God intended to work through him in a special way. God's calling on Samson's life was for him to lead Israel and give her deliverance from her enemies. This was quite a calling.

There have only been four Nazarites spoken of in all of biblical history. There have only been four men who were set apart and called to God's special purpose before even being born. The first is Samson. The next is Samuel whose mother pledged him to the Lord. Next there was John the Baptist, and the last Nazarite was Jesus, the only begotten Son of God. Nazarites have a special calling on their lives and a special purpose for their lives. Samson was called to deliver Israel from her enemies. Samuel was the last judge of Israel and the prophet through whom the Lord anointed the first and second kings of Israel. John the Baptist was anointed to be the forerunner and herald of the King. John was the voice of one crying in the wilderness. The lord Jesus is the One who was called and anointed to be the Savior. The Lord Jesus is God with us. To be called and sanctified to the office of the Nazarite is something awesome and special indeed. To be set apart by God at birth will fill your life with the great potential to be used mightily in the service of God.

God not only set Samson apart but He gifted him according to his calling. Samson was gifted with incredible strength. All the world knows of Samson's feats of strength and his mighty exploits. Samson once killed a lion with his bare hands. Samson once slew one thousand Philistines with nothing more than the fresh jawbone of a donkey. Samson broke down the mighty gates of Gaza and carried them to the top of a mountain. God gifted Samson with super-human strength.

Many people imagine that Samson may have looked like

Hercules or the incredible Hulk, but Samson did not look any different than the average man. Why? Because Samson's strength did not lie in his muscles. Samson's strength did not have anything to do with him at all. Samson's strength was the outworking of the power of God revealed in and through his life. The Philistines plotted with Delilah to discover the source of Samson's great strength and this was because from all outward appearances he didn't look like a strong man. He did not look any different than anyone else.

"And it came to pass afterward, that he loved a woman in the valley of Sorek, whose name was Delilah. And the Lords of the Philistines came up to her, and said unto her, Entice him and see wherein his great strength lieth, and by what means we may prevail against him, that we may bind him to afflict him." Judges 16:4-5 KJV

Samson was called, anointed, and blessed with spiritual gifts. Samson's life was full of potential and it is the same for every believer. In Christ Jesus we are called, anointed, sanctified, and given spiritual gifts which fills our lives with nothing but potential. In Samson's case he never realized his full potential. Samson was brought into the world by God in a miraculous way. The believer is born again into this world in a miraculous way. Samson was set apart by God before birth to be used by God and to be blessed by God in a mighty way. The believer has been predestined in Christ Jesus to bring glory to God through our lives in a mighty way. Samson was gifted by God to be Israel's champion and her deliverer. Every believer in Jesus Christ has been gifted by and through the Holy Spirit with everything he or she needs to be successful in the calling God has called him or her to. Samson never realized his full potential and in the same way many who are born again in Christ Jesus never realize their potential either.

The reason Samson never reached his full potential is because he completely disregarded the calling on his life. Samson never treated the fact that he was a Nazarite as something significant or important. Samson had no respect or regard for what he had been given by God and it is the very same with many believers. Samson took God, the calling of God, and the gifts from God for granted and in so doing, on more than one occasion, he dishonored the holy nature of the calling on his life and he dishonored God. When Samson should have been leading Israel to victory over her enemies he was playing games with the Philistines. Where Samson should have been setting the example for others to follow he acted like a child and a buffoon. Samson was a womanizer. At times, when Samson should have been leading Israel he was visiting prostitutes or shacking up with foreign women. Samson was called to deliver Israel from the oppression of the Philistines. Samson was called to go to war with the Philistines. He chose instead to marry into them, to flirt with them, and to play games with them like some sort of overgrown child.

Samson's special calling on his life came with conditions. As a Nazarite Samson was not allowed to eat or drink anything that came from the fruit of the vine. Samson was not allowed to drink anything that might ferment and become intoxicating. A Nazarite was also prohibited from touching a dead body, including those of animals. There is also the one condition most everyone knows about and this is: a Nazarite was not allowed to cut his hair. The Bible reveals that Samson violated two of these conditions. Samson touched a dead carcass of a lion in order to retrieve some honey and he allowed Delilah to cut his hair. It is not too difficult to imagine that Samson violated the prohibition against drinking wine as he was given to feasting with the Philistines. What this reveals is that Samson did not respect or regard the sanctified nature of his calling. Samson took his calling and the gifts that came with it for granted. Samson expected that he could do whatever he wanted and God would simply continue to bless him.

Samson's life is a testament to the tragedy of self-will. Samson's life is a testament to what happens to the man or woman of God who has no self-discipline and makes a habit of continually falling short of the standard of conduct that God has called His children to live to. Samson was called to be an example. Samson was supposed to be a model of commitment that others could follow. This is what it means to be a leader. In whatever capacity people are called to lead in, it doesn't matter who you are, you will set an example for someone else to follow. If you are a parent you are setting the example your children will follow. If you are an elder or a deacon in the church you do well to remember that others are looking to you as a model for what Christian living should look like. If you are a supervisor on the job others are looking to you for leadership. Samson was called to be a leader and yet he had no regard for God's standards and so he fell short. Samson did not truly respect God or His calling and so he often fell short. Samson lacked true commitment and self-discipline and this is what kept him from realizing his full potential.

"And Delilah said to Samson, Tell me, I pray thee, wherein thy great strength lieth, and wherewith thou mightest be bound to afflict thee. And Samson said unto her, If they bind me with seven green withs that were never dried, then shall I be weak, and be as another man. Then the lords of the Philistines brought up to her seven green withs which had not been dried, and she bound him with them. Now there were men lying in wait, abiding with her in the chamber and she said unto him, The Philistines be upon thee, Samson. And he break the withs, as a thread of tow is broken with it toucheth the fire. So his strength was not known. And Delilah said unto Samson, Behold, thou hast mocked me, and told me lies: now tell me, I pray thee, wherewith thou mightest be bound. And he said unto her, If they bind me fast with new ropes that never were occupied, then shall I be weak, and be as another man. Delilah therefore took new ropes, and bound him therewith, and said unto him, The Philistines be upon thee, Samson. And there were liers in wait abiding in the chamber. And he brake them from off his arms like a thread. And Delilah said unto Samson, Hitherto thou has mocked me, and told me lies: tell me wherewith thou mightest be bound. And he said unto her, If thou weavest the seven locks of my head with the web. And she fashioned

it with the pin, and said unto him, The Philistines be upon thee, Samson. And he awakened out of his sleep, and went away with the pin of the beam, and with the web. And she said unto him, How canst thou say, I love thee, when thine heart is not with me? Thou hast mocked me these three times, and hast not told me wherein thy great strength lieth. And it came to pass, when she pressed him daily with her words, and urged him, so that his soul was vexed unto death; that he told her all his heart, and said unto her, There hath not come a razor upon mine head; for I have been a Nazarite unto God from my mother's womb: if I be shaven, then my strength will go from me, and I shall become weak, and be like any other man. And when Delilah saw the he had told her all his heart, she sent and called for the lords of the Philistines, saying, Come up this once, for he hath shewed me all his heart. Then the lords of the Philistines came up unto her, and brought money in their hand. And she made him sleep upon her knees; and she called for a man, and she caused him to shave off the seven locks of his head; and she began to afflict him, and his strength went from him. And she said, The Philistines be upon thee, Samson. And he awoke out of his sleep, and said, I will go out as at other times before, and shake myself. And he wist not that the LORD was departed from him." Judges 16:6-20 KJV

What was it that led Samson to believe that God would never allow him to suffer defeat? It was the fact that time and again the Lord allowed Samson to have victory over the Philistines. Samson had grown so accustomed to being blessed that it never occurred to him that God would allow him to suffer defeat or allow him to suffer due to his poor decisions. Maybe Samson was not very smart. How many times does a woman have to set you up before you realize that she doesn't love you? Samson thought he could never be defeated. The Bible presents that Samson was shacking up with Delilah and playing games, flirting with disaster, never once considering that this woman was out to destroy him or that God might actually let her destroy him. Samson was not dumb, however. Samson was arrogant. Samson was proud and his pride led to his downfall.

How many professed believers in Christ act in the very same way? Only these men and women are not flirting with disaster by shacking up with someone who wants to destroy them, these men and women are on the cusp of ruin because they keep flirting with sin and continue to do what they know God doesn't want them to have anything to do with. Time and again these believers will engage in some sin that God has delivered them from, knowing full well that the believer has been delivered from sin.

"What shall we say then? Shall we continue in sin that grace may abound? God forbid. How shall we, that are dead to sin, live any longer therein?" Romans 6:1-2 KJV

"Because sentence against an evil work is not executed speedily, therefore the heart of the sons of men is fully set in them to do evil." Ecclesiastes 8:11 KJV

When a person does something wrong and they do not receive immediate punishment they are emboldened to greater acts of wrongdoing. This is the attitude of the heart found in sinful mankind. Some people even imagine that God does not care about humanity and how we choose to live, but the Bible tells us otherwise.

"He that being often reproved hardeneth his neck, shall suddenly be destroyed, and that without remedy." Proverbs 29:1 KJV

What happened in the case of Samson?

"But the Philistines took him, and put out his eyes, and brought him down to Gaza, and bound him with fetters of brass; and he did grind in the prison house." Judges 16:21 KJV

The Lord allowed Samson to suffer defeat. The Lord allowed Samson to be humiliated by his enemies because this is what he was playing games with. You can mark this down and know it will happen: when you play games with God by flirting with sin, being a child of God, God will humble you. God will bring you to a place where you will learn not to disregard Him or the gifts and calling He has placed on your life.

So many people today take God for granted. So many believers are neglecting the calling on their lives. So many Christians are not using the gifts God has given them through the Holy Spirit, or even worse, many believers are using their spiritual gifts to glorify and enrich themselves as they live lives filled with sin. If you are ignoring God as a child of God, God will get your attention.

In my own life I often imagine that I have made so many mistakes that I may have already crippled my potential just as Samson did, but with the Lord Jesus there is always hope. While Samson was grinding in the dungeon his hair did begin to grow.

"Howbeit the hair of his head began to grow again after he was shaven." Judges 16:22 KJV

Samson's great strength did not lie in his hair. Samson's great strength came from God, but Samson's hair was symbolic of the calling on his life. Samson's hair growing back means that God had not cut him off or forgotten him. Samson may have made a mess of his life but his potential remained because God was with him. God had never abandoned Samson though he allowed Samson to be humbled. It is never too late with God. **There is always hope with God.** There is always potential in God. If you are struggling in life draw hope from this truth. If God did not completely write off Samson, there is hope for everyone. There is always hope in the Lord Jesus.

We do well to remember that we are all broken people and we are prone to making mistakes. No one knows this more than the Lord Jesus. God loves to fix broken people. So, maybe you have made a mistake or two over the years. When you come to the Lord Jesus in repentance and faith you will once again find hope and strength. When you come to the Lord Jesus in repentance and faith seeking forgiveness and restoration you will find that you are once again on your way to realizing your full potential. If there is hope for Samson there is hope for you and me. There is always hope in the Lord Jesus.

CHAPTER SIX

Naomi

In life we must interact with people. There is no avoiding it unless you choose to live as a hermit in a cave or under a bridge. The people we encounter and interact with will display a variety of dispositions and attitudes. Some people are happy. Some people are sad. Some people are worried and seem overwhelmed with life, while at times there are others who are angry and there are always men and women who are completely out of touch. Our reactions to these different types of people and their personalities and dispositions will vary. With the angry we often attempt to appease. With the sad and worried we often attempt to bring a measure of comfort. Most people probably prefer their company to keep a cheery disposition. This is because a cheerful person brings sunshine into our lives. There is one attitude or disposition found in a person that no one enjoys encountering, and it is seen in the man or woman who is bitter. No one truly desires to have a relationship with a bitter person.

I once happened upon a documentary that chronicled the life of a lady as she was going through a weight-loss program. The experts on the show had determined that the main cause of this lady's weight problem had to do with being raised in a family that used food as a source of comfort. When she felt sad, or as was often the case, bitter, she would eat to make herself feel better. One episode this lady shared had to do with her involvement in church. At one point when she and her husband were experiencing marital discord she became more active in church and joined the choir. She explained how singing made her feel better but one evening when she showed up for choir practice the choir director took her aside and asked her to stop coming. Of course she was hurt and perplexed about this request. She asked the director if it was because she was not a good musician. The director told her that the request did not have anything to do with her talents and abilities but that she was a very bitter and negative person and nobody wanted to endure her attitude any longer. Being negative and bitter will absolutely drive people out of your life.

This brings us to the story of Naomi that is found in the book of Ruth. Naomi is a woman who becomes so bitter about life that she goes so far as to change her name to reflect her disposition.

"So they two went until they came to Bethlehem. And it came to pass, when they were come to Bethlehem, that all the city was moved about them, and they said, Is this Naomi? And she said unto them, <u>*Call me not Naomi, call me Mara: for the Almighty hath dealt very bitterly with me*</u>*."* Ruth 1:19-20 KJV (Underline mine)

The name Naomi means pleasant, sweet, or happy. Mara means bitter. Clearly Naomi is displaying much bitterness. Naomi is a broken woman who has become poisoned by her own bitterness, but God loves to fix broken people. Naomi is not the only person who has experienced bitterness. If there is one attitude that is prevalent in the world today it is bitterness and resentment. The world has more than its fair share of complainers. There are many people in the world today who are in the same place as Naomi. These men and women are poisoned by bitterness. These men and women are broken. When Naomi tells her friends and family to stop calling her Naomi and to start calling her Mara she was declaring that she was no longer the sweet and pleasant woman they once knew, but now because she had suffered in this world she is Mara; bitter. Naomi is so bitter about life she changed her name to reflect her heart.

How is it possible that someone could become so bitter?

Life can be difficult and many people suffer with hardship, but life also comes with its fair share of blessings. Everyone endures bad circumstances from time to time but the bad times never last. It may well be that some people are easily disappointed by life and become bitter because this person has unreal expectations about life. A complaint is an expression of dissatisfaction. When a person complains he or she is operating from a position that believes and expresses that he or she deserves satisfaction. A person who is prone to complaining is someone who erroneously believes everything in his or her life ought to suit them perfectly. A person who continually complains about everything presents that he or she believes the world and everything in it exists to bring them complete satisfaction and when they are not happy, by God no, one else will be happy either. How did Naomi become so bitter? She claimed it was all God's fault.

"It grieveth me much for your sakes that the hand of the LORD is gone out against me." Ruth 1:13 KJV (Underline mine)

"And she said unto them, Call me not Naomi, call me Mara: for the Almighty hath dealt very bitterly with me. I went out full, and the LORD hath brought me home again empty: why then call me Naomi, seeing the LORD hath testified against me, and the Almighty hath afflicted me?" Ruth 1:20-21 KJV (Underlines mine)

How many people blame God for all the troubles they face in life? I have heard this old song and dance many times over, being the pastor of a church; *"The Almighty hath dealt very bitterly with me."* (Vs. 20) or, *"The Almighty hath afflicted me."* (Vs. 21). What I often hear is, "Preacher, I sometimes think God must hate me." From Naomi's testimony you would think that only bad things come from God and not the opposite. The truth is every good thing we experience comes from God.

"Do not err my brethren. Every good gift and every perfect gift is from above, and cometh down from the Father of lights, with Whom is no variableness, neither shadow of turning." James 1:16-17 KJV

Was God the cause of Naomi's suffering or was it her own poor choices and bad decisions? Let us drive to the heart of this issue because in the greater context of this discussion we are not focusing on Naomi. We are examining and exposing the truth about men and women who spend their life complaining about every circumstance and ultimately blaming God.

The meaning of names is key to understanding the book of Ruth. Naomi's husband's name was Elimelech. His name means, "My God is king." Elimelech's name identifies him as a man who was, or should have been, fully devoted to God. Elimelech and Naomi with their two sons lived in the region of Bethlehem. The name Bethlehem means, "House of provision." Bethlehem is the birth place of our Savior, Jesus, and rightly so because He is our provision.

There was a famine in the land of Bethlehem. This is what caused Elimelech and Naomi to decide to leave. Elimelech and Naomi were looking for sustenance and provision. The severity of this famine is questionable, seeing as there was no great exodus of people from the region of Bethlehem. Elimelech decided that it would be a good idea to leave his home to find a place that might make living life a little easier. On the surface this may sound like a good plan because this is what many people do. When life gets tough in one place they move to a place where life is a little easier. The problem with Elimelech and Naomi's decision is that they did not receive word from God telling them to leave. Matthew Henry's comments about what is happening are fitting. He writes, "The famine was not severe enough to drive others to remove themselves from the promised land, thus Elimelech's actions could have weakened the resolve of his brethren to inhabit the promised land." Bethlehem was the promised land. Bethlehem was the place of God's provision. To leave looking for greener pastures was a poor testimony coming from a man whose name means, "My God is King."

Neither Elimelech nor Naomi took any time to seek the Lord's will when they made their plans. Elimelech and Naomi simply took it upon themselves to make this move; and why? For comfort's sake. Elimelech and Naomi believed life would be better in the land of Moab and they left God out of the equation. Elimelech and Naomi were only concerned with their level of comfort and so they based their decisions solely on this lone parameter, just like so many other people do, but devising plans for our lives without regard to God is a sin.

"Go to now, ye that say, Today or tomorrow we will go into such a city, and continue there a year, and buy and sell, and get gain: Whereas ye know not what shall be on the morrow. For what is your life? It is even a vapor, that appeareth for a little time, and then vanisheth away. For that ye ought to say, If the Lord will, we shall live, and do this, or that. But now ye rejoice in your boastings: all such rejoicing is evil. Therefore to him that knoweth to do good and doeth it not, to him it is a sin." James 4:13-17 KJV

Making plans without regard to God's will is a sin. If you know that it is right to include God in your decision-making and yet you do not, you have just made yourself into a practical atheist. What is a practical atheist? It is someone who claims to believe and trust in God and yet lives as if God doesn't really exist. To plan your life without thought to the will of God is to live presumptuously and it is a sin and yet this is exactly what Elimelech and Naomi did. These two made and implemented their plans without any regard to God.

When you leave God out of your plans then you cannot blame God for the results. If believers fail to seek the Lord Jesus' direction for their life, calling, and mission the responsibility for the consequences of our lives are directly proportional to the decisions that we have made and therefore, we are responsible for the circumstances of our lives. When you leave God out of your plans you step out from under His authority and you also step away from His protection, which means what ever happens at this point is on you and not on God.

Still, when a child of God makes a mistake, God does not

abandon him or her and leave him or her to suffer the consequences. God is still omnipotent and very often He steps in and protects His children from their own bad choices and mistakes, but there are also times when God allows His children to suffer from a poor decision made without regard to His will so that he or she will learn from his or her mistakes and learn to trust Him more. The circumstances that led to Naomi's bitterness were brought about by her own poor decisions, not by God.

What happened to Naomi in the land of Moab?

"And Elimelech Naomi's husband died: and she was left, and her two sons. And they took them wives of the women of Moab; the name of one was Orpah, and the name of the other Ruth: and they dwelt there about ten years. And Mahlon and Chilion died also both of them; and the woman was left of her two sons and her husband." Ruth 1:3-5 KJV

In the course of her time spent in Moab, Naomi lost her husband and both of her sons. Naomi's circumstances in Moab grew far worse than they ever were in Bethlehem. When Naomi lost her husband and her sons she was cut off from any help she may have received from her extended family. It doesn't matter if everything you are doing "feels" right. Without God in your life, any situation can turn bad in a heartbeat.

"Then she arose with her daughters-in-law, that she might return from the country of Moab: for she had heard in the country of Moab how that the LORD had visited His people in giving them bread." Ruth 1:6 KJV

In light of this verse I am prone to believe that Naomi is a little self-serving. She is always following the bread. In cowboy parlance Naomi is, "following the grub line." When things got a little difficult in Bethlehem she moved to Moab. When things got bad in Moab and things were better in Bethlehem she moves back to Bethlehem and yet upon her return she is one bitter woman. Bitterness is usually the result of pursuing the world and not pursuing God. In verse 21 it is recorded that Naomi said, *"I went out full, and the LORD hath brought me home again empty."* If I could ask Naomi one question it would be, "If you were full before you went out, why did you go?"

How often is it the case, concerning angry and bitter people, that they direct their fury at other people? Why do angry and bitter people direct their wrath at others? Because, bitter and angry people often fail to recognize their own hand being involved in their own difficult circumstances. Not every bad situation is caused by a person's own poor decisions but many are and with almost every bitter person I have met, they were the cause of their own suffering. What is more, their complaining simply made their suffering worse. Bitterness is an acid that will eat its own container. There has never been one problem facing any person that complaining ever made better. When we dwell on the wrongs we believe we have suffered, this doesn't make life better for us. Being bitter will only make you more miserable.

"I remembered God, and was troubled: I complained and my spirit was overwhelmed." Psalm 77:3 KJV

Being bitter and constantly complaining will cause a person to become overwhelmed.

"I went out full, and the LORD hath brought me home again empty: Why then call ye me Naomi, seeing the LORD hath testified against me, and the Almighty hath afflicted me?" Ruth 1:21 KJV

Can you hear the bitterness in the things Naomi is saying as she is laying the blame for all her troubles at the feet of God? God did not cause Naomi's problems. Naomi brought all this on herself; but how many men and women are just like Naomi? How many people are bitter and angry and blame God for all their troubles? How many people today believe any difficulty they may experience in life is due to some grand conspiracy put in place by God to rob them of their happiness? Many people today are buying into Satan's lies and are calling evil good and good evil. This is what is fueling the racism and bigotry that is on the rise among the very people who claim to oppose racism and bigotry. Believing Satan's lies is what is fueling envy and animosity in the world. Too many people today have misplaced anger and this is causing their issues. Misplaced anger is giving rise to a generation of extremely bitter people.

The only way a person will rid his or her life of bitterness is to come to terms with who it is that is making your life bitter, and more often than not, that person is you. If you are a bitter and angry person, you need to recognize the part you have played in your own bitterness. If you are a bitter and angry person, you have to recognize the decisions you have made in life apart from the will of God that have led to your life being right where it is today. Stop blaming the Lord for all the things you have done. Don't hang on to the tired and false belief that other people are responsible for your happiness. The only way other people can affect your attitude and disposition is if you allow it. To get away from being bitter you have to recognize and own the part you played in your life that put you right where you are today. To get free from being bitter, stop blaming God and other people for your life and start counting your blessings.

Naomi only focused on all the negative things in her life and this is what caused her to miss all the positives. Naomi claimed that she went out full but came home empty, but this woman did not know just how blessed she truly was. Naomi did not return home empty. She came home with Ruth. God worked through Ruth to change every circumstance in Naomi's life. God worked through Ruth to preserve Naomi's family and her posterity, and it is through Ruth that Naomi is in the lineage of King David and the lineage of King Jesus.

"And the women her neighbors gave it a name, saying, There is a son born to Naomi; and they called his name Obed: he is the father of Jesse, the father of David." Ruth 4:17 KJV

Naomi's friends and neighbors pointed out to Naomi just

how blessed she was by Ruth.

"And the women said unto Naomi, Blessed be the LORD, which hath not left thee this day without a kinsman, that his name may be famous in Israel. <u>And he shall be a restorer of thy life, and a nourisher of thine old age</u>." Ruth 4:14-15 KJV (Underline mine)

God brought Ruth into Naomi's life to restore her life. Ruth married Naomi's brother-in-law and through this, God restored Naomi's family, her life, and her posterity in Israel. God brought Ruth into Naomi's life because **God fixes broken people**. God can and will change your spirit today if you will let Him. You will have to take your eyes off of your circumstances and start looking to Jesus. Stop complaining, it will only leave you overwhelmed, and besides this no one really wants to hear it. Count your blessings. If you will identify three or four things to thank God for at the beginning of each day you will see your disposition growing brighter. Most importantly, if you do not have a living relationship with the Lord Jesus, pray and ask Him to save you today. He will save you, and His presence in your heart and life will begin a process of transformation. Nothing gets rid of a bitter spirit quicker than the indwelling presence of the Holy Spirit. Nothing gets rid of bitterness faster than letting God change your life.

CHAPTER SEVEN

Ruth

Elimelech and Naomi made some poor choices which resulted in Elimelech's death and in Naomi developing an angry and bitter disposition. Naomi was a broken woman. Naomi was a woman who was truly disappointed and embittered by life, but as God fixes broken people He restored Naomi's life. It may be better stated that in Naomi's case God rescued her from despair and restored her life and posterity by bringing a true friend into her life in Ruth.

How often is it the case that when God brings blessings into our lives He does so by bringing true friends into our lives? These friends truly are more than friends. These friends are in reality family. It is funny how sometimes your friends seem more like family than your own family does. I have family members that I have not spoken with in years. I try to keep in touch, but our interaction is limited and I suppose this is due to the fact that the relationship we have with each other is not important enough for them to return any effort I may make, but I have friends who are always willing to make the effort. These friends call me often. These friends write and exchange emails. These friends stop by for a visit when they are close. Truthfully I am closer to some of my friends than I am with my extended family. Isn't it funny how sometimes friends are more like family than some family?

"A friend loveth at all times, and a brother is born for adversity."
Proverbs 17:17 KJV

"A man that hath friends must shew himself friendly: and there is a friend that sticketh closer than a brother." Proverbs 18:24 KJV

Ruth is a very good example of the kind of friend the Bible describes. She is a friend who sticks closer than family. God worked to restore Naomi's life through the friendship she shared with Ruth. God fixed Naomi's broken spirit through the relationship she had with Ruth and from this we understand that friends are important.

Some theologians discount the importance of the book of Ruth, but if this little book were not important we would not find it in the Bible. These men claim the only importance to the book is found in the chronicle of the lineage of king David and of course the lineage of King Jesus. One commentator I happened upon described the book as one of "minor importance." There are no books of the Bible that are of minor importance. The cannon of scripture is all the Word of God. The story of Ruth and her interaction with Boaz and Naomi is important in that it clearly displays that all people, from rich to poor, from those who are popular to those who may be painfully shy, from the highest born to the lowest, all people matter to God. God cares and God is involved in every person's life even to the smallest of details. God is concerned with humanity. God cares about how each and every one of us fare in life. The story of Ruth and Naomi lets us know that, even if no one else ever thinks we are important, God does. God considers our lives and our eternity to be so important that He sent His only begotten Son to die, in our place, on the cross, bearing our sins, so that we may be redeemed, saved, and secure for eternity.

"And as Moses lifted up the serpent in the wilderness, even so must the Son of man be lifted up: That whosoever believeth in Him should not perish, but have eternal life. For God so loved the world, that He gave His only begotten Son, that whosoever believeth in Him should not perish, but have everlasting life. For God sent not His Son into the world to condemn the world; but that the world through Him

might be saved. He that believeth on Him is not condemned: but he that believeth not is condemned already, because he hath not believed in the name of the only begotten Son of God." John 3:14-18 KJV

Our eternal salvation is found only in Jesus which makes Jesus the greatest friend to all mankind. God at times restores our lives and fixes our brokenness through the friends He brings into our life. Which means having friends and being a friend to others is important. Friends are important. This then begs the question: What does it mean to be a true friend?

There is a friend that sticketh closer than a brother." Proverbs 18:24 KJV

A true friend is that person who will stick by your side through thick and thin and this is exactly the type of character Ruth puts on display.

"And Ruth said, Entreat me not to leave thee, or to return from following after thee: for whither thou goest, I will go; and where thou lodgest I will lodge: thy people shall be my people, and thy God my God: Where thou diest, will I die, and there will I be buried: the LORD do so to me, and more also, if ought but death part thee and me." Ruth 1:16-17 KJV

Ruth declares that nothing but death will separate her from Naomi. This is the measure of a true friend. As I stated in the last chapter, names and their meanings are important to understanding the significance of the book of Ruth. The name Ruth means "companion." The name Ruth means "friend." The name Ruth comes from the primitive root **Ra-ah** which is a word that is used to describe something that sticks. The root word **Ra-ah** describes someone who grasps hold of something or someone and then holds on with all his or her might. This is the measure of a true friend.

"A friend is someone who walks in when the rest of

the world walks out." -Walter Winchell

A true friend is someone who will remain your friend no matter what. A true friend will never leave you or forsake you. This is the very promise we have from the Lord Jesus.

"Let your conversation (way of life) *be without covetousness; and be content with such things as ye have: for He hath said, I will never leave thee, nor forsake thee."* Hebrews 13:5 KJV (Parenthesis and underline mine)

Many people who presume to be friends with others are, in truth only connected to their friends for the benefits they might receive by the association. Proverbs 19:4 says, *"Wealth maketh many friends."* Rich people find they have a lot of friends and this is because they are rich. In this world you will find many fair-weather friends. This is the type of friends the prodigal son encountered after he journeyed away from his home and family.

"And not many days after the younger son gathered all together, and took his journey into a far country, and there wasted his substance with riotous living. And when he had spent all, there arose a mighty famine in that land; and he began to be in want. And he went and joined himself to a citizen of that country; and he sent him into his fields to feed swine. And he would have fain filled his belly with the husks that the swine did eat: and no one gave unto him." Luke 15:13-16 KJV (Underline mine)

When the prodigal had something to offer, wasting his inheritance, sporting an outrageous lifestyle, and being the life of the party he found himself surrounded by many people who claimed to be his friends, but the minute the money ran out so did his fair-weather friends. The Bible says, *"and no one gave unto him."* (vs16) which means no one helped him in any way. A true friend will be a true friend no matter what your circumstances. You can clearly ascertain who your friends truly are when or if you find yourself reduced to nothing and they are still around.

When Naomi found herself with nothing Ruth was right by her side.

Ruth is an excellent example of what it means to be a true friend. She consistently displays the character of a person who genuinely cares. Ruth did not even think about abandoning Naomi in her hour of need. Ruth cared and she sought to bless Naomi in whatever way she could wherever they went and whatever they encountered. Ruth cared for Naomi and probably did so until Naomi's dying day.

"And the women said unto Naomi, Blessed be the LORD, which hath not left thee this day without a kinsman, that his name may be famous in Israel. And he shall be unto thee a restorer of thy life, and a nourisher of thine old age: for thy daughter-in-law, which loveth thee, which is better to thee than seven sons, hath born him." Ruth 4:14-15 KJV (Underline mine)

Naomi now had a relative who could and would care for her until the day she died. Elimelech now had an heir because Ruth chose to stay with Naomi even though in so doing, Ruth's own future became uncertain. The reason Ruth decided to stay with Naomi is because Ruth is self-less not selfish. Ruth was willing to put someone else's needs before her own. Orpah, Naomi's other daughter-in-law displayed a character which was opposite of Ruth's. When Naomi released Orpah from any obligation and allowed her to return to her family she left without hesitation. The name, "Orpah" describes someone who is apt to turn back. The name, "Orpah" describes someone who is prone to taking flight when faced with adverse circumstances. "Orpah," is literally translated as flighty and unstable.

What is the nature of many of the friendships we encounter in the world today? Are they not more akin to Orpah than to Ruth? Many people know someone, whether they are family or not, who may be defined as a fair-weather friend. These are the people who will feign friendship as long as you have something to offer, but the minute all you have to offer is friendship they are nowhere to be found. This is the kind of friend who, when they are in need, you will be the first person they will call, but if you have a need arise with which they might be able to help, well, they simply cannot be bothered because they just don't have the time. (Do you want to know who your true friends are? Ask them to help you move.)

A true friend is someone who will stick by your side through thick and thin. Along this line of argument we could clearly identify that a true church is one that will love you and stick with you in the same way as a true friend. Genuine brothers and sisters in Christ should always stick together, love each other, and when needed, rescue one another.

"Is any sick among you? Let him call for the elders of the church; and let them pray over him, anointing him with oil in the name of the Lord: and the prayer of faith shall save the sick, and the Lord shall raise him up; and if he have committed sins, they shall be forgiven him. Confess your faults to one another, and pray one for another, that ye may be healed. The effectual fervent prayer of a righteous man availeth much. Elias was a man subject to like passions as we are, and he prayed earnestly that it might not rain: and it rained not on the earth by the space of three years and six months. And he prayed again, and the heaven gave rain, and the earth brought forth her fruit. Brethren, if any of you do err from the truth, and one convert him; Let him know, that he which converteth the sinner from the error of his way shall save a soul from death, and shall hide a multitude of sins." James 5:14-20 KJV

A Christian friend ought to be a real friend. A Christian friend ought to be someone God can work through to restore life just as He did for Naomi through Ruth.

Consider carefully what it means to have friends and also to be a friend. When God brings a true friend into your life He is blessing you. When God brings real friends into your life He may well be working at restoring your life because true friends will look out for you and seek your well-being. True friends desire your happiness and joy. A true friend does not like to see his or her friends hurting, sad, down, or depressed. Which means that person who may claim to be a friend, if he or she gossips, spreads lies and rumors and is trying to stir you up and make you angry, this is no real friend. Any person who imagines ways to get you into trouble or keep you in trouble, or may suggest doing things which might affect your health and well-being, or in some way may leave you without and hurting, this person is no real friend; but the man or woman in your life who cares enough to check on you when you are not feeling well, or who may step in to help you when you need it, or that church that is willing to help you keep your electric turned on, or your water running, or helps you to feed your family, these are true friends and they are a real blessing from God. These friends are the people God brings into our lives to restore our lives. Working at blessing and restoring others is what defines someone who truly cares. True friends will seek to bless you. True friends will not want to hurt you.

What should we do about the people who claim to be our friends and yet are really not? These are the people who never think to be a blessing. These are the people who are always taking and never giving. Consider Naomi: what may we discern about her from the book of Ruth? She is bitter and negative. Bitter and negative people tend to drive others away from them. I don't imagine that Naomi was easy to get along with. What did she say to her friends who were happy to see her? She said, "Don't call me Naomi. Call me Mara." Naomi means pleasant and Mara means bitter. This is not what I would describe as a happy reunion. Ruth lived with Naomi for ten years before her husband died. Ruth knew what kind of woman Naomi was. Living with Naomi could not have been easy and yet in spite of this Ruth chose to stay with her. It is one thing to have true friends in our lives that are a blessing and it is another thing to choose to be a friend and to be a blessing to someone else, especially when the person you choose to befriend is negative and bitter. The plain truth is there are some people with whom it is difficult to be a friend, but there are times Christians should step up and be-friend difficult people because the Christian should strive to be a friend to the friendless.

Christians ought to reach out and care for everyone because it is in our new nature in Christ to do so, and this even includes difficult people. The way of the world is to eliminate negative people from your life, but the Christian is called upon to love the loveless and befriend the friendless.

"A man that hath friends must shew himself friendly." Proverbs 18:24 KJV

If you desire to have real friends in your life then you must be friendly to others. In addition to this the Lord Jesus instructed us to love our enemies. Most people will leave the ungodly and unfriendly all to themselves, but the Christian should not because God can work through us and our befriending others to restore lives. By choosing to be a friend to a difficult person, and then stepping up and acting in the manner of a real friend, God may bring the person you are friends with to the point of repentance and faith in the Lord Jesus. After your friend starts walking with Jesus, the Lord Jesus will bring change into his or her life. God can and will restore his or her life. God can and will change your friend from the inside out through the indwelling presence of the Holy Spirit, and this man or woman will become a real and true friend in the manner of friendship you have shown him or her. This may not always be the case, but it can be.

I like Will Rogers and what he said, "I never met a man I didn't like." I often feel the same way. Even when a person wrongs me personally I have a hard time holding a grudge, and this is a true blessing from God. As I was growing up I had this tendency to try and befriend everyone I met, but especially those who seemed to be outcast and friendless. One year while attending a Christian summer camp, one of the campers in our cabin was a young man who was recently paroled from a juvenile detention facility. It was apparent after speaking with him that he was suffering from some form of mental illness. No one wanted anything to do with him because, in truth, everyone was scared of him. He spent most of his time alone. I couldn't handle this situation. I don't care to see people being treated like an outcast so I made an attempt to befriend him. I took the time to talk to him. He enjoyed running in the mornings and so I would get up and go running with him and try to keep up, but he was too fast for me. After camp was over our youth group was sharing our experiences with the church in the Sunday evening service. This young man stood up to share testimony. He said, "The only person in this church who really took the time to talk to me was Chris." This meant something to him and it meant something to me. This young man, on the surface, was an intimidating individual, but he needed a friend.

I once had a conversation with my dad concerning the friends I kept at school. He was cautioning me about the nature and character of the people I chose to hang out with. Many of the people I call friends some might consider unacceptable. My dad asked me, "Why would you want to be friends with any of those guys?" The only thing I could think to say in response was, "Because they need a friend." As believers in Jesus there are situations in which we should reach out to be a friend to someone else, not because they have a great personality and it seems as if they would make a great friend, but especially because they are difficult and outcast and alone, because even difficult people need a friend. Everyone should, at the very least, have one good friend.

Today I am still the same as I was when I was a teenager. When I see someone I think could use a friend I am going to try to be that friend. Why? Because God may use me offering to be a friend to someone else to restore a life. God can use believers reaching out to others with genuine care and in friendship to fix a broken person and to set his or her life on the right track just as He did for Naomi through Ruth.

Why would someone, Christian or not, want to continue

in a friendship with someone who doesn't seem to really care? Why would someone desire to continue in a friendship with someone who may only be looking to take advantage of their friendship? Can anyone truly take advantage of a Christian? Our God is the Creator of everything who has complete authority over all of His creation. The Bible explains that Father God has now placed everything under the authority of our Lord Jesus.

"And hath put all things under His feet, and gave Him to be head over all things to the church." Ephesians 1:22 KJV

This means that everything in the world is under the Lord Jesus' authority for the express purpose of supporting the church and her ministry in the world today. This means that no one can really take advantage of a believer or the church. Whatever we do or whatever we may give reaching out in friendship and love, even if the person we are being kind and generous to is only thinking about himself or herself and what he or she might be profited, God can replace anything we might lose with an abundance. No one will ever out give God and God will never run short of supplying the believer's needs. Additionally, God intends for His children to be a channel of blessing.

What happened in Ruth's life? Ruth stood by Naomi and took care of her and God in turn took care of Ruth. This is how things work in God's kingdom.

"Be not deceived; God is not mocked: for whatsoever a man soweth, that shall he also reap." Galatians 6:7 KJV

Everyone will reap what he or she has sown which includes all the good things we may sow with our lives.

"But this I say, He which soweth sparingly shall reap also sparingly; and he which soweth bountifully shall reap also bountifully." 2 Corinthians 9:6 KJV

This Bible principle doesn't just apply to tithes and offerings. This Bible principle applies to every area of our lives in which we can give, even if it is realized in the giving of our very selves. If you sow good things with your life you will reap good things in return. If you sow bountifully then you will reap bountifully. If you are a friend to the friendless God will fill your life with good friends. If you live your life seeking to be a blessing God will fill your life with blessings. God will take care of His children. Which means no one will ever be able to take advantage of us.

God loves to fix broken people and mend broken lives and sometimes He does this by calling on His children to go out and be a friend to others, to love our neighbors, and even to love our enemies. How amazing is it to know that the Holy Spirit could use you and your life to impact someone else? How amazing it is to know that your friendship could be the vehicle through which another person's life is restored? Go out and be a friend to others. Be a true friend by telling your friends about Jesus. He is the true friend who sticks closer than a brother.

CHAPTER EIGHT

David's Heart

"And Samuel said unto Saul, Thou hast done foolishly: Thou hast not kept the commandment of the LORD thy God, which He commanded thee: for now would the LORD have established thy kingdom upon Israel forever, but now thy kingdom shall not continue: _The LORD hath sought Him a man after His own heart_, and the LORD hath commanded him to be captain over His people, because thou hast not kept that which the LORD hath commanded." 1 Samuel 13:13-14 KJV (Underline mine)

"And afterward they desired a king: and God gave unto them Saul the son of Kish, a man of the tribe of Benjamin, by the space of forty years. And when He had removed him, He raised up unto them David to be their king; to whom also He gave testimony, and said, I have found David the son of Jesse, _a man after Mine own heart, which shall fulfill all My will_." Acts 13:21-22 KJV (Underline mine)

How often is it, that when we imagine the kind of person our heroes might be we overlook their flaws? How often do we imagine our heroes of the faith being superhuman? How often do we imagine these men and women do not have the capacity to stumble and fail? How often do we transcribe the same attributes onto preachers and pastors and onto those who hold public office? If there is one thing I have never understood it is the tendency in people to believe that the pastor of a church is somehow above being tempted or even falling prey to temptation. Why do we lift people up and put them on a pedistal? Has there ever been any person who has ever lived that has not made a mistake? Has there ever been anyone who did not stumble at one time in his or her life? There is only one man in all of human history who was, is, and will always be perfect and this is the Lord Jesus. If there is one scripture that will put our minds in the right place when it comes to acknowledging human frailty it is Ecclesiastes 7:20

"For there is not one just man upon the earth, that doeth good, and sinneth not." Ecclesiastes 7:20 KJV

There is no one who is righteous before the Lord. There is not one single person who has ever lived, except for the Lord Jesus, who has never committed a sin. Clearly the Bible establishes this truth that there is no frail sinful human being who will always do what is right. We are all broken people. Everyone's life has been affected by sin. Which means everyone makes mistakes. There are no perfect people in the world though there are many who might imagine that they are.

Why then was God disposed to showing grace, patience, and mercy to king David when he stumbled, and not so inclined when it came to king Saul? This is an important question to ask, especially when investigating the subject of mankind's brokenness. All humanity has sinned and fallen short of the glory of God and the believer has come to Christ Jesus by faith having become aware of his or her sinful condition, and also having the desire to be in right standing with God. The believer's desire is for the Lord Jesus to step into our lives and make up what we lack due to our shortcomings and failures and in so doing fix our brokenness. This is why the Lord Jesus is my Lord and Savior. I am a broken and sinful man who is prone to stumble. I need the Lord Jesus in my life. I desire the guidance of the Holy Spirit because without the Lord Jesus I am in serious trouble and in case you, dear reader, do not understand this, without the Lord Jesus you too are in trouble. Everyone is prone to fall prey to temptation and to engage in sin. So why is it that David found forgiveness and grace and Saul did not?

Saul was called and anointed by God the very same as David.

"Then Samuel took a vial of oil, and poured it upon his head, and kissed him, and said, Is is not because the LORD hath anointed thee." 1 Samuel 10:1 KJV

Saul was sanctified by God and set apart to be the king of Israel and though Saul made many mistakes so too did David. Saul was disobedient at times, but again, so too was David. Saul tried to murder David on several occasion and he also had the priest of God killed in his murderous lust, but David also had a man killed in an attempt to hide his sins, and David took this murdered man's wife to be his own wife. If you were to lay both men's mistakes and sins side by side you would have to admit that neither man was the epitome of morality. Both David and Saul were prone to stumble. Both men committed terrible offenses against their fellow man and against God. The only difference between the two is that David found grace and forgiveness while Saul was rejected as king. The question that remains is why?

"And he tarried seven days, according to the set time that Samuel had appointed: (This is speaking about Saul) *but Samuel came not to Gilgal; and the people were scattered from him. And Saul said, Bring hither a burnt offering to me, and peace offerings. And he offered the burnt offering. And it came to pass, that as soon as he made an end of offering the burnt offering, behold, Samuel came; and Saul went out to meet him, that he might salute him. And Samuel said, What hath thou done? And Saul said, Because I saw that the people were scattered from me, and that thou camest not within the days appointed, and that the Philistines were gathered together at Micmash; therefore said I, The Philistines will come down now upon me to Gilgal, and I have not made supplication unto the LORD: I forced myself therefore, and offered a burnt offering."* 1 Samuel 13:8-12 KJV (Parenthesis mine)

This is the first recorded instance of Saul being disobedient. After Saul had been anointed king, Samuel instructed Saul that after seven days he would meet him at Gilgal to present an offering before the Lord and to pray to seek God's will and then afterwards Samuel would instruct Saul in the will of God. Saul went to Gilgal but Samuel did not arrive at the agreed upon time. Although the truth is that it was probably on the seventh day that Saul presented the offering and he did so because he did not have the patience to wait until the end of the day to allow Samuel the time needed to arrive and make the offering. When Samuel did not arrive at Gilgal when Saul thought he should have he made the offering himself.

[1]"Perhaps he began to reproach Samuel as false to his word, careless of his country, and disrespectful of his prince, and thought it more fit that Samuel should wait for him that he for Samuel, and nothing appears to the contrary but that he did it himself, though he was neither priest or prophet, as if, because he was a king, he might do anything." -Matthew Henry

Saul may have presumed that he could do anything he desired because he was the king which included disobeying the instructions from a man of God or even disobeying God. The excuse Saul made for his disobedience clearly indicates that he knew he was in the wrong when he made the sacrifice.

Another occasion of Saul's disobedience, which is probably the most well known, is Saul's failure to complete the task given to him to destroy the Amalekites.

"Now go and smite Amalek, and utterly destroy all that they have, and spare them not; but slay both man and woman, infant and suckling, ox and sheep, camel and ass." 1 Samuel 15:3 KJV

God commanded Saul to destroy everyone and everything concerning the Amalekites. Saul went to war with the Amalekites but he did not carry out his orders in full. Saul and his army saved the best of Amalek's cattle. Saul could not bring himself to destroy everything.

"And Samuel came to Saul: and Saul said to him, Blessed be thou of the LORD: I have performed the commandment of the LORD. And Samuel said, What meaneth then this bleating of sheep in my ears, and the lowing of the oxen which I hear? And Saul said, They have brought them from the Amalekites: for the people spared the best of the sheep and of the oxen, to sacrifice unto the LORD thy God; and the rest we have utterly destroyed. Then Samuel said unto Saul, Stay, and I will tell thee what the LORD hath said to me this night. And he said unto him, Say on. And Samuel said, When thou was little in thine own sight, wast thou not made the head of the tribes of Israel, and the LORD anointed thee king over Israel? And the LORD sent thee on a journey, and said, Go and utterly destroy the sinners the Amalekites, and fight against them until they be consumed. Wherefore then didst thou not obey the voice of the LORD? And Saul said unto Samuel, Yea, I have obeyed the voice of the LORD, and have gone the way which the LORD sent me, and have brought Agag the king of Amalek, and have utterly destroyed the Amalekites. But the people took of the spoil, sheep and oxen, the chief of the things which should have been utterly destroyed, to sacrifice unto the LORD thy God in Gilgal. And Samuel said, Hath the LORD as great delight in burnt offerings and sacrifices, as in obeying the voice of the LORD? Behold, to obey is better than sacrifice, and to hearken than the fat of rams. For rebellion is as the sin of witchcraft, and stubbornness is as iniquity and idolatry. Because thou hast rejected the word of the LORD, He hath also rejected thee from being king." 1 Samuel 15:13-23 KJV

In every way Saul failed to do what the Lord required of him. He was proud. He was presumptuous and he was disobedient and yet so was king David. What is king David's most well-known failure? It is his sin with Bathsheba, which was an act filled with rebellion, presumption, and pride. In the same way that Saul believed that a king could do whatever he desired with whomever he desired David did too when he presumed to take another man's wife.

"And it came to pass, after the year was expired, at the time when kings go forth to battle, that David sent Joab, and his servants with him, and all Israel; and they destroyed the children of Ammon, and besieged Rabbah, but David tarried still at Jerusalem. And it came to pass in an evening tide, that David arose from off his bed, and walked upon the roof of the king's house: and from the roof he saw a woman washing herself: and the woman was very beautiful to look upon. And David sent and inquired after the woman. And one said, Is not this Bath-Sheba, that daughter of Eliam, the wife of Uriah the Hittite? And David sent messengers, and took her; and she came in unto him, and he lay with her; for she was purified from her uncleanness: and she returned unto her house." 2 Samuel 11:1-4 KJV

Another occasion of David's willfulness and disobedience is found when he ordered a census which God had never instructed him to do.

" And again the anger of the LORD was kindled against Israel, and he moved David against them to say, Go number Israel and Judah." 2 Samuel 24:1 KJV

David's pride was the thing that moved him to take census and thereby bring trouble upon Israel. There was no good reason to take a census of the people and God did not call for him to do it. Taking this census was done in willful disobedience to the Lord.

"And David's heart smote him after that he had numbered the people. And David said unto the LORD, I have sinned greatly in that I have done: and now, I beseech Thee, O LORD, take away the iniquity of Thy servant; for I have done very foolishly." 2 Samuel 24:10 KJV

What difference did the Lord see between David and Saul? The difference is found in how each man reacted to the rebuke of God. Saul did not respond in repentance but with remorse and he made excuses. Saul tried to lay the blame for his actions upon others. Saul fought to justify himself and his sin when there was no justification. When David is made aware of the sinfulness of his actions and is brought under conviction he immediately repents. The difference between Saul and David is what was found in their heart. The reason God rejected Saul and yet showed grace, mercy, and patience with David is because David honestly loved the Lord with all his heart. This is what made David a man after God's own heart. Saul held very little regard for the Lord.

What actions and attitudes defined David being a man after God's heart and defined Saul as a man who disregarded the Lord? When instructed by God, David offered complete obedience while Saul only offered partial obedience. When obeying God, David listened and received God's instruction. In his disobedience Saul relied upon his own opinions. David listened to God. Saul listened to men. David feared God. Saul feared men. David took the blame for his own mistakes. Saul blamed others. David had a contrite and broken spirit before the Lord. Saul was defensive. David was honest with himself and honest before God. Saul would rationalize his actions, not being honest with himself or others. Saul was focused on his own resources. David was focused on what God was able to do. To understand God's rejection of Saul and His grace toward David you have to look at each man's heart and the way to know what lies in a man's heart is to see how they react when confronted with their sin and their mistakes. Then it becomes evident that David cared for his relationship with God to the point that he would earnestly and immediately beg to be forgiven while Saul would not. Being convicted by sin drove David to repent. Being called out for his sin led to Saul becoming angry and dismisive.

What does this tell us about people's reactions when falling under conviction over sin? What does this tell us about people's reactions to their own brokenness? A person who reacts to the gospel bringing him or her under conviction will display whether or not he or she truly has a heart for God. The question we are left to answer for ourselves is: what will be my response when being exposed to the truth that I am a sinner before God? What happens inside your heart when you are reminded of your faults and mistakes by the Holy Spirit? How do you respond to God, especially when you suffer the consequences for your own poor choices and mistakes?

There are many people who are a lot like Saul. Which is, being filled with pride they do not like to be called out for their mistakes. Many people like Saul, being self-willed will act in direct disobedience to God. Men and women like this are pre-sumptuous and though many of them are church members and attend worship regularly, they live their lives according to the way of the world and according to the design of Satan. Satan does whatever he desires in sinful rebellion against God and he always has an excuse. There are many men and women who call themselves Christians who dare to live the very same way. Though you cannot live like Satan and call yourself a child of God this is exactly what these men and women try to do. These same men and women when falling under conviction and being confronted with their sin get annoyed and angry and offer a ready list of justifications and excuses. They will say things such as, "This is what I had to do. I had no other choice." This being the same thing Saul said to Samuel about making the sacrifice. The problem is that Saul made a move before God gave him any direction. Which means Saul disregarded the word of God.

It is exactly the same when people operate according to their own opinions and according to their own devices. People who love God live their lives according to the word of God. People who do not love God disregard His word with impunity doing exactly what they want when they want, and when they are rebuked for their enmity toward the Lord they offer up some pathetic excuse such as, "I did what I had to do." A person who displays this kind of attitude doesn't love God, neither does he or she hold any true respect for God. You cannot dismiss the word of God and expect anyone to honestly believe that you love God. You cannot live your life as you choose according to your own opinions absent of the word of God and expect anyone to believe that you love and respect the Lord Jesus. You cannot live life how you choose apart from the word and according to your own devises and imagine that you are honoring God with your life. A person who loves the Lord Jesus does not disregard Him or His word at every turn.

You must also understand that incomplete obedience is simply disobedience. What did Saul say when he was rebuked by Samuel for not completely fulfilling the command of God?

"For the people have spared the best of the sheep and of the oxen, to sacrifice unto the LORD thy God." 1 Samuel 15:21.

Every time I read this verse I imagine Saul acting like a little child who has been caught with his hand in the cookie jar. A mother says to her child, "What do you think you are doing?" And the child replies, "I was just getting you a cookie." This is how pathetic Saul's excuse truly is. Do you suppose Samuel or even God bought into Saul's nonsense? Do you think God believes the nonsense we frail human beings say when we are caught engaging in sin?

"O generation of vipers, how can ye, being evil, speak good things? For out of the abundance of the heart the mouth speaketh. A good man out of the good treasure of the heart bringeth forth good things: and an evil man out of the evil treasure bringeth forth evil things." Matthew 12:34-35. KJV

Whatever resides in the heart will make it to the surface of a person's life in how he or she lives. It is exactly as my dad used to say, "What's down in the well will come up in the bucket," but the Lord Jesus does not have to examine our lives to know what resides in our hearts. He already knows because, though man can only look on the outward appearance, God looks upon the heart. However, the true desire of our hearts may be exposed to other people by how we are living. Any person who knows the truth of God's word can identify when someone has a real heart for God or not. Everybody can see how we are living, but most people will not call us out for our presumption. This doesn't mean they believe we are sincere it just means they are being polite. Though most people will not call us out on our sinful attitudes and the games we play we should take the time to do some serious introspection and we should be calling ourselves out on our own hypocrisy? Maybe it is far past time that we got honest with ourselves? Ask yourself: "How do I honestly feel about the Lord Jesus?" Ask yourself: "What is in my heart? Do I truly love the Lord Jesus, or not?" Saul was rejected because his heart was not true. Saul played games and acted the part of a genuine believer but his heart was not true. After Samuel informed Saul that he had been rejected by God, Samuel began to depart. Saul then chased Samuel down and begged him to stay.

"I have sinned: yet honor me now, I pray thee, before the elders of my people, and before Israel, and turn again with me, that I may worship the LORD thy God." 1 Samuel 15:30 KJV

Even after hearing that he had been rejected Saul's greatest concern was his standing before the people. Saul was more concerned about his reputation than he was with his relationship with God. Saul continued to play games, but when you play games with God the only person who will suffer is you. If you try to play games with the Lord Jesus the results will be disastrous. Your relationship and standing with the Lord Jesus is not a game. Your relationship to the Lord Jesus is reality and it is a reality that will affect your eternity.

Our hearts must be right before God. The question is, how do we get our hearts right before God? The only way is to allow the Holy Spirit to change the person you are in your heart. The only way the Holy Spirit can take up residence in your heart is by you coming to the Lord Jesus in faith seeking to be forgiven and delivered from sin. This is exactly what David did every time the Lord placed him under conviction. When David was exposed to the nature of his sin he turned away from his sin and gave his heart back to the Lord.

You cannot love sin and love the Lord Jesus at the same time. The inward regeneration that comes from the indwelling presence of the Holy Spirit is the only person who can affect the changes in our lives we desire, if we honestly desire to be changed. So it comes down to this: do you honestly desire the Lord Jesus to save you and change your life? Do you honestly want God to give you a new heart? The only way to have this is to come to the Lord Jesus and call on His name in faith and asking for these very things.

CHAPTER NINE

Elijah

"Is any among you afflicted? Let him pray. Is any merry? Let him sing psalms. Is any among you sick? Let him call for the elders of the church; and let them pray over him, anointing him with oil in the name of the Lord: and the prayer of faith shall save the sick, and the Lord shall raise him up; and if he have committed sins, they shall be forgiven him. Confess your faults one to another, and pray one for another, that ye may be healed. The effectual fervent prayer of a righteous man availeth much. Elias (Elijah) was a man subject to like passions as we are, and he prayed earnestly that it might not rain: and it rained not on the earth by the space of three years and six months. And he prayed again, and the heaven gave rain, and the earth brought forth fruit." James 5:13-18 KJV (Parenthesis mine)

The context of the above cited passage allows the reader to discern that James was not writing to people whom we may consider superheroes of the faith. Often we read the accounts of people in the Bible who have endured great trials and we might imagine that they have some sort of super anointing by the Holy Spirit, or that there might be something special about them, but James is not calling these kinds of people to prayer. It is the prayers of the normal or average faithful believer that works effectively in this physical realm. James calls on believers to, *"Call for the elders of the church; and let them pray over him."* (vs 14) James writes that the prayer of faith will save the sick and the Lord will raise him up. It is not the person who is praying that makes the difference. It is not the person praying who makes things happen. It is the outworking of genuine faith that moves God to act on our behalf. When we pray it is the Lord Jesus who moves and answers. When we pray it is the Lord Jesus through the Holy Spirit who acts to heal or provides. It is not the person doing the praying that makes the difference. It is the faith of the person praying that matters. When it comes to prayer, faith matters. When it comes to prayer, belief is what matters.

Using high sounding words attempting to impress God doesn't mean anything. Using the same words over and over again in empty repetition will not move God to do something. In His instruction to us about prayer the Lord Jesus made these truths clear.

"And when thou prayest, thou shalt not be as the hypocrites are: for they love to pray standing in the synagogues and in the corners of the streets, that they may be seen of men. Verily I say unto you, They have their reward. But thou, when thou prayest, enter into thy closet, and when thou hast shut thy door, pray to thy Father which is in secret; and thy Father which seeth in secret shall reward thee openly. But when ye pray, use not vain repetitions, as the heathen do: for they think that they shall be heard for their much speaking." Matthew 6:5-7 KJV

For prayer to be effective it must be presented in faith. The question we need an answer to is: how do you exercise a genuine faith that results in having a powerful prayer life? The short answer is that you must believe that God exists and that He is listening. You must also know with all your heart that He cares and that He will answer your prayers in such a way that serves your best interest while at the same time being answered in a way that brings Him glory. All this is summed up in this one word: belief.

"But without faith it is impossible to please Him (God)*: for he that cometh to God must believe that He is, and that He is a rewarder of them that diligently seek Him."* Hebrews 11:6 KJV (Parenthesis

mine)

Too many people believe that prayer is a ritual that must be observed. This is where all the nonsense the Bible dismisses comes from. Consider the existence of prayer books. Books filled with prayers for people to read in some sort of offering up to God. These books often cause me to wonder, how does reading something someone else has written amount to interacting in fellowship with the Lord? How does reading someone else's prayer build a relationship? If prayer is a vital part of our relationship with the Lord Jesus how could reading someone else's thoughts and prayers result in a growing and vibrant relationship? Reading prayers is not engaging in a living relationship with the Lord Jesus. Is may be nothing more than religion and religion is what people believe they must do in order to gain God's favor. Religion is nothing more than a worthless attempt to appease an angry God. What if God is not angry with His children? What if the sacrifice necessary to atone for our sins and necessary to bring restoration has already been made? In addition to this, why would the righteous God of heaven and earth be appeased by empty rituals? Many people engage in worthless rituals believing that this is what God desires from them, but what does God honestly want from mankind?

"Thou shalt love the Lord thy God with all thy heart, and with all thy soul, and with all thy mind. This is the first and greatest commandment. And the second is like unto it, Thou shalt love thy neighbor as thyself. On these two commandments hang all the law and the prophets." Matthew 22:37-40 KJV

God desires to have a genuine living and loving relationship with His children. The Lord Jesus desires to be involved in our lives in every way possible. God loves us and He wants us to **genuinely** love Him in return. How then does genuine love express itself? Is it found in worthless religious rituals? Is love present in meaningless conversation? It would be prudent to examine the manner of our prayer with these things in mind.

How do we interact with the people we love? Must we force ourselves to talk to our loved ones? Or, do we willingly converse with those we love, openly sharing our heart?

I once heard it said that God's children should not treat Him the same way people treat the Internal Revenue Service. How do most Americans interact with the I.R.S.? We only deal with the I.R.S. once a year, if we can get by with that. When we do interact with the I.R.S. we try to keep them from knowing too much about us so they will not take too much from us. When filling out our tax forms we look for every opportunity to cut our taxes. Most people do not trust the government or the I.R.S. Which keeps them guarded and makes them want to have as little to do with it as possible. There are people who treat God in the very same way. Which is to say that they are guarded and keep their distance. They think they are paying their dues to God through their empty and worthless religion and even with that they want it to be as little as they can possibly get by with. Many people want to have as little interaction with the Lord Jesus as they possibly can and this doesn't really present that they love the Lord. What their actions say is that in truth they loathe Him. Where do you see love and trust in actions like these? And yet, the very same people who treat God with contempt through their vain religion are hoping that God will step up and answer their prayers making their dreams come true, and that He will be disposed to pouring out bountiful blessings on their lives, and if He does not they will not hesitate to accuse God of being unloving and uncaring and unworthy of any worship at all.

When you honestly love a person you make an effort to establish a relationship and you make an effort to keep the relationship moving forward. When you honestly love someone you keep the lines of communication open. When you honestly love someone you desire to be with that person spending as much time as possible with them. Can anyone honestly say they truly love someone they have no desire to be around?

Imagine yourself in the place of God. God is love and He

loves us to unimaginable degrees. The Lord Jesus is Lord of lords and King of kings and desires to be the Lord of our lives in order to bring blessing into our lives. The Lord Jesus honestly desires to have a real and living relationship with all people. How do you think you might feel if your very own creation that you love treated you like an obligation, or worse, as some undesired responsibility you have been called to bear? Some people do not have to imagine how this feels because they have family and friends upon whom they have poured out their love and affection and yet these same people never find any time to be a part of their lives. How does it make you feel when the people who are constantly taking advantage of your good nature and your loving heart only come calling when they are looking for a blessing? How do you feel about people who only want anything to do with you when they need something from you, and after getting what they wan you will not hear from them until the next time they need something? I.E. An elderly woman asks her husband, "When was the last time the kids came for a visit?" The man says, "I don't recall. Hang on a minute and I'll look in the checkbook." Now, is this not the same way many people treat God?

At one time God was put out with Israel and her idolatry and spiritual adultery. The people of Israel were prone to wandering away from faith in God. The people of Israel would forget all about God and go out and worship pagan gods and practice idolatrous religions, but only until things got bad. When life would take a turn for the worse the people would come back to God looking for Him to rescue them.

"And the children of Israel did evil again in the sight of the LORD, and served Baalim, and Ashtaroth, and the gods of Syria, and the gods of Zidon, and the gods of Moab, and the gods of the children of Ammon, and the gods of the Philistines, and forsook the LORD, and served not Him. And the anger of the LORD was hot against Israel, and He sold them into the hands of the Philistines, and into the hands of the children of Ammon. And that year they vexed and oppressed the children of Israel: eighteen years, all the children of Israel that were

on the other side of Jordan in the land of the Amorites, which is in Gilead. Moreover the children of Ammon passed over Jordan to fight also against Judah, and against Benjamin, and against the house of Ephraim; so that Israel was sore distressed. And the children of Israel cried unto the LORD, saying, We have sinned against Thee, both because we have forsaken our God, and also served Baalim. And the LORD said unto the children of Israel, Did not I deliver you from the Egyptians, and from the Amorites, from the children of Ammon, and from the Philistines? The Zidonians also, and the Amalekites, and the Maonites, did oppress you; and ye cried unto Me, and I delivered you out of their hand. Yet ye have forsaken Me, and served other gods: <u>Wherefore I will deliver you no more. Go and cry unto the gods which ye have chosen; let them deliver you in the time of your tribulation.</u>" Judges 10:6-14 KJV (Underline mine)

Is this not how any parent might treat a wayward child? Is this not how a good parent would treat a prodigal? These children walk away from home without looking back thinking that they will find blessing and fulfillment in the things of the world. These wayward children listen to false prophets and evil affected preachers coming out of Hollywood and preaching modern culture and dismissing the good words of parents and family, but then after being beat up by the world they want to make their way back home to find healing and blessing. After so many times we are prone to say, "You made your bed now you go and lie in it." The Lord God says the same in this way, *"Go and cry unto the gods ye have chosen; let them deliver you in the time of your tribulation."* Judges 10:14 KJV

Even within this culture there are men and women who do genuinely love God. There are men and women who have a real and active relationship with the Lord Jesus through faith and these same men and women are honest in their prayers, and because of their real relationship with God when they pray things happen. These are the people others seek out to share their prayer request because they know that when these men and women pray God moves. We call these men and women prayer warriors.

"Is any sick among you? <u>Let him call for the elders of the church; and let them pray over him, anointing him with oil in the name of the Lord:</u> and the prayer of faith shall save the sick, and the Lord shall raise him up; and if he have committed sins, they shall be forgiven him." James 5:14-15 KJV (Underline mine)

This passage identifies that many mature Christians who are called into leadership are genuine prayer warriors. It is in this situation that some might be inclined to believe that God hears the prayers of some while ignoring the prayers of others. It is this situation that might make people think some people are special while others are not, but this is the thinking you might find in someone who is new to the faith and unlearned in scripture. The kind of thinking that leads someone to believe that God plays favorites among His children is not rooted in sound doctrine. It is rooted in immaturity and lack of Bible knowledge. Effective prayer is not inherent in any person in particular, but effectiveness is found in the faith and the fervency found in the person who is praying.

"Confess your faults to one another, and pray for one another, that ye may be healed. <u>The effectual fervent prayer of a righteous man availeth much.</u>" James 5:16 KJV (Underline mine)

The prayer that is effective is found coming from the person who is in a right relationship with God through faith in the Lord Jesus Christ and is constant and fervent in prayer being guided by the presence of the Holy Spirit. As an example of this kind of person James points to the prophet Elijah.

"Elias (Elijah) was a man subject to like passions as we are, and he prayed earnestly that it might not rain; and it rained not on the earth by the space of three years and six months. And he prayed again, and the heaven gave rain, and the earth brought forth her fruit." James 5:17-18 KJV

Do not get caught up with the effect of Elijah's prayer. Too many people look at the result of his prayer and miss the most important information being provided by these verses. The Bible makes this point abundantly clear, Elijah was a normal human being just like every other person on this planet. James points out that Elijah was subject to like passions which means he suffered with the very same trials and afflictions, temptations, tribulations, and shortcomings everyone else does. Elijah was not a super-human person. Elijah had a powerful prayer life because he lived in a real and close relationship with the Almighty God.

Here is what I desire to emphasize in this chapter: God does not call extraordinary people to do extraordinary things in His name. God does extraordinary things through ordinary people like me and you. God does mighty works through ordinary people, and through His moving and working in us and in our lives; our lives then become something extraordinary. God moving and working in and through us through the power of the Holy Spirit takes our ordinary lives and transforms them into something vibrant, powerful, and exciting. God can and will do amazing and extraordinary things with our lives if we will simply submit to His will and let Him move and work in and through us, because in Him we live and move and have our being as the apostle Paul has written.

"For in Him we live, and move, and have our being." Acts 17:28 KJV

Elijah was no different than any other person and yet at times God put His power on display through him. James points to the power that was revealed through Elijah's prayer life because this is fitted to the context of what James was addressing, but God put His power on display in and through Elijah's life in other ways too.

One of my favorite stories in all the Bible is when Elijah squared off with Jezebel's 400 prophets of Baal at Mount Carmel. God challenged Israel to decide who they would worship.

"How long halt ye between two opinions? If the LORD be God, follow Him: but if Baal, then follow him." 1 Kings 18:21 KJV

Elijah issued the challenge. The God who answers by fire would be God.

"Then said Elijah unto the people, I, even I only, remain a prophet of the LORD; but Baal's prophets are four hundred and fifty men. Let them therefore give us two bullocks; and let them choose one bullock for themselves, and cut it in pieces, and lay it on wood, and put no fire under it: and I will dress the other bullock, and lay it on wood, and put no fire under: And call ye on the name of your gods, and I will call on the name of the LORD: and the God that answereth by fire, let him be God. And all the people answered and said, It is well spoken." 1 Kings 18: 22-24 KJV

The prophets of Baal built their altar and laid their bull on it and then they proceeded to call upon the name of Baal. These prophets of Baal prayed and chanted and cut themselves all day but nothing happened. At the time of the daily sacrifice Elijah prepared his altar and his sacrifice before praying; however, Elijah had his people pour water on the sacrifice, not once, or twice, but three times until the altar and sacrifice was completely soaked, and then he prayed.

"And it came to pass at the time of the offering of the evening sacrifice, that Elijah the prophet came near, and said, LORD God of Abraham, Isaac, and of Israel let it be known this day that thou art God in Israel, and that I am Thy servant, and that I have done all these things at Thy word. Hear me, O LORD, hear me, that this people may know that Thou art the LORD God, and that Thou hast turned their heart back again. Then the fire of the LORD fell, and consumed the burnt sacrifice, and the wood, and the stones, and the dust, and licked up that water that was in the trench. And when all the people saw it, they fell on their faces: and they said, The LORD, He is the God; the LORD, He is the God." 1 Kings 18:36-39 KJV

Elijah's actions resulted in the power of God being put on display and this is because the Lord was working in and through Elijah's life because of faith. God worked in and through Elijah's life to gain great spiritual victories because Elijah was a man who prayed in faith, and yet Elijah was a man who was subject to like passion as we all are. This same spiritual giant who saw such a great victory at Carmel also ran away when threatened by Jezebel.

"And Ahab told Jezebel all that Elijah had done, and withal how he had slain all the prophets with the sword. Then Jezebel sent a messenger unto Elijah saying, So let the gods do to me, and more also, if I make not thy life as the life of one of them by tomorrow about this time. And when he saw that, he arose, and went for his life, and came to Beer-sheba, which belongeth to Judah, and left his servant there, but he himself went a day's journey into the wilderness, and came and sat down under a juniper tree: and he requested for himself that he might die; and said, It is enough; now, O LORD, take away my life; for I am not better than my fathers." 1 Kings 19:1-4 KJV

Why did Elijah run? Because he was human just like anyone else. Elijah was a man who was subject to like passions the same as all of humanity. Even witnessing a great victory at Carmel he ran when his life was threatened, and who wouldn't? Which means, even though Elijah was a man of great faith, and even though Elijah was a man who lived within a close relationship with God, at times he could be filled with doubt. How then is Elijah different than any other human being? The answer is, he was not, and yet he was a man in right standing with God because of his genuine love and honest faith. Elijah was a man in right standing with God because he lived by faith. Elijah was a child of God having faith that his Messiah would come and this provided his real and living relationship with God, and it was this relationship that made his prayer life effective and powerful. Living in a right relationship with the Lord Jesus will also serve to make your prayer life effective and powerful because living in a right relationship affects everything.

Elijah may have run away and given up when someone threatened his life, but the truth is God never gave up on Elijah and it is the same for every child of God. When we stumble and make mistakes God doesn't cast us away or give up on us. God never quits anyone.

"Let your conversation be without covetousness; and be content with such things as ye have: for He hath said, I will never leave thee, nor forsake thee. So that we may boldly say, The Lord is my helper, and I will not fear what man shall do unto me." Hebrews 13:5-6 KJV (Underline mine)

God will never give up, so don't give up on God. Maybe you have been praying but you cannot see God moving and working in your life, and maybe you are thinking that God doesn't care and that He is not listening. I challenge you, dear reader, to keep praying, but don't just go through the motions. Call on the Lord with a true heart of faith. Mean it when you pray, and if you cannot realize true faith and you begin to doubt, thinking, "There is nothing at all to this." At this point you must pray and ask the Lord to give you the faith you need to pray. Yes, you can do this. Realize however that the point to prayer is not to bend God to our will, but it is to establish a genuine living relationship with God through the Lord Jesus. If you get real with the Lord Jesus you will be amazed at what God will do in and through your life. The challenge then is to get real with God. You can do this by reaching out to the Lord Jesus in prayer asking Him to be real in your life.

CHAPTER TEN

Isaiah

There are not too many people who have been born saved. There are not too many who have been born righteous. As a matter of fact, no person has ever been born who did not need to be born again in Christ Jesus to receive eternal life. The Lord Jesus being the only exception. Nicodemus, the man who came to see Jesus at night for fear of being seen by his peers, was a pharisee of pharisees. Nicodemus had been a very religious man I imagine for all of his life, and yet when he encountered the Lord Jesus, the Lord Jesus confronted him with his need to be born again.

"Verily, verily, I say unto thee, Except a man be born again, he cannot see the kingdom of God." John 3:3 KJV

The Lord Jesus informed Nicodemus that he must be born again because being righteous in the eyes of the world doesn't mean anything to God. The world looks upon the outward appearance, but God looks upon the heart.

One difficulty the church is often confronted with today is a culture that dismisses the message we preach by pointing to our flaws. When doing this, people are revealing an attitude that says, "I don't have to listen and I will not listen because I may not be perfect, but neither are you." One person challenged me as I was sharing the gospel to her in this way, "What makes someone like you believe that you can and should be speaking for God?" I would like to offer a response to the question.

Why do Christians presume to preach and teach the gospel of Jesus Christ and why should the church engage in the practice of trying to lead people to Christ? Who are we to speak for God? Are we not sinful, fallen, and broken people just like everyone else in the world? What makes someone like me believe that I can and should be speaking for God?

The first thing we must do in response to this question is rid ourselves of a few presuppositions. The question itself presupposes that only someone who is perfect, sinless, and righteous should be able to bring God's message. This false assumption is easily countered with truth. The truth is absolute. Truth is true for everyone and does not depend on the righteous or unrighteous nature of the messenger. The message and the messenger are not one and the same. No matter who is preaching the truth, the truth remains constant which is why the apostle Paul can say, *"Notwithstanding, every way, whether in pretense, or in truth, Christ is preached; and I therein do rejoice, yea, and will rejoice."* Philippians 1:18 KJV

"And many of the brethren in the Lord, waxing confident in my bonds, are much more bold to speak the word without fear. Some indeed preach Christ even of envy and strife; and some also of good will: The one preach Christ of contention, not sincerely, supposing to add affliction to my bonds: but the other of love, knowing that I am set for the defense of the gospel. What then? Notwithstanding, every way, whether in pretense, or in truth, Christ is preached; and I therein do rejoice, yea, and will rejoice." Philippians 1:14-18 KJV

The motivation and disposition of the messenger does not take away from the truth of the message. Paul rejoiced in the preaching of the gospel because people were being saved regardless of who was bringing the message of the gospel. This is the very reason all believers can rejoice over mega-churches and their mega-pastors as men and women are coming to Christ through these things. Even if there is something wrong with the messenger the message of "Jesus saves," remains true.

The second presupposition in the question of, "What

makes me believe I can and should speak for God," is that by preaching the message of Jesus we are attempting to speak for God Himself, which is just not true. Christians are not speaking for God. He has His own voice which is clearly revealed in the Word, by the Spirit, and through the message of His only begotten Son. We are not trying to speak for God. The church is simply preaching and teaching the message we have received, and the reason we presume to take this message from God to others is because God has ordained that man will preach the message of salvation to man. God speaks to human beings through other human beings. This is the precedent and rule brought out in scripture. There are a few exceptions to this rule, such as when God spoke to Balaam through a donkey, but this is the exception not the rule. God speaks to people through other people. This is why God spoke to Israel and led Israel through Moses, and also through the judges, and the kings, and the prophets, and today through the church. The rule is presented to the astute student of scripture in the book of Acts through the apostle Peter's interaction with Cornelius the centurion.

"There was a certain man in Caesarea called Cornelius, a centurion of the band called the Italian band. A devout man, and one that feared God with all his house, which gave much alms to the people, and prayed to God always. He saw in a vision evidently about the ninth hour of the day an angel of God coming to him, and saying unto him, Cornelius. And when he looked on him, he was afraid, and said, What is it Lord? And he said to him, Thy prayers and thine alms are come up for a memorial before God. And now send men to Joppa, and call for one Simon, whose surname is Peter." Acts 10: 1-5 KJV

Cornelius was praying when an angel came to him in a vision and told him to send for Peter in Joppa. The Lord then convinced Peter that he should go to Cornelius' home. When Peter arrived he realized that he had been sent to preach the message of Jesus to Cornelius and his friends and family so that they could hear and respond in faith.

"And the morrow after they entered into Caesarea. And Cornelius waited for them, and had called together his kinsmen and near friends. And as Peter was coming in Cornelius met him, and fell down at his feet, and worshiped him. But Peter took him up, saying, Stand up; I myself also am a man. And as he talked with him, he went in, and found many that were come together. And he said unto them, Ye know how that it is an unlawful thing for a man that is a Jew to keep company, or come unto one of another nation; but God hath shewed me that I should not call any man common or unclean. Therefore came I unto you without gainsaying, as soon as I was sent for: I ask therefore for what intent ye have sent for me? And Cornelius said, Four days ago I was fasting unto this hour; and at the ninth hour I prayed in my house, and, behold, a man stood before me in bright clothing, and said, Cornelius, thy prayer is heard, and thine alms are had in remembrance in the sight of God. Send therefore to Joppa, and call hither Simon, whose surname is Peter; he is lodged in the house of one Simon a tanner by the sea side: who, when he cometh, shall speak unto thee. Immediately therefore I sent to thee; and thou hast well done that thou art come. Now therefore we are all here present before God, to hear all things that are commanded thee of God." Acts 10:24-33 KJV

From this point in the narrative Peter begins to preach the message of salvation in Jesus and the Holy Spirit falls on Cornelius and his family confirming His presence in the house and upon them all, Jew and Gentile alike.

"And as I began to speak, the Holy Ghost fell on them, as on us at the beginning. Then remembered I the word of the Lord, how that He said, John indeed baptized with water: but ye shall be baptized with the Holy Ghost. Forasmuch then God gave them the like gift as He did unto us, who believed on the Lord Jesus Christ; what was I, that I could withstand God? Acts 11:15-17 KJV

Consider carefully the interaction between the angel and Cornelius and the apostle Peter. Take note that the angel never spoke a word to Cornelius about redemption and salvation being in Christ Jesus. Why didn't the angel simply tell Cornelius and his family about Jesus? It is because angels are not ordained to preach the gospel to humanity; this calling belongs to men. The church has been called, equipped, and commissioned by the Lord Jesus to make disciples of all nations and to baptize them in the name of the Father, and the Son, and the Holy Spirit.

"And Jesus came and spake unto them, saying, All power is given unto Me in heaven and in earth. Go ye therefore, and teach all nations, baptizing them in the name of the Father, and of the Son, and of the Holy Ghost: teaching them to observe all things whatsoever I have commanded you: and, lo, I am with you alway, even to the end of the world. Amen." Matthew 28:18-20 KJV

"And He said unto them, Go ye into all the world, and preach the gospel to every creature. He that believeth and is baptized shall be saved; but he that believeth not shall be damned." Mark 16:15-16 KJV

The church is called and commissioned to preach the message of Jesus to all the world and to all of humanity. Men are called to preach the gospel not angels.

"God who at sundry times and in divers manners spake in time past unto the fathers by the prophets, hath in these last days spoken unto us by <u>His Son</u>, whom He hath appointed heir of all things, by whom also He made the worlds." Hebrews 1:1-2 KJV (Underline mine)

In what way did the Lord Jesus present Himself to the world? As a man. Why did the Lord Jesus present Himself to the world as a man? Because God speaks to humanity through humanity. At present all power and authority has been delegated to the Lord Jesus and He has delegated the authority to preach to the church. The church made up of human beings is the body of Christ in the world today and as such she has full authority to preach and teach the Word. People dismissing the church and her message due to the very obvious character flaws of the people who make up the church does not remove the church's authority or her responsibility, but people pointing out our failures will make some doubt his or her calling. People pointing out our flaws and failures may cause us to respond in fear which then may cause us to shrink back in the face of the challenge being issued.

There is no use denying that we are affected when others judge us for our shortcomings. We may profess that these things do not bother us, but this is not a factual statement. No one likes their flaws to be made an issue. No one likes their failures being used to criticize them, often unfairly, and being critical of others because they are flawed is unfair. Everyone is flawed and everyone has had failures and defeats in life. Our flawed and sinful nature is not the starting point when it comes to our calling and commission. The gospel is the focus of our attention. For this reason the church must press forward preaching the gospel even when we are called out for our faults. Presenting Christ to the lost is not a competition to prove who is more righteous before God. The object of being a Christian is not to prove to the world how righteous we may believe ourselves to be, because the Christian ought to know better than those who are not believers just how unrighteous we are apart from Christ, and though many outside of faith in Christ believe we are standing in judgment over them we must press on with preaching the gospel for the eternal well-being of those who will hear and respond in faith.

There is much believers can learn about our circumstances in this current evil age, and how to face up to them, and how to continue in our calling, from the calling God placed on Isaiah. Isaiah was a frail human being. Isaiah was a broken man and yet God worked in and through him.

"In the year that king Uzziah died I saw also the Lord sitting upon a throne, high and lifted up, and His train filled the temple. Above it stood the seraphims: each one had six wings; with twain he covered his face, and with twain he covered his feet, and with twain he did

fly. And one cried unto another, and said, Holy, holy, holy, is the
LORD of hosts: the whole earth is full of His glory. And the posts of
the door moved at the voice of him that cried, and the house was
filled with smoke. Then said I, Woe is me! For I am undone; because
I am a man of unclean lips, and I dwell in the midst of people of un-
clean lips: for mine eyes have seen the King, the LORD of hosts. Then
flew one of the seraphims unto me, having a live coal in his hand,
which he had taken with the tongs from off the altar: and he laid it
upon my mouth, and said, Lo, this hath touched thy lips; and thine
iniquity is taken away, and thy sin purged." Isaiah 6:1-7 KJV

What was Isaiah's reaction to being in the presence of the
holy God? His immediate response is to pronounce a woe on
himself. " *Woe is me! For I am undone; because I am a man of un-*
clean lips, and I dwell in the midst of people of unclean lips: for mine
eyes have seen the King, the LORD of hosts." (Vs 5) What is a woe?
It is a proclamation of disaster. When someone pronounces a
woe upon themselves it means they know that they're in trouble.
Isaiah's self evaluation in the presence of God is that he is in
trouble. Isaiah's self-evaluation in the presence of God is that he
is a dead man which is the literal translation of, "I am undone."

Not only does Isaiah know he is in trouble, he also begins
to confess his sins. In the presence of perfect righteousness.
Isaiah understands the degree to which he is flawed. He knows
he is broken and he confesses, *"I am a man of unclean lips, and I*
dwell in the midst of people of unclean lips." (Vs 5) Here Isaiah is
confessing to having a dirty mouth. Isaiah, though a prophet of
God, is a man who has a propensity for using colorful language
and he confesses to socializing with people of the same nature
and character. What does this reveal about Isaiah? Just that he
loves God, but sometimes he cusses. Though he loves the Lord
there are times when things come out of his mouth that should
not. I know of no one who cannot identify to some degree with
Isaiah's shortcoming. It doesn't matter who you are or how you
have lived your life, you will feel completely undone in the presence of our Holy God. The Bible describes Job as a man who was

upright in all his ways and yet when he stood in the presence of God he repented of his ways.

"There was a man in the land of Uz, whose name was Job; and that man was perfect and upright, and one that feared God, and eschewed evil." Job 1:1 KJV

"Then Job answered the LORD, and said, I know that Thou canst do everything, and that no thought can be withholden from Thee. Who is he that hideth counsel without knowledge? Therefore have I uttered that I understood not; things too wonderful for me, which I knew not. Hear, I beseech Thee, and I will speak: I will demand of Thee, and declare Thou unto me. I have heard of Thee by the hearing of the ear: but now mine eye seeth Thee. <u>Wherefore I abhor myself, and repent in dust and ashes</u>." Job 42:1-6 KJV (Underline mine)

The task given to the church that is made up of human beings, is a holy task. What the Lord Jesus has asked of His church is more than we are able to do and this is on purpose. Our God-sized task of preaching the gospel keeps us connected to Christ. The only way we are able to answer the calling on our lives is to be connected to Christ.

"I am the vine, ye are the branches: He that abideth in Me, and I in him, the same bringeth forth much fruit: <u>for without Me ye can do nothing</u>." John 15:5 KJV (Underline mine)

Still, what are we to do with those shortcomings of ours? No matter where we go or what we do our failures remain. No matter who we speak to about the Lord Jesus our reputation precedes us and it is speaking too. Though we may run from our reputation we will only get so far before it catches up to us. I have often tried to run from my mistakes, but there is no running. The Lord informed me that I must live them down because this is the only thing you can do with your past. The only thing you can do with the life you have lived up to this point is learn to live with it and continue moving forward with Christ, and the only way to live with your mistakes is to seek the Lord's forgiveness and then forgive yourself and move on. Either you will allow your past to cripple you or you will keep moving forward with the Lord Jesus and leave your past in the past. When it comes to those people you may encounter who are determined to never let you forget your mistakes and through their constant criticism seek to cripple your walk with the Lord Jesus; just leave them to the Lord. Only the Lord can humble the proud and the Lord knows just what to do with someone that cannot bring himself or herself to let go of his or her past.

The thing about our sinful failures when it comes to God is this: He doesn't overlook them and He certainly doesn't justify them, but He will remove them from our record. God cleanses us from our sins and thereby makes us fit for His service.

"Then flew one of the seraphims unto me, having a live coal in his hand, which he had taken with the tongs from off the altar: and he laid it upon my mouth, and said, Lo, this hath touched thy lips; and thine iniquity is taken away, and thy sin purged." Isaiah 6: 6-7 KJV (Underline mine)

In Christ Jesus the believer is made into a new creation. In Christ Jesus the believer is redeemed, born-again, made whole, made new, and made fit for the Lord's service.

"Therefore if any man be in Christ, he is a new creature: old things are passed away; behold, all things are become new." 2 Corinthians 5:17 KJV

You will never move forward in your walk with the Lord Jesus, neither will you ever truly answer His call on your life until you grasp hold of this truth with all your heart and keep it there; this is especially true when someone is trying to call you out on your past; God has cleansed you of all sin. In the eyes of God you do not have a past. In Christ you only have a future.

What can the believer do when someone is reliving our past mistakes for us? What should the believer do when we are trying to tell someone about Jesus and all they do is accuse us of being judgmental, while at the same time calling us out on our past? In the film <u>Oh Brother Where Art Thou</u> there is one particular scene where the heroes encounter a church group heading down into a body of water to baptize. One character, Delmar, runs up to the man baptizing the others and whispers something in his ear and then the preacher baptizes him. After this Delmar comes back to his friends and says, "Well its all over for me now boys! I've been redeemed. I've been forgiven of all my sins including knocking over that Piggly-Wiggly in Yazoo city." To this Ulysses says, "I thought you said you were innocent of that?" Then Delmar says, "Well, I lied, and I've been forgiven for that too." This is exactly the attitude we should have when it comes to others not letting go of our mistakes. We have been forgiven. God will never hold our mistakes and failures against us and so we should not let anyone else do it either; and honestly, the only way anyone can use your past to keep you down is if you let them.

Other people's judgment can only keep you from fulfilling your calling if you let what they say or think paralyze you and keep you from answering the call. Remember, however, that other people's estimation of you and their judgment upon you is not God's estimation nor His judgment. When God calls you into His service there is nothing or no one that will ever be able to keep you from fulfilling your calling.

I cannot recall how many times people have told me that they were going to keep me from continuing as a pastor or keep me from preaching the gospel. I suppose it never occurred to them that they are not God and what happens in my life has little or nothing to do with them. No one can stop you from fulfilling your calling, because you belong to the Lord Jesus. He is your Savior. He has redeemed you. He is your righteous King and Almighty God. If He has determined that you will serve Him and bring glory to His name through your life, nothing and no one will ever get in the way. Which means, the only person who can ever keep you from reaching your potential is you. The only person who will keep you from obtaining everything God has planned for your life and all the blessings that are waiting is you.

God brought Isaiah into His presence and seeing God in His holiness and glory moved Isaiah to immediately repent. God cleansed Isaiah of his sins and made him fit for service and then after this God issues the call.

"Also I heard the voice of the Lord, saying, Whom shall I send, and who will go for us." Isaiah 6:8 KJV

This is the same calling that God issues to every one of His children. "Whom shall I send? Who will go for Us?" When you come to Christ Jesus in faith He forgives you for all your sins and He cleanses you of all unrighteousness. You become a whole new creation that is fit for service and then He calls you into His service. As a believer in Christ you are a part of the church which is commissioned to make disciples and preach the gospel. You are called to go into the world and proclaim the good news. The only thing left for you to do is to answer the call. How did Isaiah respond?

"Also I heard the voice of the Lord, saying, Whom shall I send, and who will go for us? Then said I, Here I am send me." Isaiah 6:8 KJV (Underline mine)

The calling God has placed on your life will not mean anything nor will it accomplish anything if you are not willing to go.

"And He said, Go, and tell this people, Hear ye indeed, but understand not; and see ye indeed, but perceive not. Make the heart of this people fat, and make their ears heavy, and shut their eyes; lest they see with their eyes, and hear with their ears, and understand with their heart, and convert, and be healed. Then said I, Lord, how long? And He answered, Until the cities be wasted without inhabitant, and the houses without man, and the land be utterly desolate, and the LORD have removed men far away, and there be a great forsaking in the midst of the land." Isaiah 6:9-12 KJV

The Lord told Isaiah to keep preaching even though

people will not listen and though they will never understand. The Lord told Isaiah to keep preaching though no one will perceive and they will continue to grow dull. The Lord told Isaiah to keep preaching until they grow weary of hearing the message. Some will see. Some will hear. Some will come to Christ and they will be saved. The Lord told Isaiah to keep preaching until every city and town is desolate and every person has been carried away into captivity. Why was Isaiah to keep preaching? Because when God was finished doing what He will, everyone would fully understand that a prophet, a true man of God, was in their midst.

In the same way we must continue to preach the gospel in the world. We must continue to preach though it looks as if the entire world is turned away from the truth. We must continue to preach until kingdom come so that when the Lord Jesus returns they will know the children of God have been among them preaching the good news and they will know the answer to their own question, "What makes you believe that you should speak for God?"

CHAPTER ELEVEN

Jeremiah: Uniquely
Called and Gifted

"I will praise thee: for I am fearfully and wonderfully made." Psalm 139:14 KJV

      Every person is a unique creation of God. The word translated as "wonderfully" in Psalm 139:14 is the Hebrew word **Pawlah** (Strong's: 6395) and its literal definition is, "Distinguished." Each one of us is fearfully and wonderfully made which makes us distinguished. We are the unique and distinguished creations of God and we are all individuals. This is why the Lord Jesus interacts with everyone differently. God deals with each one of us as an individual and unique creation. This is why everyone's salvation experience is different. No one's personal interaction with the Lord Jesus is exactly the same. No one comes to faith in Christ in exactly the same way as someone else. Furthermore, because every person is individually unique every person has a unique and personal calling from God on his or her life.

"Before I formed thee in the belly I knew thee; and before thou camest forth out of the womb I sanctified thee, and I ordained thee a prophet unto the nations." Jeremiah 1:5 KJV

      Just as God created Jeremiah with a unique and individual calling and ministry He has done the very same for you. This means, before you were born God had a plan and a purpose in mind for you and your life. The scriptural evidence which supports this doctrine is many and varied.

"I therefore, the prisoner of the Lord, beseech you that ye walk worthy of the vocation wherewith ye are called." Ephesians 4:1 KJV

"And He gave some apostles; and some prophets; and some evangelists; and some, pastors and teachers; for the perfecting of the saints, for the work of the ministry, for the edifying of the body of Christ." Ephesians 4:11-12 KJV

"Having then gifts differing according to the grace that is given to us, whether prophecy, let us prophesy according to the proportion of faith; or ministry, let us wait on ministering: or he that teaches, on teaching; or he that exhorteth, on exhortation: he that giveth, let him do it with simplicity; he that ruleth, with diligence; he that sheweth mercy, with cheerfulness." Romans 12:6-8 KJV

Every person being a unique creation of God has been created with a specific and individual calling and ministry in mind. We are the special creation of God. We are the unique creations of God. We have been created with purpose in mind and we have been gifted for this purpose. Though everyone has a calling and in ways everyone's calling may be similar, it is still unique to the individual and unique as the individual. The apostle Peter was called from being a fisherman to become a fisher of men. The apostle Paul was called out of worthless and dead religion to a living faith in the Lord Jesus. The account of Barnabas' conversion is not recorded in the pages of the Bible, but we do have the account of his calling.

"Now there were in the church that was at Antioch certain prophets and teachers; as Barnabas, and Simeon that was called Niger, and Lucius of Cyrene, and Manaen, which had been brought up with Herod the tetrarch, and Saul. As they ministered to the Lord, and fasted, the Holy Ghost said, Separate me Barnabas and Saul for the work whereunto I have called them. And when they had fasted and prayed, and laid their hands on them, they sent them away. So they, being sent forth by the Holy Ghost, departed unto Seleucia." Acts 13:1-4 KJV

Everyone's calling may have similar characteristics. Such as, the Lord places the call on men and women's hearts through the conviction and moving of the Holy Spirit. Just about every believer understands that it is God who is calling, and in addition to this, the calling God places on the believer's life will be recognized by others. These are the things that will be similar, but what is unique and individual is exactly how God gets our attention.

For Moses it was a burning bush. For the apostle Paul, he encountered the Lord Jesus on the road to Damascus. Barnabas received his call from the Holy Spirit through the church at Antioch. How each one is called and how your individual ministry within the body is revealed by God will be as personal to you as when the Lord Jesus came into your life and saved you. The calling God has placed on your life has to do with you, therefore, it will be very personal to you. The individual way in which God calls His children has to do with the fact that we are not all the same and so naturally we are not all called to do the very same things. God created everyone with a unique purpose in mind and God has created and called all His children to do something specific which is suited to who you are and is in accord with the gifts and talents He has developed in you.

"But of those who seemed to be somewhat, (whatsoever they were, it maketh no matter to me: God accepteth no man's person:) for they who seemed to be somewhat in conference added nothing to me: <u>But contrariwise when they saw that the gospel of uncircumcision was committed to me, as the gospel of circumcision was unto Peter;</u> (for he that wrought effectively in Peter to the apostleship of the circumcision, the same was mighty in me toward the Gentiles:)" Galatians 2:6-8 KJV (Underline mine)

God called and equipped Peter to preach to the Jews. God called and equipped Paul to preach to the Gentiles. Both men had a specific and unique calling from God because every one of God's children has been uniquely created with a specific calling and purpose in mind, and though everyone's calling may share similarities our calling and gifting is as unique to us as the individuals that we are, because the Lord interacts with each one of us on a individual and personal level.

In addition to our calling, sharing similarities and yet remaining individual and unique, so too is the equipping that we receive through the gifts of the Holy Spirit, gifts that are to be used to fulfill our calling and purpose. In some ways our gifts may be similar but these are nonetheless unique to each person.

"Before I formed thee in the belly I knew thee: and before thou camest forth out of the womb I sanctified thee, and I ordained thee a prophet to the nations." Jeremiah 1:5 KJV

This verse informs the reader to this truth: before we were born God knew us. Before you were born God knew you and before I was born God knew me. How is this possible and what does it mean? Does this mean that we existed before we took on this corporeal form at birth? No, this is not what the Bible is saying. What this verse is stating is that God knows everything there is to know about us. God knew when and where we would be born. God knew who our parents would be. God knew how we would be raised because He was in control of all these things. Why did God bring you into the world in the way He did? Why did God allow you to be raised in the way you were? Because God had a purpose in mind when He created you and everything that God has allowed into your life has everything to do with the calling He has placed on your life. Which means your life is the way it is on purpose.

God had a purpose in mind for your life when you were nothing more but a thought in His mind. God had a purpose in mind for your life before you were created. In my case God may have said to Himself, "I desire to create someone who loves to study My word. I desire to create someone who loves to preach the gospel and to teach. I will create Christopher Dysinger to pastor Cross Trail Church and Mission." God may have said to

Himself, in my case, "I will fashion for Myself and My purposes Christopher Dysinger. He will be born to Robert and Judy. He will be born in Oklahoma. He will call on My name and be saved in July of 1995. He will attend this school. He will serve in certain ways until He fulfills completely My calling on his life to be My pastor in Blackwell, Oklahoma." Everything about my life has to do with the calling of God on it. Everything about my life has to do with God's divine appointment. This is how God relates to each and every one of us in a very personal way and all of these things were ordained before we were even created. We were conceived in the mind of Christ with a purpose in mind. We were conceived in the mind of God to fulfill a calling.

"Before thou camest forth out of the womb I sanctified thee, and I ordained thee." Jeremiah 1:5 KJV (Underline mine)

Everyone has a specific calling from God on his or her life. Every believer is equipped, gifted, and strengthened to fulfill his or her calling by the Holy Spirit. This means every believer is sanctified by the Holy Spirit. This means all believers have been set apart by the Holy Spirit to fulfill a ministry. All believers have been ordained by the Holy Spirit to fulfill a ministry.

"I beseech you therefore, brethren, by the mercies of God, that ye present your bodies a living sacrifice, holy, acceptable unto God, which is your reasonable service. And be not conformed to this world: but be ye transformed by the renewing of your mind, that ye may prove what is that good, and acceptable, and perfect will of God. For I say through the grace given unto me, to every man that is among you, not to think of himself more highly that he ought to think; but to think soberly, according as God hath dealt to every man the measure of faith. For as we have many members in one body, and all members have not the same office: So we being many, are one body in Christ, and every one members one of another. Having then gifts differing according to the grace that is given to us, whether prophecy, let us prophesy according to the proportion of faith; Or ministry, let us wait on our ministering: or he that teacheth, on teaching; Or he

that exhorteth, on exhortation: he that giveth, let him do it with sim-plicity; he that ruleth, with diligence; he that sheweth mercy, with cheerfulness." Romans 12:1-8 KJV (Underline mine)

You were created by God with a specific purpose in mind and this specific purpose is in accord with the calling of God on your life and the gifts of the Holy Spirit are also in accord with your calling. You are uniquely equipped to fulfill your calling through the indwelling and personal presence of the Holy Spirit who also works to strengthen, guide, and inspire you and all of this was in the mind of God before you were born. Therefore, fulfill your calling! In other words, God has taken care of every-thing you need in order for you to do what He created you to do. Now it is up to you to go out and do what you were made for.

Where the truths of God's word short circuit in many people's lives is when they fail to answer the call of God on their lives. Why do so many believers fail in answering the call? Many will say, "I cannot figure out just what it is I am supposed to do." These people claim that they cannot discern the will of God and they use this excuse to keep from ever doing anything. For any-one who is genuinely struggling when it comes to discerning the will of God, I want to offer this instruction from the Word.

"I beseech you therefore, brethren, by the mercies of God, that ye pre-sent your bodies a living sacrifice, holy, acceptable unto God, which is your reasonable service." Romans 12:1 KJV

In order to discern God's will for your life you must first present yourself for service. Ask yourself if you are honestly sold out to do God's will. If you are not, you will have a diffi-cult time recognizing God's will for your life because you cannot conform to the world while trying to submit to God at the same time.

"And be not conformed to this world: but be ye transformed by the renewing of your mind, that ye may prove what is that good, and ac-ceptable, and perfect, will of God." Romans 12:2 KJV

In seeking God's will you must renew your mind through scripture which allows the Holy Spirit to enact a real transformation in your life. It is this transformation which will allow you to discern what is the good and acceptable will of God. Nothing happens without real transformation.

There are also men and women who never answer the call of God on their lives, claiming that they do not possess any spiritual gifts.

"Then said I, Ah, Lord GOD! Behold, I cannot speak: for I am a child." Jeremiah 1:6 KJV

The truth is that sometimes God calls us to serve in the capacity in which we believe we are at our weakest because His strength is made perfect in weakness.

"And lest I should be exalted above measure through the abundance of the revelations, there was given me a thorn in the flesh, the messenger of Satan to buffet me, lest I should be exalted above measure. For this thing I besought the Lord thrice, that it might depart from me. And He said unto me, My grace is sufficient for thee: for My strength is made perfect in weakness. Most gladly therefore will I rather glory in my infirmities, that the power of Christ may rest upon me." 2 Corinthians 12:7-9 KJV

"But we have this treasure in earthen vessels, that the excellency of the power may be of God, and not of us." 2 Corinthians 4:7 KJV

There are times God calls us to serve where we believe we are at our weakest so that His power will be on display. Then again, where God leads He will provide.

"But then I said, Ah, Lord GOD! Behold I cannot speak: for I am a child. But the LORD said unto me, Say not, I am a child: for thou shalt go to all that I shall send thee, and whatsoever I command thee thou shalt speak. Be not afraid of their faces: for I am with thee to deliver thee, saith the LORD. Then the LORD put forth His hand, and touched my mouth, and the LORD said unto me, Behold I have put My

words in thy mouth." Jeremiah 1:6-9 KJV

If you are someone who is looking for something easy to do, something that you can accomplish in the power of your own strength, you may be missing what it is God has called you to do. There are times God calls upon His children to do difficult things, frightening things, but even in this do not shrink back or think that serving the Lord is nothing but misery and woe.

Too many ministers want people to believe the Lord's work is toil, drudgery, and heartbreak. This is so that they might appear to be more hard-working than they truly are. God did not create humanity to serve as His slaves. The work He has created us to do is not drudgery. In fact, the very thing that is dearest to your own heart is more than likely the area of life God has called you to serve in.

If a young mother were to come to me as her pastor, heartbroken because she did not feel as if she had a calling from God, because her heart is inclined to be with her children and she wants to be a good and godly wife and mother, and she truly desires to be a home-maker, but all she hears from outside the home is that being a home-maker is nothing more than indentured servitude, I would assure her that being a wife, a mother, and a home-maker is a glorious calling from God. What God calls you to do with your life will almost always have to do with the inclination of our heart, and if it doesn't, in time it will.

"Delight thyself also in the LORD; and He shall give thee the desires of thine heart." Psalm 37:4 KJV

God has called no one into slavery. God calls His children to minister in His name and whatever ministry God has called you to will not be a burden. It will be the exact opposite. Though at times it will be difficult and challenging it will always bring true satisfaction and joy to your life.

All God's children have been created by God to be unique individuals and to have unique experiences, and gifts, and talents, and loves, and hates. All these have been given to allow us to fulfill our calling. You and I have been created with God's purpose in mind. You and I have been called to be a blessing to the church.

"But unto everyone of us is given grace according to the measure of the gift of Christ. Wherefore He saith, When He ascended up on high, He led captivity captive, and gave gifts to me." Ephesians 4:7-8 KJV

To what end did the Lord Jesus give gifts unto men?

"And He gave some apostles; and some, prophets; and some, evangelists; and some, pastors and teachers; for the perfecting of the saints (To equip the saints), *for the work of the ministry, <u>for the edifying of the body of Christ</u>."* Ephesians 4:11-12 KJV (Parenthesis and underline mine)

The church is of great significance to God. The church is not some Sunday morning social club. The church is not a fraternal organization. The church is not another community outreach. The church is the living body of Christ. The church is the bride of Christ. The church is that living entity through which the Holy Spirit moves and operates as we preach the gospel of Jesus to the world. The church is significant. The church is also that vessel through which the believer will find God's blessings being poured out upon him or her. Then again, the men and women, the families and children, the believers God brings together are the blessings and God's gifts to the church. Which means, you dear believer, are the blessing and you, dear believer, are what makes for a gifted church. You are a gift and a blessing from God when you are serving the Lord Jesus in the calling He has prepared for you in the church.

Which means, you cannot forsake the calling of God on your life, and forsake the congregation and expect to find your life fulfilling and blessed.

"For we shall be of little use to God if we know only our salvation, and have caught no glimpse of the purpose for which He has brought us into relation with His Son." - Watchman Nee

Can a believer say "no." when the Lord comes calling? Yes he or she can, but what happens when he or she says no? Are they lost? Are they cast aside? The answer is no.

"If we believe not, yet He abideth faithful: He cannot deny Himself." 2 Timothy 2:13 KJV

When a believer says "no" to God's calling on his or her life the Lord simply raises up another believer to fulfill that ministry. The Lord will give the position to someone else along with all the blessings and the glory. The work of the ministry will continue, but those who refuse will miss out on the blessings God intended for them through that ministry and as those who refuse continue to live life they might find their lives falling short of what they hoped it might be. In addition to this, his or her worship will grow stale. At whatever point you say "no" to the Lord, this is the place in your life where you stop growing as a Christian and this is the point where you stop growing closer to the Lord Jesus. Worship will become nothing more than going through the motions. Prayers will become empty and heartless. Why does this happen? Because, instead of pursing the Lord and His will for your life, you said, "no thank you. I will not go. Do not send me." When you say "no" to God you cannot help but to lose heart because your heart will be distant from where it truly longs to be.

Say, "yes," to the Lord Jesus. Serve the Lord with gladness. It may at times be challenging, but you will never regret it.

CHAPTER TWELVE

Hosea

All men and women are born with free will. Which means every individual will have the final word on every decision he or she makes in life and these decisions culminate in how he or she lives. Having a free will means we decide the character we will live by and how we will relate to each other. Our free will is involved in how we live. Our free will is involved in who we choose to love or not to love. There are many people who express the sentiment that you do not have any control over who you love. They say, "The heart wants what it wants," and other nonsense to excuse themselves from their commitments, when the truth is that love is a choice we make. You and I choose who we will love and we also choose who we don't care for. Keeping our commitments to those we choose to love is not always easy. Keeping our commitments can, at times, be difficult. I am speaking to you as a man who has struggled with loving people. Loving the people God brings into our lives, our spouses, our children, our extended family and friends, and even our church family can be difficult. This is due to the fact that we are broken people. Everyone has his or her own flaws to contend with.

There are times when we are not at our best. There are times when we are selfish and self-centered. There are times we can be inconsiderate. There are times, and this is true even of believers, that we can be real jerks. Which means that everyone can be someone who is not easy to love; but does this mean that we should stop loving people? Does the fact that some people are not easy to live with mean we should stop being loving toward others? The answer: certainly not.

"This is My commandment, That ye love one another, as I have loved you." John 15:12 KJV

"These things I command you, that ye love one another." John 15:17 KJV

"A new command I give unto you, That ye love one another; as I have loved you, that ye also love one another. By this shall all men know that ye are My disciples, if ye have love one to another." John 13:34-35 KJV

The Christian is identified through being a loving person. The question is: can a believer truly love an unfaithful and unloving person? Can Christians respond in love to men and women who do not reflect good or godly character? How should Christians respond and react to unfaithful and unloving people? The plain truth is Christians encounter unloving people on a daily basis and everywhere we go. This situation will only grow more prevalent as the end of the age approaches.

"Then shall they deliver you up to be afflicted, and shall kill you: and ye shall be hated of all nations for My name's sake. And then shall many be offended, and shall betray one another. And many false prophets shall rise, and shall deceive many. And because iniquity shall abound, the love of many shall wax cold." Matthew 24:9-12 KJV

Clearly the church is living in a loveless age and yet, because we have a living relationship with the Lord Jesus by faith, and because we have the commandment from our Savior and Lord to love, we must love the unlovable. The prophet Hosea's life stands as a testimony and example of how to love the unlovable. This prophet of God was given instruction to marry an unfaithful woman. This prophet was commanded by God to love an unloving and uncommitted woman. Hosea is a perfect example of how to love the unlovable with the love of God.

"The word of the LORD that came unto Hosea, the son of Beri, in the days of Uzziah, Jotham, Ahaz, and Hezekiah, kings of Judah, and in the days of Jeroboam the son of Joash, king of Israel. The beginning of the word of the LORD by Hosea. And the LORD said to Hosea, <u>Go, take unto thee a wife of whoredoms and children of whoredoms: for the land hath committed great whoredom, departing from the LORD.</u> So he went and took Gomer the daughter of Diblaim; which conceived and bare him a son." Hosea 1:1-3 KJV (Underline mine)

Hosea was a man of God who had to contend with a wife who, from all the biblical evidence, did not practice any faith whatsoever and who was uncommitted to her husband and her marriage; and in this Gomer was a picture of the faithlessness of Israel in her relationship with God. Can a believer truly love a faithless person? By faithless I mean to define a person who has no faith in the Lord Jesus and also struggles with being faithful in his or her relationships to others.

Lets get the preliminary questions out of the way first. Can a believer be married to an unbeliever? The answer is yes.

"But to the rest speak I, not the Lord: If any brother hath a wife that believeth not, and she be pleased to dwell with him, let him not put her away. And the woman which hath an husband that believeth not, and if he be pleased to dwell with her, let her not leave him. For the unbelieving husband is sanctified by the wife, and the unbelieving wife is sanctified by the husband: else were your children unclean, but now they are holy." 1 Corinthians 7:12-14 KJV

This does not mean that an unbeliever is saved by being married to a believer. What this means is that an unbelieving spouse will receive blessings by the fact that he or she is married to a believer. Unbelievers receive blessings by living in close proximity to believers, but the blessings he or she may receive are residual. In addition to this when Paul writes, *"Else were your children unclean, but now they are holy,"* (Vs. 14) he is speaking to children having the benefit of a two parent household, and he

123

is also speaking about the benefit of having, at least, one believing parent. This passage allows us to understand that there are situations in which a believer may find himself or herself in a relationship with an unbeliever, but this is not tacit permission from God for believers to marry unbelievers. The fact is a person can marry whomever he or she pleases as long as the other party is agreeable, but the Bible clearly presents that believers should not be unequally yoked.

"Be ye not unequally yoked together with unbelievers: for what fellowship hath righteousness with unrighteousness? And what communion hath light with darkness? And what concord hath Christ with Belial? Or what part hath he that believeth with an infidel? 2 Corinthians 6:14-15 KJV

God commanding Hosea to marry an unfaithful woman is not permission for believers to run out and marry the first person, believer or not, who will have them. The primary reason a believer should not marry an unbeliever is because being married to an unbeliever will make your life even more difficult than it already is by proxy of being a child of God in the midst of a wicked generation. Living by faith in the world today will try you, and being a believer married to an unbeliever will make your life exponentially more difficult.

Here then is the Bible's position clearly stated. If you are married to an unbeliever and he or she is disposed to continue in the marriage then do not seek a divorce. If you become a believer and find yourself married to an unbeliever and this person decides that he or she doesn't want any part of your faith and leaves, and seeks a divorce, there is really nothing you can do about it. If you are single and desire to be married and you are a believer the best course of action is to marry another believer. If you desire a truly God-honoring marriage, then you will allow the Holy Spirit to bring the right person into your life.

"But as God hath distributed to every man, as the Lord hath called everyone, so let him walk." 1 Corinthians 7:17 KJV

Believers should continue through life living by faith in the Lord Jesus in the situation and circumstances they find themselves, in trusting that God will change those circumstances as He sees fit. The believer lives by faith trusting in the Lord that He will work everything according to His will. Therefore, we must let Him do it.

There is another consideration which concerns marriage and divorce that is appropriate to address in this chapter. There are some people who wonder if it is OK with God for someone who is divorced to re-marry. There are some ministers who will not oversee a marriage between divorced people and the reason they will not is found in the book of 1 Corinthians.

"And unto the married I command, yet not I, but the Lord. Let not the wife depart from her husband: but and if she depart, let her remain unmarried, or be reconciled to her husband: and let not the husband put away his wife." 1 Corinthians 7:10-11 KJV

Many people who are divorced and now single may wonder about the righteous or unrighteous nature of being married again. According to my understanding based upon scripture, and also according to my own opinion, I do not think it is a sin for someone who is divorced to remarry. I base this opinion on three scriptures.

"I say therefore to the unmarried and widows, it is good for them if they abide even as I. But if they cannot contain, let them marry: for it is better to marry than to burn." 1 Corinthians 7:8-9 KJV (Underline mine)

"I will therefore that the younger women marry, bear children, guide the house, give none occasion to the adversary to speak reproachfully. For some are already turned aside after Satan." 1 Timothy 5:14-15 KJV

"But the younger widows refuse: for when they have begun to wax wanton gainst Christ, they will marry." 1 Timothy 5:11 KJV

A strong and godly marriage will encourage a strong faith in the family. Strong and godly families lead to a strong and godly nation. It is better for the unmarried, whether through being made a widow or widower, or through divorce, to marry instead of burning with desire. If you find yourself disagreeing with my position, this is your prerogative. Having a disagreement is fine, but if you believe, based upon your position that your calling is to interfere in other people's lives and their marriages, and their families, you are operating outside your sphere of authority. Other people's lives are none of your business. So, when it comes to other people's lives mind your own business. This brings us back to the situation Hosea was in. Hosea was a man of God who was married to a harlot. Hosea was a man who had a calling on his life and had a mission to perform and he was unequally yoked. **Family will affect your ministry.**

When it comes to all believers, we are saved. We are sanctified. We are called and equipped for ministry. Every single child of God is called no matter what his or her past contains. All believers have a calling on their lives no matter if they are single, married, divorced, remarried. All believers have a calling on their lives no matter if their past is full of sinful mistakes and failures or their past is pristine. Every believer has a calling and a ministry and family affects ministry.

Family will affect your ministry as it affects the resources you have to perform the work of the ministry. Family will affect your ministry as in the direction your life will takes either toward a greater fulfillment of ministry or toward fulfilling your obligations to family. Family will affect your ministry in how others will view your ministry and calling in light of how they view your family; and what others think about the minister's family is probably the most difficult situation to have to contend with for a lot of ministers. What I am saying is that how others view and judge your family as a minister will affect your ability to fulfill your calling. This is not how it should be, but this is how it is.

The most obvious way being unequally yoked will affect a person's ministry is in this: a house divided cannot stand. When a believer is married to an unbeliever this man and wife will always have two minds about everything. I would go so far as to say, in a marriage which consists of a believer and an unbeliever, any time there is agreement it will come at the expense of the believer's convictions. The only time there is real agreement between an unbeliever and a believer is when the believer allows the unbeliever to have his or her way and more often than not this is just to keep the peace. I.E. My wife and I agree most of the time, but in reality my wife is just letting me have my way because it is just not worth fighting about.

Being unequally yoked will also affect how others view you and your family. Unscrupulous men and women will find ways to use your family against you in any attempt to tear apart your ministry.

"This is a true saying, If a man desire the office of a bishop, he desireth a good work. A bishop then must be blameless, the husband of one wife, vigilant, sober, of good behavior, given to hospitality, apt to teach; not given to wine, no striker, not greedy of filthy lucre; but patient, not a brawler, not covetous; <u>*One that ruleth well his own house, having his children in subjection with all gravity*</u> (Meaning having their respect) *(for if a man know not how to rule his own house, how shall he take care of the church of God?)"* 1 Timothy 3:1-5 KJV (Parenthesis and underline mine)

Here we have Paul's guidelines for leadership in the church. This is the type of character a church should look for in a pastor, but you will never find a man in this age who is the perfect pastor according to the Bible because the picture is one of perfection, but no person is perfect; neither will anyone ever be. It is enough if a man desires to have this kind of character and is working toward it, allowing the Holy Spirit to make strides in his life to bring about this kind of character.

The last part of verse five calls on the man of God to rule

his own house well. The last part of verse five calls upon the man of God to keep his own children in subjection. This means a pastor's children should not be unruly. A pastor's children should show respect for others and they certainly should show respect for God, but no matter how diligent you may be to raise your children in the training and admonition of the Lord they have a free will and they will do what they will do. Still, in this ministry of being a pastor there have been no shortage of men and women who have attempted to use this verse as a means of disqualifying me from the ministry. In the 22 years that I have served as a pastor many people have tried to use my family against me and against the work of the ministry and this is because family affects ministry, but the relationships you have in your life do not disqualify you from your calling and ministry. The family you have does not remove God's calling from your life. Based upon the calling on Hosea's life we see that you can fulfill your calling in spite of your family's failings and short-comings. You do not have to have the perfect family in order to fulfill your calling.

I do not know where the idea that a minister must have the perfect family originated, seeing as how no one I know has ever had a perfect family. I have endured many complaints and suffered many criticisms concerning my family from church members who have, at times, called upon me to visit their children in jail. This seems a bit hypocritical in my humble estimation. When it comes right down to it, criticizing others because of their family relationships is illegitimate.

"And why beholdest thou the mote that is in thy brother's eye, but considerest not the beam that is in thine own eye? Or how wilt thou say to thy brother, Let me pull out the mote out of thine eye; and, behold, a beam is in thine own eye? Thou hypocrite, first cast out the beam out of thine own eye; and then shalt thou see clearly to cast out the mote out of thy brother's eye." Matthew 7:3-5 KJV

Imagine the kind of abuse Hosea endured because of the

actions he took with his wife? Consider this too, that God instructed Hosea to marry this woman. Hosea's marriage to Gomer was all a part of God's plan and Hosea's marriage to Gomer was a part of his ministry. God used Hosea's relationship to his unfaithful wife as a picture of His own relationship to unfaithful Israel. God used Hosea's family, including the very names he named his children, to highlight and punctuate what was happening between the people of Israel and Him. Which means Hosea's family was all a part of God's plan for Hosea's life. The beautiful thing about Hosea's relationship to his unfaithful wife, which is also an apt description of the manner in which God loves us, is that no matter how wrong Gomer treated her husband, Hosea loved her in return.

"Then said the LORD unto me, Go yet, love a woman beloved of her friend, yet an adulteress, according to the love of the LORD toward the children of Israel, who look to other gods, and love flagons of wine. So I bought her to me for fifteen pieces of silver, and for a homer of barley, and a half-homer of barley: and I said unto her, Thou shalt abide for me many days; thou shalt not play the harlot, and thou shalt not be for another man: so will I also be with thee." Hosea 3:1-3 KJV

Hosea's wife ran off and sold herself into prostitution. Hosea had to go and find her, and when he did, he then had to buy her out of prostitution in order to bring her home. Why did he do this? Because he loved his wife even though she was unfaithful.

The Lord told Hosea to love his wife in the same way that He loves Israel. This is the very same way the Lord loves me and you. We know this because the Lord Jesus ransomed us out of the bondage of sin. The Lord Jesus paid the necessary price so that we could be saved. If the Lord Jesus can love me enough to forgive my adultery and enough to rescue me from the bondage of sin, then I believe I can reach out and love the loveless even when I find a loveless attitude among those in my own family.

Everything the Lord does is on our behalf. Everything the Lord allows into our lives is according to His plan and purpose for our lives and these things will ultimately result in blessings. How am I assured of this? Because the Bible tells us that all things are working together for the benefit of all who love Jesus and are called by Him. You find this truth illustrated time and again in the pages of scripture. Can we love unfaithful people? Yes we can because we all have been unfaithful to the Lord Jesus at one time or another and He has forgiven us, and He continues in His love for us. It is this love that now resides within our hearts.

CHAPTER THIRTEEN

Jonah

Just about everyone knows the story of Jonah. If you have spent any time in church as a child you have probably heard the tale more than once. Many have taken this story and presented it as a fairy tale rather than as a historical event, but let me assure you the story of Jonah is entirely and absolutely true. Though some people may be skeptical, any skepticism should be put to rest in the knowledge that the Lord Jesus Himself referenced Jonah being swallowed by a great fish, and the Lord spoke in such a way that would not allow someone to believe He was telling a fairy tale.

"Then certain of the scribes and of the Pharisees answered saying, Master, we would see a sign from Thee, but He answered and said unto them, An evil and adulterous generation seeketh after a sign; and there shall no sign be given to it, but the sign of the prophet Jonah: for as Jonah was three days and three nights in in the whale's belly; so shall the Son of man be three days and three nights in the heart of the earth. The men of Nineveh shall rise in judgment with this generation, and shall condemn it: because they repented at the preaching of Jonah; and, behold, a greater than Jonah is here." Matthew 12:38-41 KJV

If the Lord Jesus were referencing a fabricated story He certainly would not have mentioned the results as genuine. If the story of Jonah and the whale was nothing more than a fairy tale, the Lord's statement about the men of Nineveh standing in judgment of others would be a false statement because men in fairy tales do not exist. The story of Jonah and all the events that took place in his life are true. Jonah was a real person. Jonah was called to be a prophet of God.

"He restored (He being Jeroboam the king of Israel) *the coast of Israel from the entering of Hamath unto the sea of the plain, according to the word of the LORD God of Israel, which He spake by the hand of His servant, Jonah, the son of Amittai, the prophet, which was of Gath-Hepher."* 2 Kings 14:25 KJV (Parenthesis mine)

The Jonah who is mentioned in the historical book of 2 Kings is the same Jonah spoken of in the book of Jonah. Jonah took it upon himself to write an account of what happened to him when the Lord gave him direction and he refused to follow. What we have in the book of Jonah is a first-hand account of what happens to a child of God when he or she decides that he or she does not want to do what God asks. The question I am posing through this chapter and that I will attempt to find an answer to in the story of Jonah is: what happens when a person doesn't want to do what the Lord asks?

Can someone say "no" to the Lord Jesus? The answer is, yes. All human beings have been created with free will. Can a person say, "No thank you," to the calling the Holy Spirit has placed on his or her life? Again, the answer is yes, because we have free will. God will not make you do something you really do not want to do, but God can make you willing. The Lord Jesus can and will move you in the direction He desires for your life. It is good to know, however, and to remember; the direction the Holy Spirit has for your life will always be what is best for you. Which begs the question, why say "no" to the Holy Spirit when we understand that He knows what He is doing and it will always be in our own best interest?

"And we know that all things work together for good to them that love God, to them who are the called according to His purpose." Romans 8:28 KJV

What happened in the case of Jonah? The Lord called Jonah to be a prophet and it appears that Jonah did not have a problem with answering this call. Jonah served as a prophet in Israel. Where Jonah encountered problems is when the Lord called upon Jonah to go and preach in Nineveh.

"Now the word of the LORD came unto Jonah the son of Amittai, saying, Arise, go to Nineveh, that great city, and cry against it; for their wickedness is come up before Me. But Jonah rose up to flee unto Tarshish from the presence of the LORD, and went down to Joppa; and he found a ship going to Tarshish: so he paid the fare thereof, and went down into it, to go with them unto Tarshish from the presence of the LORD." Jonah 1:1-3 KJV

Jonah refused to go to Nineveh because he did not care for Nineveh. Jonah did not mind ministering in Israel, but he was not willing to bless Nineveh. Why did Jonah have a problem with Nineveh? Because, Nineveh was the capital city of Assyria and the Assyrians were the avowed enemies of Israel and the Assyrians had committed many atrocities in Israel and had committed many crimes against the Hebrews. Jonah harbored resentment against the Assyrians and because of this he did not want God to bless them. Jonah wanted God to punish them. Jonah's refusal to preach repentance stemmed from his personal desire to see his enemies destroyed.

Matthew Henry in his commentary on Jonah postulates that Jonah may have believed that the gospel was only meant for Israel and that it was an abomination to preach repentance to anyone other than the children of Israel. This may well have been the case as this attitude was present within the early church.

"Now they which were scattered abroad upon the persecution that arose about Steven traveled as far as Phenice, and Cyprus, and Antioch, preaching the word <u>to none but the Jews only</u>." Acts 11:19 KJV (Underline mine)

133

The gospel, however, is for everyone so that as many as have ears to hear may hear and respond in faith and be saved by the Lord Jesus.

"And this gospel of the kingdom shall be preached in all the world for a witness unto all nations; and then shall the end come." Matthew 24:14 KJV

"Go ye into all the world, and preach the gospel to every creature." Mark 16:15-16 KJV

We believers do not get the luxury of deciding who will hear the gospel and who will not. It does not matter if we believe we have a good excuse for not telling someone about Jesus, we should not refuse to fulfill our calling and responsibility before God. The major emphasis behind the calling on every Christian's life is that the gifts and the calling and the empowering of the Holy Spirit is in place to enable the believer to effectively present the Lord Jesus to everyone. Which means that it doesn't matter if we like the people we are witnessing to or not and it also doesn't matter what they have done, or have not done. What matters is that the Lord Jesus desires all men and women to be saved and come to a knowledge of the truth.

"I exhort therefore, that, first of all, supplications, prayers, intercessions, and giving of thanks, be made for all men; for kings, and for all that are in authority; that we may lead a quiet and peaceable life in all godliness and honesty. For this is good and acceptable in the sight of God our Savior; who will have all men to be saved, and to come unto the knowledge of the truth." 1 Timothy 2:1-4 KJV (Underline mine)

In addition to our calling requiring us to preach the gospel to all nations, the Lord Himself has instructed us to love our enemies.

"Ye have heard that it hath been said, Thou shalt love thy neighbor, and hate thine enemy. But I say unto you, Love your enemies,

bless them that curse you, do good to them that hate you, and pray for them that despitefully use you, and persecute you." Matthew 5:43-44 KJV

Can you think of a better way to, "love your enemies," than to present the gospel? Jonah's prejudice and bigotry did not in any way remove the calling of God from his life nor did it relieve him of his responsibility before God as a prophet. When it comes to Christians who are prone to being bigoted and prejudicial, he or she should take the time to consider that it is possible and likely that God doesn't feel the same way that you do when it comes to others.

The Hebrews could be a very bigoted people. They often let the fact that they were God's chosen nation go to their heads. Israel is God's chosen in this capacity: they were chosen to present Christ to the world. Israel was ordained by God to bring the Messiah into the world to be the Savior of all mankind. Many Hebrews wrongly believed that salvation was only offered to Israel and that the Messiah was the Savior of Israel alone. This is the reason the Jews did not travel through Samaria in Jesus' day. This is why the Lord had to convince Peter, through a vision, to go to the Gentile Cornelius' home to present the gospel. This is the reason Paul rebuked the apostle Peter for acting like a bigot while in Antioch by refusing to dine at the same table as the Gentiles. Jonah's bigotry was the reason the Lord's instruction to preach to Nineveh was anathema to him and would make him think to run away, but Jonah's bigotry did not give him a reason to shirk his responsibility before God nor to disobey God's command.

The church today faces similar circumstances especially among men and women who claim Calvinism. Calvinists wrongfully believe that they were, in fact, chosen before the foundation of the world to be saved. They believe in a roundabout way that they were born saved and that the irresistible grace of the Lord Jesus through the drawing of the Holy Spirit has brought them to Christ and made them aware of their eternal state. Calvinists believe they were created to be saved and all others were created for no other reason than to be condemned. This false doctrine is nothing less than a cloak for bigotry and an excuse to ignore the Bible and the great commission. Why would there be a great commission if everything was predestined?

There are many professed believers in Christ who are a lot like Jonah. These men and women despise others to the point that they would never think to approach them with the good news of Jesus. While it was not overt in any way and no one would have dared to confess that this was the truth of things, there was an undercurrent of bigotry in a church I once pastored in Arkansas. It was just understood that there was a certain part of the population who were not welcome. It truly puzzled me how there were people who professed to have a living relationship with the Lord Jesus and believed that they indeed did love everyone with the love of Christ and yet allowed their unloving attitudes to rule them at the same time. The reason is because we are broken people and our lives continue to be influenced to some degree by sin. Jonah was God's prophet who refused to take God's word to a certain group of people because he hated them. Jonah was a broken man. Jonah had his issues and yet God still worked through Jonah. Jonah with all his issues was still a man of God.

We have to step back and realize that no one has a perfect and righteous nature. Everyone has his or her idiosyncrasies that show up from time to time. Which means, not only should we practice love, and grace, and patience with everyone the Holy Spirit moves us to reach out to, but we should also seek to exercise the same love, grace, and patience with men and women who may just react to the mission of the church in the same way Jonah did. Not only should Christians work to overcome our inherited prejudices and bigotry and what the world may define as racism, but we should also extend our grace, patience, and love toward those people who may be having a difficult time getting beyond these things. Loving our enemies extends to everyone, even those we believe that we possess the moral high ground over. Jonah refused to follow the direction of the Lord and yet he was still God's prophet. Jonah had issues related to bigotry and prejudice but he continued to have the calling of God on his life.

Jonah did more than refuse to obey God. He also tried to run away.

"But Jonah rose up to flee unto Tarshish from the presence of the LORD, and went down to Joppa; and he found a ship going to Tarshish: so he paid the fare thereof, and went down into it, to go with them unto Tarshish from the presence of the LORD." Jonah 1:3 KJV

Jonah put himself on a boat going in the opposite direction from Nineveh. I have heard that when it was said by someone in Jonah's day, that they were heading to Tarshish, what they were really saying is that they were going somewhere far away where no one could find them. Jonah so did not want to minister to Nineveh that he attempted to flee from the Lord. Jonah was trying to get to a place that even God could not find him. Is there any place you could go where the Lord could not find you?

"Whither shall I go from Thy Spirit? Or whither shall I flee from Thy presence? If I ascend up into heaven, Thou art there: if I make my bed in hell, behold, Thou art there. If I take the wings of morning, and dwell in the uttermost parts of the sea; even there shall Thy hand lead me, and Thy right hand shall hold me." Psalm 139:7-10 KJV

One belief in Israel among many of the Hebrews was that God only operated within the borders of Israel. When the nation of Judah was carried away captive to Babylon the captives believed they had been cut off from God because they had been carried outside of the borders of Israel. Jonah attempted to run away from God by getting as far away from Israel as he possibly could, but what happened?

"But the LORD sent out a great wind into the sea, and there was a mighty tempest in the sea, so that the ship was like to be broken."

Jonah 1:4 KJV

Here is what is to be learned from this: when you say "no" to God and break fellowship with Him often you find yourself running headlong into a mighty tempest. When you say "no" to the leading of the Holy Spirit, life will often get rough and you may think that God is simply being a bully, but you have to understand, what God has prepared for your life is better than anything you might imagine for yourself. When a person says "no" to the Lord, for whatever reason, what he or she is truly saying is, "I don't trust You Lord."

We often imagine that we know what is best for our lives. We believe that we are the masters of our own fate. We want to believe that we make our lives all that they are or will be without ever really considering that everything that exists beyond ourselves is beyond the limits of our control. You cannot run from God and expect your life to be blessed. When you run away from God you are running away from the source of all good and blessings in your life.

"Do not err, my beloved brethren. Every good gift and perfect gift is from above, and cometh down from the Father of lights, with Whom is no variableness, neither shadow of turning." James 1:16-17 KJV

"What man is there of you, whom if his son ask bread, will he give him a stone? Or if he asks a fish, will he given him a serpent? If ye then, being evil, know how to give good gifts unto your children, how much more shall your Father which is in heaven give good things to them that ask Him?" Matthew 7:9-11 KJV

God is the source of all good things. When I was in the Army I was posted at Fort Carson in Colorado. Often, on long weekends I would drive to see my family in Oklahoma City and to do so I had to drive through the panhandle of Oklahoma and many times I made my way through the small town of Turpin. Turpin is little more than a collection of houses on the prairie with a convenience store and a school system. The Oklahoma panhandle has rolling hills and tall grass prairie but not too many trees. There is just not a lot to look at in this part of the country and many times as I was making my way through I would look out over the expanse and think to myself, "Why would anyone want to live here?"

In June of 1999 Turpin Baptist Church called me to be their pastor and my first thought was, "Really Lord?" But, my family and I made the move and began to serve. I found the work I did there to be very fulfilling. I discovered that the people who lived in the area were good people who loved the Lord Jesus. The Lord revealed to me that there was a lot there that made living in the panhandle worthwhile and it was contingent upon this one fact: this is where the Lord wanted me to be. It is the Lord Himself who is the source of our joy and fulfillment. When you are living your life walking with the Lord Jesus in obedience and by faith, where you are located doesn't matter and who you are ministering to doesn't matter. What matters is that you are found in God's will and by being in God's will you are operating according to a living and vibrant relationship with the Lord Jesus. This is what makes life worth living. This is what brings fulfillment.

When Jonah said, "no," to the Lord he put himself in a position of being out of fellowship with God. God did not move away from Jonah. Jonah moved away from God which is exactly where a lot of Christians find themselves today. Many believers move away from God by virtue of the fact that they refuse to fall in line with God's will for their lives. Many Christians have moved away from God and because of this their fellowship with God is strained, and what is more they know it and they are feeling it. Being estranged from the Lord leads to worship that is empty and meaningless. Being estranged leads to prayer that is nothing more than going through the motions. Being out of fellowship with God affects Bible reading in this way, when you read the word God doesn't speak to you. All of this happens when God calls and the believer says, "no thank you."

There is something else the Christian should understand

about being estranged from the Lord. When you say "no" to the moving of the Holy Spirit the results will affect more than just your life. Saying "no" to God doesn't only affect your life. Jonah tried to run away from God and ran right into the heart of a storm, but Jonah was not alone on that ship.

"Then the mariners were afraid, and cried every man unto his god, and cast forth the wares into the sea, to lighten it of them, but Jonah was gone down into the sides of the ship; and he lay, and was fast asleep." Jonah 1:5 KJV

Saying "no" to God doesn't just move your life into a place of turmoil it also affects everyone who is on the ship with you. In other words, your relationship with the Lord Jesus will have an affect on everyone who is a part of your life. Jonah's actions cost the ship owner, as he had to throw his cargo into the sea. Jonah's actions placed the sailor's lives in danger. Jonah saying "no" to God didn't just affect his life. While the sailors were in fear for their lives Jonah was asleep. The reason Jonah could sleep in the middle of this storm is because he knew that God's will always comes to pass. Jonah knew he was going to preach in Nineveh because this is what God said he was going to do. No storm will change the will of God, therefore Jonah did not fear this storm and so all his running away really amounted to nothing. Running away from God did not remove the call of God on Jonah's life. Running away from God did not change God's mind or His will. It didn't work for Jonah and it will not work for anyone else.

There are times when I have, figuratively speaking, run away from God, but I knew that I would do what God asked of me and this is because God is always going to move His children to the place of obedience. Why? Because this is the place where God pours out His blessings on His children.

God convinced Jonah that he should go and preach to Nineveh. Jonah went to Nineveh and preached and a great revival took place. Many people repented and called on the Lord seeking forgiveness and salvation. 120,000 children were saved from judgment. What a blessing. Fulfillment comes in a relationship with the Lord Jesus. If you desire to know this kind of blessing in your life is begins by saying "yes" to the Lord Jesus when He calls.

CHAPTER FOURTEEN

Jonah 2

"And the word of the LORD came unto Jonah the second time, saying, Arise, go unto Nineveh, that great city, and preach unto it the preaching that I bid thee. So Jonah arose, and went unto Nineveh, according to the word of the LORD. Now Nineveh was an exceedingly great city of three days journey. And Jonah began to enter into the city a days journey, and he cried, and said, Yet forty days, and Nineveh shall be overthrown. So the people of Nineveh believed God, and proclaimed a fast, and put on sackcloth, from the greatest of them even to the least of them. For word came unto the king of Nineveh, and he arose from his throne, and he laid his robe from him, and covered him with sackcloth, and sat in ashes. And he caused it to be proclaimed and published through Nineveh by the decree of the king and his nobles, saying, Let neither man nor beast, herd nor flock, taste anything: let them not feed, nor drink water: but let man and beast be covered with sackcloth, and cry mightily unto God: yea, let them turn every one from his evil way, and from the violence that is in their hands. Who can tell if God will turn and repent, and turn away from His fierce anger, that we perish not? And God saw their works, that they turned from their evil way; and God repented of the evil, that He had said that He would do unto them; and He did it not. But it displeased Jonah exceedingly, and he was very angry." Jonah 3; 4:1 KJV

In teaching believers how to pray the Lord Jesus instructs,

"After this manner therefore pray ye: Our Father which art in heaven, Hallowed be Thy name. <u>Thy will be done in earth, as it is in</u>

heaven." Matthew 6:9-10 KJV

The first priority in prayer is for the believer to seek God's will and yet how many Christians actually do? I would postulate that many people mistakenly believe that prayer is an attempt to bend God to our will and not the other way around. The first priority of prayer is to seek God's will which is why believers are called followers. Christians follow God. He leads and we follow, but what do people define as living by faith in the Lord Jesus? What do many people consider following the Lord Jesus?

From what I have witnessed in my years serving in the ministry some people think the Christian faith is pretending to obey the rules while giving lip service to God through feigned prayers so that He will pour out blessings, while for the most part, what these men and women really desire is for the Lord Jesus to stay out of their lives unless of course He intends to give them blessings. Something along the lines of, "bless me Lord and then just leave me alone." This is the impression I get when I see some Hollywood star or famous musician receiving some worthless award where they stand up and say, "I want to thank my friends and my family, and everyone who had a part in making this happen, and, oh yeah, I also want to say thank you to the Man upstairs." This is the impression I get from some famous country singer who makes millions of dollars writing and singing songs praising beer drinking and womanizing and then decides to put Amazing Grace on their latest album. Their homage to God just doesn't seem sincere, but this particular brand of hypocrisy is not limited to the rich and famous. Just about everybody plays this game at one time or another.

We make a pretense of loving God and living by faith when the truth is, we, for the most part, are going through the motions and mouthing words we do not mean hoping this will result in God's blessings on our lives. I am not trying to appear cynical about people's faith. I am trying to present an honest assessment of the games people play when it comes to God. I personally do not buy into people's baloney even when I am the

143

person slinging the baloney; especially when I am the person slinging the baloney and so I assess people with the same measure that I assess my own life and if I see hypocrisy within my own life I am certainly not going to believe that I am the only hypocrite in the world.

What is the point? The manner of most people's lives, according to my estimation, is that people are not honest when it comes to genuinely seeking God and seeking God's will for their lives. I believe when it comes to religious machinations, most people are trying to bend God to their will and they call this following Jesus. What makes me believe this? The number of people who claim to live by faith in the Lord Jesus and how uninvolved they are in the Lord's work. I'm not doubting that these men and women have a form of love for the Lord Jesus or that they honestly desire to receive eternal life, but I do doubt the extent and the depth of their love and faithfulness. The Lord Jesus expressed what I am saying best in the parable of the sower.

"He also that received the seed among thorns is he that heareth the word; and the cares of this world, and the deceitfulness of riches, choke the word, and he becometh unfruitful." Matthew 13:22 KJV

I believe the Bible expresses the same idea in the book of Isaiah.

"Wherefore the Lord said, Forsasmuch as this people draw near to me with their mouth, and with their lips do honor me, but have removed their heart far from me, and their fear toward me is taught by the precept of men." Isaiah 29:13 KJV

"Ye hypocrites, well did Isaiah prophesy of you, saying, This people draweth nigh unto me with their mouth, and honoreth me with their lips; but their heart is far from me. But in vain do they worship me, teaching for doctrines the commandments of men." Matthew 15:7-9 KJV

There are many people like Jonah in that they are all right with God's will as long as it aligns itself with what they want to do. There are many people who suppose themselves to be all right with God's will as long as it adheres to their particular brand of theology, but the minute God calls upon him or her to move in a direction they do not want to go they flee. What did Jonah do the minute God's will for his life took a turn he was unwilling to take? He ran in the opposite direction. Do you suppose that if Jonah prayed according to the Lord's prayer, "Our Father who art in heaven, Thy will be done," that he genuinely meant it? I do not doubt that Jonah loved God and I do not doubt that Jonah had a real desire to serve, but what I do have doubts about is Jonah's resolve, and looking at Jonah's example I have surmised that if Jonah struggled when it came to following the Lord's direction for his life then the rest of us may have a few struggles of our own as well.

Jonah made a mistake when he decided he was not going to do what God had willed for his life and he broke fellowship with God and the very same thing happens when a believer leaves off pursuing God's will. The thing about this is, just about everyone at one time or another has said "no" to God. By writing this I am not standing in judgment of anyone because I include myself in this estimation. I know my own shortcomings and failures all too well. I know the times I have left off what I knew the Holy Spirit was calling me to do to pursue my own stubborn will. I know the depths of my own sin more than any other person, but I also know that I am not alone in the world. Everybody makes mistakes. Everyone has done something stupid and sinful at one time or another and we say "no" to God and break fellowship with Him, and with family, and with the church, and we try to run away, and though we may imagine that we have abandoned God, He has not nor ever will abandon us.

"But if we believe not, yet He abideth faithful: He cannot deny Him-self." 2 Timothy 2:13 KJV

"Let your conversation be without covetousness; and be content with such things as ye have: for He hath said, I will never leave thee, nor

forsake thee." Hebrews 13:5 KJV

God does not abandon His children. This is what we can see in God's interaction with Jonah. God instructed Jonah to go to Nineveh but he refused. Jonah ran away, but then he ran right into the heart of a storm. The mariners cast Jonah into the sea where he was swallowed up whole by a great fish. Jonah was in the belly of that great fish for three days and three nights and while there Jonah had a change of heart and he prayed.

"But I will sacrifice unto Thee with the voice of thanksgiving; I will pay that that I have vowed. Salvation is of the LORD. And the LORD spake unto the fish, and it vomited out Jonah upon the dry land. And the word of the LORD came unto Jonah the second time, saying, Arise, go unto Nineveh, that great city, and preach unto it the preaching that I bid thee." Jonah 2:9- 3:1-2 KJV

In response to Jonah's repentance the Lord renewed the calling on Jonah's life. When Jonah was in the belly of that great fish he had a "come to Jesus," moment, which is exactly what he did. Jonah did not believe he was going to make it and in his despair he called out to God and God answered. The fish spit Jonah up on dry land. Jonah found deliverance from death and Jonah also found God renewing the call on his life, in effect giving Jonah a second chance; a second chance at life and a second chance to fulfill his calling. In the very same way the believer will find redemption and salvation in a relationship with the Lord Jesus. Through repentance and faith the believer is given a second chance at life and a new opportunity to fulfill his or her calling.

In the same way that God rescued Jonah from certain death and renewed the calling on his life, God rescues the believer from the depths of sin and despair which is certain death and then issues or renews the divine calling on his or her life. Through the Lord Jesus all who call on His name are given a second chance to respond in faith and obedience and in so doing we are given the opportunity to live our lives according to God's will which is more than just having a second chance at life, because fulfilling our calling impacts our eternity. To restate: the Lord Jesus can and will rescue and redeem the repentant person and deliver him or her from the depths of sin and despair and through redemption give this person a second chance at making their lives count, and this will also impact every other person his or her life may influence. God gave Jonah a second chance and He is willing to do the very same thing for any person who desires to live for Him.

God is gracious and patient and kind and there are times He not only gives people second chances, but third chances, and fourth, and so on. God is patient and gracious and willing to work in us, through us, and with us as long as we are willing to continue forward with Him by faith and through repentance, and often through the many chances God allows us to have, these do not just lead to new opportunities to engage in the will of God, but in pursuing the will of God He often, through renewal, gives men and women the opportunity to do things he or she may have failed at the first time. There are times God allows us to do things right that we may have done wrong the first time. Here is what I am telling you. When you set your heart to answer God's call on your life, and you set your heart to do God's will with your life, not only do you receive a second chance to answer the call, but God may also give you a second chance at having a family, or a second chance at having a successful career doing something you enjoy.

All through the Bible you will find stories of God's grace leading to restoration. Naomi lost her family by doing things her own way, but God in His grace brought Ruth into Naomi's life which gave Naomi a second chance at having a family. Moses was in the wrong when he decided he was going to free Israel in his own strength, but God restored Moses and gave him a second chance to lead the nation of Israel out of bondage.

God giving His children second chances extends beyond the borders of our calling. God's second chances have to do with every aspect of our lives. When you set your heart to do things

God's way by listening to Him and following His direction for your life then God works to restore and rebuild your life. When a person genuinely desires to see God's will come to pass, all of his or her life will be blessed.

This is not to say that believers do not endure difficult circumstances. Life is difficult at times for all people, but in the difficult times the believer is assured of the presence of God through the Holy Spirit and the believer rests in the knowledge that difficult times will not last. Hard times are temporary. God is eternal. Another way to think of this is, even when times are not so good God is always good and living by faith in the Lord Jesus makes life worth living.

God rescued Jonah from the belly of the great fish and renewed the call on his life. Not only did God rescue and restore Jonah, but God also blessed Jonah's ministry with success. The people of Nineveh responded to Jonah's preaching and repented.

"So the people of Nineveh believed God, and proclaimed a fast, and put on sackcloth, from the greatest of them even to the least of them." Jonah 3:5 KJV

"And God saw their works, that they turned from their evil way; and God repented of the evil, that He said He would do unto them; and He did it not." Jonah 3:10 KJV

The true extent of God's success through Jonah's preaching is found in Jonah 4:11.

"And should I not spare Nineveh, that great city, wherein are more than six score thousand persons (120,000) *that cannot discern between their right hand and their left hand; and also much cattle."* Jonah 4:11 KJV (Parenthesis and underline mine)

In describing these 120,000 people who cannot discern between their left hand and their right the Lord is saying that there were 120,000 children in this city who were saved in addition to all the adults who were spared and the livestock. Jonah's preaching did exactly what God intended it to do. It moved men and women to repentance and faith which delivered them from the devastating judgment of God. Jonah's preaching saved a lot of people and livestock from physical and eternal destruction and delivered them to the place of living under God's grace and blessings.

It is important to note this fact: though God forgives, cleanses of sin, and restores people to their calling and ministry, there are men and women who will never allow you to forget your past and it is these same men and women who will never fail to call the legitimacy of your calling into question. These men and women have as their agenda stopping believers from fulfilling their calling and doing what God desires them to do. This is important to understand because believers also need to know that someone else's opinion does not remove or change the calling of God on their life. What is more, the opinions of other people cannot keep God's blessings from your life. If you genuinely desire to live your life to the glory of the Lord Jesus by answering the call of God on your life, exercising the gifts of the Spirit, and following God's will then you must set your heart to serve God by answering the call no matter what anyone else may think or do.

"My brethren, be not many masters, knowing that we shall receive the greater condemnation." James 3:1 KJV

Clearly any man or woman who proposes to teach the Bible must withstand greater scrutiny on their lives. Any person who sets his or her heart to follow the Lord in obedience will open himself or herself up to criticism and judgment, but as my dad used to say, "They do not build statues to honor critics, just to those who have the tenacity to withstand them." Many times I have been the object of criticism and scorn. At one time I received an instant message that said, "You should never be allowed to preach or teach the Bible ever again." God did not send that message. That message originated from a different source. Imagine if someone decided that Jonah's first reaction to God's instruction to go to Nineveh should have disqualified him from ever preaching again? What would have been the fate of those 120,000 children? Which is why I will always say to those who criticize me, "If I don't go out and preach the gospel who will? Will you?" The truth is I have never yet seen even one person who was in the habit of criticizing believers answer the call themselves.

The calling the Holy Spirit has placed on your life was not given to you to please critical people. The calling God has placed on your life is to fulfill His will and when you allow God to work in and through you in the power of the Holy Spirit, God will provide the results. **Damn the critics; God's will be done!**

The results of Jonah's preaching not only led to the salvation of a great many people, but God was preparing the way for those men and women who would be led away captive by Assyria. The northern ten tribes of Israel were defeated and captured by Assyria in 720 BC. These are the same Assyrians we see responding to the Lord in the book of Jonah. Which means there were people in Assyria, and in Nineveh who believed in, and belonged to God and these men and women would receive God's people Israel and treat them mercifully. God's reasons for sending Jonah to Nineveh were very important. Not only was God looking to save a great many people, but He was also looking out for the livelihood of His people Israel.

Here is where the light should come on for the believer because the very same situation is at work in each believer's individual ministry. What the Lord Jesus has called and empowered you to do through the Holy Spirit's presence is very important to the care and livelihood of God's people, and the church is God's people. Nothing God calls anyone to do is unimportant.

"But now God hath set the members every one of them in the body, as it hath pleased Him. And if they were all one member, where were the body? But now are they many members, yet but one body. And the eye cannot say unto the hand, I have no need of thee: nor again the head to the feet, I have no need of you. Nay, much more those

members of the body, which seem to be more feeble, are necessary; and those members of the body, which we think to be less honorable, upon these we bestow more abundant honor; and our uncomely parts have more abundant comliness. For our comely parts have no need; but God hath tempered the body together, having given more abundant honor to that part which lacked: that there should be no schism in the body; but that the members should have the same care one for another. And whether one member suffer, all the members suffer with it; or one member be honored, all the members rejoice with it. Now ye are the body of Christ, and members in particular."
1 Corinthians 12:18-27 KJV

1 Corinthians 12 is the apostle Paul's way of saying that we are all in this together and everyone in the church and what he or she does is important. The calling on your life is very important to the mission of the church. The calling on your life is important to the continued care, blessing, and livelihood of God's people. You are important and what you do has a real impact for God's glory and for the good of God's people.

God gave Jonah a second chance and God blessed Jonah's preaching in Nineveh, but Jonah was not happy about the results.

"But it displeased Jonah exceedingly, and he was very angry." Jonah 4:1 KJV

Unfortunately Jonah could not let go of his animosity toward the people of Nineveh.

"And he prayed unto the LORD, and said, I pray thee, O LORD, was this not my saying, when I was yet in my country? Therefore I fled before unto Tarshish: for I knew that Thou art a gracious God, and merciful, and slow to anger, and of great kindness, and repentest Thee of evil. Therefore now, O LORD, take, I beseech Thee, my life from me; for it is better for me to die than to live." Jonah 4:2-3 KJV

Jonah would rather die than to see God's blessings on the

people of Nineveh. Jonah was so invested in his bigotry and prejudice that he could not even enjoy the blessings God was pouring out through his life and calling. Some men and women, though they are serving according to the will of God cannot or will not let go of their old hatred and animosity and this will absolutely steal their joy.

CHAPTER FIFTEEN

Jonah 3

"And God saw their works, that they turned from their evil way; and God repented of the evil, that He had said that He would do unto them; and He did it not. But it displeased Jonah exceedingly, and he was very angry." Jonah 3:10; 4:1 KJV

The prophet Jonah presents us with an interesting example of a believer. Jonah loved the Lord and he was a man called to be a prophet of God. Jonah ministered in the name of God and in this capacity he proclaimed God's judgment as well as God's grace. When God moved Jonah to preach he was either an instrument of grace and blessings or he could be an instrument that would strike fear and trepidation into the hearts of men. Which displays that a calling from God is in no way a minor thing no matter how it manifests itself in those who are called. It is important to note that all believers have a calling from God on their lives. God works in His children, who are surrendered to His will, as an agent of grace or to strike fear into the hearts of the unrepentant. This is exactly how the Lord Jesus described the ministry of the Holy Spirit who operates in and through the church.

"Nevertheless I tell you the truth; It is expedient for you that I go away: for if I do not go away the Comforter will not come unto you; but if I depart I will send Him unto you. <u>And when He is come, He will reprove the world of sin, and of righteousness, and of judgment</u>: Of sin, because they believe not on Me; Of righteousness, because I go to My Father, and ye see Me no more; Of judgment, because the

prince of this world is judged." John 16:7-11 KJV (Underline mine)

The Comforter the Lord sent at Pentecost is the Holy Spirit who now resides in all believers who now comprise the church. Thus the ministry of the believers through the church is marked by the ministry of the Holy Spirit Who reproves the world of sin, of righteousness, and of judgment. The church made up of men and women who minister in the name of Jesus will either be received as a blessing from God or it will remind people of God's immanent judgment. This does not mean that believers are to tower over others preaching hell fire and brimstone. What this means is that as believers live their lives to glorify the Savior the Holy Spirit will use our testimony to show grace and be a blessing or He will use our testimony to convict the unrepentant of sin and the coming judgment of God.

The interesting thing about Jonah is that he does not really seem to desire that his ministry find success. Matthew Henry has made this observation in his commentary on the book of Jonah. [2]"What a strange sort of man was Jonah, to dread the success of his ministry."

"And he prayed unto the LORD, was this not my saying, when I was yet in my country? Therefore I fled before unto Tarshish: for I knew that thou art a gracious God, and merciful, slow to anger, and of great kindness, and repentest Thee of the evil." Jonah 4:2 KJV (Underline mine)

The very reason Jonah ran away from God is because he knew God is merciful and he also knew that his preaching in Nineveh would be successful. Which means Jonah did not desire the people of Nineveh to experience the grace of God. Jonah did not desire the people of Nineveh to have the opportunity to repent and thereby experience God's mercy and to receive salvation. This same thing could be said of any man or woman who refuses to answer the call of God on his or her life. By neglecting to present the gospel of the Lord Jesus a person is displaying that he or she does not truly desire for people to be saved. Jonah was more fixated on his hatred and animosity toward Nineveh than he was focused on his calling and ministry. Jonah was more interested in practicing hate than he was in doing the Lord's work. Jonah hated the people of Nineveh so much that he became angry at the thought of any of them being redeemed and when a great revival took place, instead of rejoicing in the Lord, he became angry.

"But it displeased Jonah exceedingly, and he was very angry." Jonah 4:1 KJV

The question I would ask of Jonah, if possible, is the very same question God puts to him in verse 4.

"Then said the LORD, Doest thou well to be angry?" Jonah 4:4 KJV

An honest answer to this question will help us to think twice when we get angry. An honest answer to this question will serve to guide the believer when he or she gets put out with God, because this does happen. There are times when, through our own misconceptions and unreal expectations, or unrealized expectations, we imagine that God has failed us in someway which leads to getting put out with God. In all honesty there have been times that I have gotten angry with God. This doesn't mean that God has ever wronged me or failed me. What this means is that there have been times in my life when I have made a mistake or had a misconception and in those times when things did not work out in the way I had imagined they should, I chose to believe that God had dropped the ball, or worse that He didn't truly care; but the truth is that God was working all things out according to His perfect and pleasing will. The truth is that God was working all things to His glory which then led to blessings on my life. It was just that God was doing His will in His own way, which He can because He is God, but in-between my prayers and my circumstances and God's answer I got myself all out of sorts by letting my imagination run away with me. Still, at the conclusion of the matter after God has enacted His will in His way, and I see the perfection in which God has done something, and see how everything works out for my good and God's glory, I find myself repenting for my poor attitude and the resulting reaction. No matter what I may imagine about God I always find myself coming to the place of realizing that God is God and I am not and that His way will always be the best way. I always come to this place because this is the place the Holy Spirit is always going to lead the believer. The Holy Spirit will always lead us home to our Lord. The Holy Spirit always guides prodigals back to the Father.

When first coming to the Lord Jesus I had many misconceptions concerning the Lord's will for my life and as a consequence I spent a lot of time being angry with God, but as I have grown older and having spent time walking with the Lord, and growing in spiritual maturity, and seeing the Lord at work in my life I am now less prone to getting bent out of shape when I cannot reconcile the direction the Holy Spirit is moving as opposed to what I might imagine God should do. In other words, after many years of struggle I am now able to simply lift my concerns and circumstances up to God and trust Him as He moves in whatever way He will. Still, there have been some times over the years when I have prayed some prayers filled with anger much as Jonah does, but in those times we find ourselves getting angry with God and in those times we find ourselves praying in a way that is not good; God can handle it. Listen to the tenor of Jonah's prayer.

"And he prayed unto the LORD, and said, I pray thee O LORD, was not this my saying, when I was yet in my country? Therefore I fled before unto Tarshish: for I knew that Thou art a gracious God, and merciful, slow to anger, and of great kindness, and repentest Thee of the evil. <u>Therefore, now O LORD, take I beseech Thee, my life from me; for it is better to die than to live.</u>" Jonah 4:2-3 KJV (Underline mine)

Jonah told the Lord that he would rather die than to see Nineveh saved from destruction. This prayer is not in accord with the will of God. It is not God's will or intention to destroy people's lives, not Nineveh's or Jonah's, not even if Jonah is angry with Him.

"And it came to pass, when the time was come that He should be received up, He steadfastly set His face to go to Jerusalem, and sent messengers before His face: and they went, and entered into a village of the Samaritans, to make ready for Him. And they did not receive Him, because His face was as though He would go to Jerusalem. And when His disciples James and John saw this, they said, Lord, wilt Thou that we command fire to come down from heaven, and consume them, even as Elijah did? But He turned, and rebuked them, and said, <u>Ye know not what manner of spirit ye are of. For the Son of Man is not come to destroy men's lives, but to save them.</u> And they went to another village." Luke 9:51-56 KJV (Underline mine)

Jonah prayed in the way that he did because he was holding on to a deep-seated hatred toward the people of Assyria and Nineveh. Jonah prayed what he did because he did not want any of these men and women saved from destruction, not even their children. Imagine a hatred so deep that it moves a person to desire to see little babies killed. This is ungodly. This is satanic and this attitude has no place in the heart of a believer. Jonah knew only hatred for Nineveh and so he prayed and told the Lord that he would rather die than to see these people delivered from destruction. This is not a righteous prayer to pray, but how did the Lord respond to Jonah's prayer? God responded to Jonah with patience and love. When you find yourself praying like Jonah and you are angry with God, God continues to love you and He often responds with patience and love.

God asks Jonah, *"Doest thou well to be angry?"* (Vs. 4). God is not being harsh with Jonah. God is exercising patience. God is as gracious and patient with Jonah as He is with the people of Nineveh. Jonah may be put out with God, but God is not put out with Jonah. Jonah in his angry state of mind leaves the city of Nineveh and builds himself a lean-to on a hill that overlooks the city. Jonah is going to watch and see what happens to this city and these people. Jonah is waiting to see if God is going to destroy this city or not, but he knows the Lord is not going to destroy Nineveh.

"And God saw their works, that they turned from their evil way; and God repented of the evil, that He had said He would do unto them; and He did it not." Jonah 3:10 KJV

"So Jonah went out of the city and sat on the east side of the city, and there made him a booth, and sat under it in the shadow, till he might see what would become of the city. And the LORD God prepared a gourd, and made it come up over Jonah, that it might be a shadow over his head, to deliver him from his grief. So Jonah was exceedingly glad of the gourd." Jonah 4:5-6 KJV

Even though Jonah was angry with God and mad at the world, and in this state of mind prayed an angry prayer, God is still showing Jonah mercy and kindness. Even though Jonah is not acting the way a man of God should God continues to love him. Even though Jonah is acting like a child stewing in his own personal hatred toward people he doesn't even know, God is still taking care of him.

There are times when we are not at our best. There are times that believers don't act according to the love of God that resides in their hearts. There are Christians who love the Lord Jesus and yet they continue to harbor resentment toward others which is according to unsound reasoning, and even in this they are still loved by God.

How often do we presume that God is just like us and in this presumption we believe that, because we don't care for someone God must not care about them either? When I look at Jonah I see a reflection of myself. There are times I have camped out on a little hillside, figuratively speaking, waiting to see if God would take care of someone I didn't really care for, and much to my consternation I find God forgives them and loves them and continues to care for and to bless them. The whole time I am waiting and hoping God will judge, all I am doing is robbing myself of joy.

What satisfaction is there in the destruction of others? The answer is: none. Any satisfaction a person may derive from seeing something terrible happen to someone else, even if we feel they deserve it, is fleeting at best. Just as soon as one person that bothers you exits your life, in walks another, and the remedy for this situation is not to hope for the destruction of our enemies; the only way to experience true joy in life is to search out God's blessings for everyone including those people we may consider something less than a friend.

"Ye have heard that it hath been said, Thou shalt love thy neighbor, and hate thine enemy. But I say unto you, Love your enemies, bless them that curse you, do good to them which despitefully use you, and persecute you; that ye may be the children of your Father which is in heaven: for He maketh His sun to rise on the evil and the good, and sendeth rain on the just and the unjust." Matthew 5:43-45 KJV

"So Jonah went out of the city, and sat on the east side of the city, and there made him a booth, and sat under it in the shadow, til he might see what would become of the city. And the LORD God prepared a gourd, and made it to come up over Jonah, that it might be a shadow over his head, to deliver him from his grief. So Jonah was exceedingly glad of the gourd. But God prepared a worm when the morning rose the next day, and it smote the gourd that it withered. And it came to pass, when the sun did arise, that God prepared a vehement east wind; and the sun beat upon the head of Jonah, that he fainted, and wished in himself to die, and said, It is better for me to die than to live." Jonah 4:5-8 KJV

The area of Syria around the city of Nineveh is hot, windy, and dry. I live in an area of Northern Oklahoma which can, at times, be hot, windy, and dry and these circumstances can make life seem miserable especially if you find yourself out in the weather all day. God gave Jonah some relief from the elements and this made him happy, but then God took away Jonah's source of comfort which made him angry all over again. God then asks again, *"Doest thou well to be angry?"* but adds, *"For the gourd?"* (Vs. 9) The question may be better phrased in this way: "Do you have any right to be angry?" When the question is put in this way it really gets to the heart of the matter. **Do you have any right to be angry?**

"And God said to Jonah, Doest thou well to be angry for the gourd? And he said, I do well to be angry, even unto death. Then said the LORD, *Thou hast had pity on the gourd, <u>for the which thou hast not labored, neither madest it grow</u>; which came up in a night and perished in a night: and should I not spare Nineveh, that great city, wherein are more than six-score thousand persons* (120,000 people) *that cannot discern between their right hand and their left hand; and also much cattle?"* Jonah 4:9-11 KJV (Underline and parenthesis mine)

The Lord rightly points out to Jonah that he has had more compassion and concern for a little vine, something that sprang up over night and was gone the next day, than for the thousands of people in Nineveh. Jonah is more concerned with his own welfare and comfort than he is concerned with the welfare and well-being of, not only the people of Nineveh, but also the livestock. Jonah did not have any right whatsoever to be angry with God. Both the vine and the people of Nineveh were God's creation and God's concern and Jonah was a part of God's plan not the master of it.

How many Christians are a lot like Jonah in their attitudes in that they find themselves more concerned about their own well-being and comfort and have more compassion for things that do not matter than they are concerned with the redemption and salvation of others? How many of God's children are angry and brooding because they do not believe their life is as good as it ought to be and they use this as an excuse to abandon their calling and ministry? How many Christians are more concerned with their comfort than they are concerned about their neighbors, their family, and their friends?

Jonah clearly had misplaced priorities but there are many others who are just the same. There are men and women who believe that all of life including the faith is all about them and what they desire for their lives and what they want to do. These men and women have no concern whatsoever with the will of God or those things that concern the Lord Jesus? Which brings us back to God's question to Jonah which all believers may rightly ask of themselves. Do we have any right to be angry about anything that God chooses to do in His own world with His own creation which includes us? Shouldn't God's children love what He loves? Shouldn't God's children be concerned with what God is concerned with?

Misplaced anger will rob you of your joy. No person has any right to be angry with God about anything because God can do whatever He desires, being that He is God. No person has any right to be angry with God when He chooses to bless instead of destroy because His grace, mercy, and kindness extend to everyone, even those people we might think don't deserve to be loved. No person deserves God's love which is why it is defined by grace. The next time you find yourself being put out with God just take a step back and ask yourself this question: do I have any right to be angry? And then give some honest thought to your answer and you will soon realize what the answer to the question is.

CHAPTER SIXTEEN

John the Baptist

Its OK to be Weird

"In those days came John the Baptist, preaching in the wilderness of Judea, and saying, Repent ye: for the kingdom of heaven is at hand. For this is he that was spoken of by the prophet Isaiah, saying, The voice of one crying in the wilderness, Prepare ye the way of the Lord, make His paths straight. And the same John had is raiment of camel's hair, and a learthern girdle about his loins; and his meat was locust and wild honey." Matthew 3:1-4 KJV

Every believer has a calling from God and every believer has been equipped and empowered for the ministry through the indwelling presence of the Holy Spirit. God has something in mind for everyone's life. God has something He desires everyone to do with his or her life which corresponds to His kingdom work that is progressing throughout the world. This means every believer matters. What you do with your life as a follower of Christ Jesus matters. The people your life will impact and influence matters. The only way to ensure that your life will have the right influence and impact on the world and on others is to genuinely live for the Lord Jesus as you use your time, your talents, and your gifts of the Spirit to further the kingdom of God.

An integral part of how much impact your life and calling with the gifts and talents will have is your own personality. God created all people to be unique and individual. Which means everyone has their own distinct personality. No two people are exactly alike. Sometimes we may imagine that because two people look similar they must have similar personalities, but to know that this is not true all you have to do is spend some time interacting with twins. They may look alike but you will soon find that their personalities are very different. Why is this? Because God does not need or desire two of the very same people in His creation. Jacob and Esau were twins and yet these two men could not have been any more different.

"And the boys grew, and Esau was a cunning hunter, a man of the field; and Jacob was a plain man, dwelling in tents." Genesis 25:27 KJV

Another reason no two people are exactly alike is because we are all individual living souls who are also created in the image of God.

"And God said, Let us make man in our image, after our likeness." Genesis 1:26 KJV

Notice that in Genesis 1:26 God says, "Let us," and not, "Let Me," and this is because God is triune in nature. What this means is that God exists in three persons. There is God the Father, God the Son, and God the Holy Spirit. Each member of the Trinity is an individual having His own personality and yet each member of the Trinity is also fully God. Mankind is also triune in nature in that we have a body, a soul, and a spirit. The spirit that now inhabits the believer is the Holy Spirit. It is our soul that makes us individually who we are. The soul is the place where our personality originates. The soul is also the place where our emotions emanate and our soul affects every part of who we are. As a child of God the Holy Spirit will have the greatest impact on your soul.

"And so it is written, The first man Adam was made a living soul: the last Adam (The Lord Jesus) *was made a quickening* (Life giving) *Spirit. Howbeit that was not first which is spiritual, but that which is natural; and afterward that which is spiritual. The first man is*

of the earth, earthy: the second man is the Lord from heaven. As in the earthy, such are they also that are earthy: and as in the heavenly, such are they also that are heavenly. And as we have borne the image of the earthy, we shall also bear the image of the heavenly." 1 Corinthians 15:45-49 KJV (Parenthesis mine)

These verses in 1 Corinthians present that the saved person's soul is now affected to a greater degree by the life-giving presence of the Holy Spirit. Though there are occasions when believers may act worldly and lean toward the flesh and stumble, this is not the overall pattern of the Christian's life. The point I wish to emphasize is that it is our soul that makes us who we are. The soul is the place where everything that makes us distinctly who we are resides and it also has an affect on the calling on our lives. Your personality is an integral part of what God has called and gifted you to do with your life. A great example of this is found in John the Baptist. John's personality and his manner of life set him apart and it affected the reach and the impact of his ministry.

John the Baptist was the prophesied forerunner of the Messiah. As such he was called and set apart by God before even being born. John the Baptist was a Nazarite from birth. The Bible informs us that he was filled with the Holy Spirit in his mother's womb.

"But the angel said unto him, Fear not, Zacarias: for thy prayer is heard: and thy wife Elisabeth shall bear thee a son, and thou shalt call his name John. And thou shalt have joy and gladness; and many shall rejoice at his birth. For he shall be great in the sight of the Lord, and shall drink neither wine nor strong drink; and he shall be filled with the Holy Ghost, even from his mother's womb." Luke 1:13-15 KJV

Being filled with the Holy Spirit while in the womb is unique. It only occurred with John. John the Baptist is a very important part of the Lord's first coming. John the Baptist was the voice of one calling out in the wilderness.

"For this is he that was spoken of by the prophet Isaiah, saying, The voice of one calling in the wilderness, Prepare ye the way of the Lord, make his paths straight." Matthew 3:3 KJV

The Lord Jesus declared that John the Baptist was the greatest of all the prophets.

"Verily I say unto you, Among them that are born of women there hath not risen a greater than John the Baptist." Matthew 11:11 KJV

The Old Testament book of Malachi paints a picture of John the Baptist and his ministry. The name Malachi means, "My messenger." The contents of this little book are focused on the message of repentance. The message of the book of Malachi is the very message John came preaching in the wilderness. This message is summed up in this: *"Repent, for the kingdom of heaven is at hand."* (Vs 2)

"Behold I will send My messenger, and he shall prepare the way before Me: and the Lord, whom ye seek, shall suddenly come to His temple, even the messenger of the covenant, whom ye delight in: behold, He shall come, saith the LORD if hosts." Malachi 3:1 KJV

The ministry of John the Baptist is unique in every way and it had a great impact. God used John and his uniqueness to get people's attention.

"Then went out to him Jerusalem, and all Judea, and all the region round about Jordan, and were baptized of him in Jordan, confessing their sins." Matthew 3:5-6 KJV

How did God use John to get people's attention? There were a lot of itinerant preachers in John's day. There were many men who placed themselves before the populace claiming to have some great authority or some great power from God.

"But there was a certain man, called Simon, which before-time in the same city used sorcery, and bewitched the people of Samaria, giving out that himself was some great one." Acts 8:9 KJV

If there is one situation you will find over and over again it is men and women trying to impress others by making themselves out to be something special when they are not. There were men in John's day that pretended to be prophets, but God doesn't work in the manner that men do. When God desires to get people's attention He sometimes does this by calling the most eccentric from among us and He will use their eccentricities to capture and hold our attention. This is so that no one will miss or mistake the message. God used the unusual personality and personal habits of John the Baptist to get Jerusalem and Israel's attention. John's personality was very important to the success of his ministry.

"For this is he that was spoken of by the prophet Isaiah, saying, The voice of one crying in the wilderness, Prepare ye the way of the Lord, make His paths straight. And the same John had his raiment of camel's hair, and a leather girdle about his loins; and his meat was locust and wild honey." Matthew 3:3-4 KJV (Underline mine)

John the Baptist was not your ordinary run of the mill sort of prophet. He was a man who dressed himself in a camel skin coat all tied up with a leather belt and his choice of cuisine was grass hoppers dipped in wild honey. In addition to this John did not care one bit about what other people thought of his manner of life. John the Baptist wore rough clothing and ate wild food. He would take a grass hopper and dip and chew right in front of you and even in his day many people found him to be a little, "off." He was unusual. He was weird and this is what God used to get people's attention. John was so different he even managed to capture the attention of the high and mighty religious leaders in Jerusalem. God gifted John with the gift of preaching, but God then tied this together with his personality and personal habits to get people's attention in order to get the message out.

John the Baptist was also the last in the order of the Old Testament prophet. John was the last prophet before the first advent of the Lord Jesus who is now our eternal Prophet, Priest, and King. John the Baptist then is the last in the Old Testament order of prophets because this ministry is now fulfilled in the Lord Jesus. Even being in the order of the Old Testament prophet John did not fit into the mold of what people in his day might consider a prophet should be. Then again, John did resemble a prophet in a way and remind people of a certain Old Testament prophet.

"And the same John had his raiment of camel's hair, and a leather girdle about his loins." Matthew 3:4 KJV

"And they answered him, He was a hairy man, and girt with a girdle of leather about his loins. And he said, It is Elijah the Tishbite." 2 Kings 1:8 KJV

The description of John and Elijah sound very similar. Why do you suppose John was moved to dress in the way that he did? Because the Lord wanted people to recognize him as the Elijah who was to come. He was not the old testament Elijah because there is only one Elijah, but John certainly reminded Israel of Elijah and why was this? God wanted to get people's attention so they would recognize him as the prophesied forerunner of the King.

John did not dress like anyone else and he did not eat like anyone else and the way he interacted with others displays that he had little to no regard for their opinions either.

"But when he saw many of the Pharisees and Sadducees come to his baptism, he said unto them, O generation of vipers, who hath warned you to flee from the wrath to come? Matthew 3:7 KJV

When all the religious leaders in Jerusalem heard about this wild man down at the river preaching and baptizing people they were moved to go and see what it was all about. When John sees these men coming his way he didn't hesitate in his estimation of their character. He called them a bunch of snakes. He didn't care at all about who they were or who they thought they were. John didn't count them as anything special because of their poise or position, but these religious leaders recognized that John was something.

"And when He (Jesus) was come into the temple, the chief priest and the elders of the people came unto Him and He was teaching, and said, By what authority doest Thou these things? And who gave Thee this authority? And Jesus answered and said unto them, I also will ask you one thing, which if ye tell Me, I in likewise will tell you by what authority I do these things. The baptism of John, when was it? From heaven, or of men? And they reasoned among themselves, saying, If we shall say, From heaven; He will say unto us, Why did ye not believe him? But if we shall say, Of men; we fear the people; for all hold John as a prophet. And they answered Jesus, and said, We cannot tell. And He said unto them, Neither tell I you by what authority I do these things." Matthew 21:23-27 KJV (Parenthesis and underline mine)

What a predicament. These men either had to affirm the testimony of John and thereby recognize Jesus as the Messiah, or offend the people and possibly lose their position in the synagogue, but one thing they did affirm is that they had heard and received John's message.

John was a fearless prophet and not just with the religious leaders in Israel. He also took the civic authorities to task over their sin.

"And many other things in his exhortation preached he unto the people. But Herod the Tetrarch, being reproved for Herodias his brother Philip's wife, and for all the evils he had done, added yet this above all, that he shut up John in prison." Luke 3:18-20 KJV (Underline mine)

The talking heads that are labeled as, "mainstream media" often thump their chest and say outlandish things claiming to speak truth to power, but they are only saying things that ensure their popularity among their peers. Saying things that win you praise and popularity is not being brave. Preaching truth that will ultimately cost you your head is true bravery. Why did John call out Herod and his wicked queen? Because this is exactly what God moved him to do. This is the reason God created John the Baptist. He was a man who got people's attention and what John's life amounts to is that it was memorable. Most everyone in the world knows who John the Baptist is and what his message was.

This is exactly the same way God has created and conditioned all His children to be. The things we do. The very things we like or dislike. How we interact in the world with others. The ability to be brave and bold. The ability to say what needs to be said or to hold our tongue in check when it is called for. The ability to not be affected by the approval or disapproval of others. The ability to live our lives in the way the Lord Jesus wants us to and the way the Holy Spirit moves us to live, which is in accordance with the dictates of our own personality; these are the things that leave a lasting impression. These are the things that make us memorable.

Though the Holy Spirit is in charge in our lives He always allows us the freedom to choose how we are going to live, but He also guides us into God's will and gives us the strength of character to live according to God's word. You can live exactly how you want to live and the truth is you will live exactly how you want to live. This means that the way you are living your life openly declares whether you are truly a child of God or not. Your desire as a child of God, being moved by the Holy Spirit, should be to live in such a way that honors the Lord Jesus, to the degree that you don't really consider what others may think or how they will react or respond to your witness or your rebuke, just like John the Baptist.

Maybe you are thinking, "I'm not John the Baptist." No, you are not, because there is only one John the Baptist, but you are who you are, having been created in the image of God for the glory of God, and you have been called and equipped, and empowered, and also engineered in the way that you are to do what

God intends for you to do with your life. So don't try to be John the Baptist. Don't run down to city hall and start calling all your city officials snakes, but do go out and be yourself as you do what it is God has called you to do. Go out and do what God has called and equipped you to do in the way you would do it, because the only person who can be you, is you.

God engineered John the Baptist in a way that he would get Israel's attention. John was a true prophet in the manner of the Old Testament prophets. He came and preached because this is what prophets do. Israel recognized and responded to John because this is what God intended to happen. John was perfectly suited for his calling and mission and in the same way, God has engineered you. By being who you are God will use your personality to capture people's attention and get His message out to people who are not you, but maybe they are somewhat like you. You are who you are because your life and who you are is going to get someone's attention.

You can really be yourself in Christ Jesus. In Jesus you are truly free. You never have to press yourself into some kind of mold to impress Jesus. You can do this to impress fallen and sinful human beings, but this is never going to impress the Lord Jesus. The Lord Jesus knows you better than you know yourself. When it comes to your living relationship with the Lord you don't have to pretend to be something you are not, and you don't have to pretend you are perfect and sinless. The Lord Jesus simply desires your love and service. He wants you to go and be what He has designed you to be, but in all this you do have to live by faith. To be a child of God you must come into a living relationship with God through faith in the Lord Jesus. To do this you call on Jesus in prayer and ask Him to save you.

CHAPTER SEVENTEEN

Joseph
(The Husband of Mary)

"Now the birth of Jesus Christ was on this wise: When as his mother Mary was espoused to Joseph, before they came together, she was found with child of the Holy Ghost. Then Joseph her husband, being a just man, and not willing to make her a public example, was minded to put her away privily. But while he thought on these things, behold, the angel of the Lord appeared unto him in a dream, saying, Joseph, thou son of David, fear not to take unto thee Mary thy wife: for that which is conceived in her is of the Holy Ghost." Matthew 1:18-20 KJV

Joseph was espoused to Mary the virgin God chose to carry Jesus His Son. Joseph was a just and a righteous man. This is what we know from the Bible.

"Then Joseph her husband, being a just man, and not willing to make her a public example, was minded to put her away privily." Matthew 1:19 KJV

The word translated "Just" in verse nineteen is translated from the Greek word ***Dikiaos***. According to the Complete Word Study Dictionary this word is used to describe, [3]"That which is expected as duty and which is claimed as a right because of one's conformity to the rules of God or society." To apply this description to a person is to describe someone who is conformable to what is just and right according to God or to society. The word "***Dikiaos***" describes the type of person who practices justice without deficiency or failure. Joseph being described as a just man means that he always did what was right in the eyes of God and in the eyes of men. Joseph lived up to God's standards. Joseph was a man who lived up to people's expectations which is a rarity among men.

Trust me when I tell you that serving in the pastorate I have found that I often fall short of God's standards and also of people's expectations. The reason I fall short of many people's expectations is due to people's expectations not aligning themselves with God's standards; neither do they conform to God's will. God's standards and His will and the things people believe about others and expect of others are not always one and the same. This became more apparent to me as I continued in my study of the word "*Dikiaos*."

This word describes someone who acts in accord with what is just and right, but where people get their ideas about what is just and right is what truly decides if a person is genuinely acting according to God's ways or in some other way. Not every person who attains to the world's label of just and right is just in the ways of God. It depends upon where a person's ideas about right and wrong come from and our ideas of right and wrong are often contingent upon what is allowed to influence our lives. There are two foundational sources of influence in our lives. There is Father God through the Holy Spirit and through the Word, or the world which lies under the influence and sway of Satan. You may parse this truth in many different ways but influence always comes down to these two foundational sources: God through His Holy Spirit and His Word or Satan through the devices and influence of the world.

"If God were your Father, ye would love Me: for I proceeded forth and came from God; neither came I of Myself, but He sent Me. Why do you not understand My speech? Even because ye cannot hear My word. Ye are of your father the devil, and the lusts of your father ye will do. He was a murderer from the beginning, and abode not in the truth, because there is no truth in him. When he speaketh a lie,

he speaketh of his own: for he is a liar, and the father of it." John 8:42-44 KJV

"Be not deceived; God is not mocked: for whatsoever a man soweth, that shall he also reap. For he that soweth to his flesh shall of the flesh reap corruption; but he that soweth to the Spirit shall of the Spirit reap life everlasting." Galatians 6:7-8 KJV (Underline mine)

The distinction between foundational influences is seen even in the church as many religious people are self-right-eous and live according to their own standards in the place of God's, and by their own standards they consider themselves to be just. These men and women do what makes them feel good about themselves and label this as living a righteous life. These people's rules are often based upon empty and worthless religious exercises and the motivation behind their works are mainly based upon feelings. Those men and women who are not religious simply compare their social values and the actions these produce as a righteous standard in order to present to the world and others that they are righteous and just. This modern day phenomena is known as, "virtue signaling." Virtue signal-ing is nothing more than people acting in accord with social standards and calling it justice, but this is not living by divine influence. We might be inclined to believe that virtue signaling is a sign of the times we are living in, but hypocrisy of this sort has been taking place since the fall of mankind in the garden.

"Take heed that ye do not your alms before men, to be seen of them; otherwise ye have no reward of your Father which is in heaven. Therefore when thou doest thine alms, do not sound a trumpet be-fore thee, as the hypocrites do in the synagogues and in the streets, that they may have glory of men. Verily I say unto you, They have their reward." Matthew 6:1-2 KJV

What the Lord Jesus is describing in Matthew 6:1-2 is nothing less than good old-fashioned virtue signaling which He calls out as hypocrisy. The struggle all people face in this world today is the temptation to succumb to the influence of the world by inventing and holding to a human-centered standard of righteousness, or to live according to the influence and direction of the Holy Spirit which is to live to a higher standard; the standard of God. This situation has been the same for all people who have ever lived throughout all of time. The way things are in the world today are the way things have been since the fall in the garden.

Joseph lived under the very same conditions and it was under these conditions that he found himself faced with a very difficult situation. Joseph found himself betrothed to a woman who was pregnant and it was for certain that he was not the father of the child. In this situation what is a just man to do? What will influence Joseph's decision? Will it be God or the world? This is exactly the same when it comes to every decision a believer must make with his or her life.

In the Hebrew wedding tradition, after the groom had met the bride price, the bride and groom were separated for a period of time from nine months to one year. This was to ensure that the marriage was not one of convenience. There was no such thing as a shot-gun wedding in Israel. Mary was with child by the Holy Spirit meaning Mary is not guilty of committing an immoral act. It is important to remember that in everything that is happening in Joseph's life that has to do with Mary, Mary is innocent. After Joseph's proposal of marriage was accepted, Mary traveled to the hill country of Ephraim to stay with her cousin Elizabeth. When Mary left her home in Nazareth Joseph was none the wiser about her condition, but when Mary returns it is obvious to everyone that she is pregnant. You might imagine the stir this caused in a small community such as Nazareth. You can imagine that a scandal is brewing in the minds of most people. Gossip spreads like a wildfire when you live in a small town.

The actions Joseph took in response to Mary's condition informs us that he was indeed a just and righteous man who was more influenced by God than he was by the world. If Joseph's righteousness was according to the way of the world he had every right to call off the wedding by bringing an accusation of infidelity against Mary. The penalty for not remaining chaste during the period of betrothal was death by stoning. Joseph could have had Mary put to death and in so doing he would have maintained his reputation as a just man in the eyes of the world, but Joseph thought to divorce Mary secretly so as not to expose her to the possibility of the death penalty.

"Then Joseph her husband, being a just man, and not willing to make her a public example, was minded to put her away privily." Matthew 1:19 KJV

Joseph chose mercy over judgment. Joseph acted in love rather than acting in righteous indignation which evidences that Joseph was more godly-minded than worldly-minded.

"But while he thought on these things, behold the angel of the Lord appeared unto him in a dream, saying, Joseph, thou son of David, fear not to take unto thee Mary thy wife: for that which is conceived in her is of the Holy Ghost. And she shall bring forth a son, and thou shalt call his name JESUS: for He shall save His people from their sins. Now all that was done, that it might be fulfilled which was spoken of the Lord by the prophet, saying, Behold, a virgin shall be with child, and shall bring forth a son, and they shall call His name Emmanuel, which being interpreted is, God with us. Then Joseph being raised from his sleep did as the angel of the Lord had bidden him and took unto him his wife." Matthew 1:20-24 KJV (Underline mine)

Clearly Joseph was more influenced by God than he was by the world and this is why he is obedient to God's instruction. Joseph's obedience and what it cost him personally evidence his genuine love for God and for his betrothed, Mary. What did Joseph being obedient cost him? It cost him his good name among his neighbors. Being obedient to God cost him his reputation.

This is a real challenge to most people when it comes to

serving the Lord and being obedient. This is a real challenge to many when it comes to living by faith because a great many people are more worried about their reputation among their peers and they are more concerned about what the world thinks of them than they are concerned about what God would have them to do with their lives. Consider carefully what Joseph took upon himself by following God's will for his life. Remember here that no one knows what is happening except for Mary and Joseph. The Lord informed Joseph as to what was happening in his dream. The angel visited Mary to bring word. Zacharias and Elizabeth, the parents of John the Baptist understood what was happening, but Mary's parents were not included in the information and not everyone in Nazareth knew the truth. It is entirely possible that Joseph's parents did not understand the circumstances. Imagine how Joseph's parents might have felt, thinking their son was marrying an unfaithful woman. The world did not learn of the miraculous birth of the Lord Jesus until the gospel began to be preached in power after the events of Pentecost. The gospel of Matthew, which has this information, was not written until sometime after 40 A.D. This is almost 40 years after the Lord's birth. People did not know that Mary was with child by the Holy Spirit, but it is certain that word got around that Mary was pregnant before she was married because when the Pharisees were arguing with the Lord Jesus they insinuated that He was an illegitimate child.

"They answered and said unto Him, Abraham is our father. Jesus saith unto them, If ye were Abraham's children, ye would do the works of Abraham. But now ye seek to kill Me, a man that hath told you the truth, which I have heard of God: this did not Abraham. Ye do the deeds of your father. Then said they unto Him, We be not born of fornication; we have one father, even God." John 8:39-41 KJV (Underline mine)

Joseph in deciding to follow the will of God for his life would destroy his own reputation among his family, his friends, and in his community. For all intents and purposes and as far as anyone knew, Joseph was marrying an unfaithful woman. Joseph was setting himself up to become the joke of the town. Not only was Joseph sacrificing his reputation with his family and in his community but he was also sacrificing his reputation in the religious community. By taking Mary to be his wife he would destroy his reputation in the synagogue. Joseph would become an outcast in his own church. Can you imagine the hushed whispers as Joseph and Mary enter the sanctuary, Mary holding this supposedly illegitimate child in her arms. Just imagine from this how many men and women with broken lives, who have destroyed their reputation, feel when they walk into the church for the first time. Some people have been in this place more than once. We would all do well to remember in these instances that we do not know the whole story.

It is difficult to live with a bad reputation when you have earned it. A deserved reputation is a difficult thing to live with because people love to talk and share rumors and gossip. For some reason people love to hear bad things about other people and it doesn't matter if they know the person they are talking about or not. Neither Joseph nor Mary deserved the reputation they took upon themselves. Neither Joseph nor Mary did anything amiss and yet these two were willing to sacrifice their good names in order to fulfill God's will for their lives. While Joseph and Mary might not have been held as just and righteous in the eyes of mankind they certainly were just and righteous in the eyes of God. Joseph and Mary did what was right in the eyes of God by allowing God to hold greater influence over their lives than the world. Joseph and Mary did what was right in the eyes of God by conditioning their lives by God's standards. Joseph was a just man because he responded to God in faithful obedience. When the Bible declares that Joseph was a just man, this is what God has to say about him. According to God, Joseph was a just man therefore it doesn't matter at all what others might think. When you are walking in lock-step with the Lord Jesus you do not need the approval of anyone.

Throughout this book I have been highlighting people whose stories we find in the Bible and their apparent flaws. The goal of this work is to present the character flaws in believers and their misdeeds that God overcame to continue to work in and through their lives in order to bring them to the place of true victorious living. This effort is to encourage all believers to continue to live by faith allowing God to work in and through our lives, good, bad, or otherwise, to bring about victory. As far as the Bible reveals, Joseph did not display any great shortcomings that God had to overcome. The Bible presents that Joseph was a man who conditioned his life according to God's standards by stating that he was a just man. What we have in Joseph's life is God asking this just man to take on a reputation of being the sort of man he clearly was not. The Lord asked the very same thing of Mary. Father God called upon Joseph and Mary to subject themselves to the unfair judgment and wrong opinions of others and the grief this would bring into their lives in order to fulfill His will and to bring Him glory. What we see in Joseph and Mary are two people who are willing to share in the shame of a reputation many people rightly bear to be obedient to God. Joseph and Mary took upon themselves the identity of brokenness to be a blessing to others. This is a true example of being Christ-like.

"Let this mind be in you, which was also in Christ Jesus: Who, being in the form of God, thought it not robbery to be equal with God: But made Himself of no reputation, and took upon Him the form of a servant, and was made in the likeness of men." Philippians 2:5-7 KJV

Joseph and Mary humbled themselves taking upon themselves the identity of brokenness to bring blessing to the world, and this is an example of true courage. What do we define as being courageous? In modern culture many people believe a man claiming to be a woman is an act of courage. Standing up and being bold in a position that causes people to cheer you on in your wickedness is not being brave. This is nothing more than being audacious in sin. Joseph and Mary acted in true bravery. Joseph and Mary put their lives in God's hands taking on reproach and shame to fulfill His will. Joseph and Mary displayed true godliness when they put their lives into God's hands, taking upon themselves shame and reproach that would lead to the salvation of many, and this is the very same thing the Lord Jesus did for all when He died upon the cross.

The Lord Jesus was crucified with sinners. The Lord Jesus took upon Himself the reproach and shame of sin in our place that humanity might be delivered from the power of sin. The Lord Jesus suffered shame in our place that we might be redeemed. That the Lord Jesus would do this for me is beyond my ability to fully comprehend. I know what sort of person I am and it is for certain that I am not worthy to have the perfect Son of God die for me. I am not worthy to receive the eternal life the Lord Jesus gives, but I am also not worthy of the shame and reproach Joseph and Mary took upon themselves in obedience to God so that the Savior could be born into this world. We often consider the great sacrifice the Lord Jesus has made on our behalf; how often do we consider the sacrifice of men and women who are like Joseph and Mary? How often do we consider the sacrifices made by men and women by being obedient to God and how that brings blessings into our lives?

"Greater love hath no man that this, that a man lay down his life for his friends." John 15:13 KJV

We often consider John 15:13 in the context of dying so that others might live. Dying would not be that difficult. The greater challenge this verse presents is in living for the good of someone else. The greater challenge in this verse is being willing to lay aside your desires and giving your life in service for the good of someone else. The Lord Jesus did more than die for us on the cross. He now lives for us eternally.

"Wherefore He is able also to save them to the uttermost that come unto God by Him, seeing He ever liveth to make intercession for

them." Hebrews 7:25 KJV

The Lord Jesus laid down His life and gave up everything that we might live and in doing this He has given us the example of what laying down our lives truly means. It is not seen in being willing to die. It is seen in being willing to die to self in order that God might work in and through our lives to be a blessing to others.

Could you make the kind of sacrifice Joseph did so that your life might be a blessing to others? Would you be willing to sacrifice your reputation with your family, in your community, and in your church if this is what God called upon you to do? How about being willing to allow God to use your life to bring other people to Him? If you already have a reputation, why not let God use this to bring people to Him? In this way God will not only overcome your brokenness, but He will transform it to use to His glory. There are times the only way God can reach broken people is through the brokenness of others, but in order for the Lord Jesus to do this you must be conformable to His will. To live for Christ means we allow Him to have the greater influence in our lives and when you live for Christ you are then a just and righteous person. It may not be so in the eyes of the world, but it will certainly be so in the eyes of God.

CHAPTER EIGHTEEN

Mary

"And in the sixth month the angel Gabriel was sent from God unto a city of Galilee, named Nazareth, to a virgin espoused to a man whose name was Joseph, of the house of David; and the virgin's name was Mary. And the angel came in unto her, and said, Hail, thou that art highly favored, the Lord is with thee: blessed art thou among women. And when she saw him, she was troubled at his saying, and cast in her mind what manner of salutation this should be. And the angel said unto her, Fear not, Mary: for thou hast found favor with God. And, behold, thou shalt conceive in thy womb, and bring forth a son, and shalt call His name Jesus." Luke 1: 26-31 KJV

"And Mary said, Behold the handmaid of the Lord: be it unto me according to thy word. And the angel departed from her." Luke 1:38 KJV

Mary and Joseph's obedience cost them. Mary and Joseph took upon themselves the shame and reproach that comes with having a child out of wedlock. There is an absence of shame when a woman finds herself in this condition in the current wicked age, but it was not so long ago that infidelity and extra-marital relations were frowned upon. In this current age with its relative ideas concerning morals not many people think twice about an unmarried couple being with child. In the age in which Mary lived being with child out of wedlock could cost more than your reputation. Mary being pregnant before she was married could have cost her, her life. Mary was willing however to pay the price in order to be obedient to God. Mary's situation serves to inform all believers that there are times that living by faith in the Lord Jesus and serving the Lord Jesus may cost us.

"And there went a great multitude with Him: and He turned, and said unto them, If any man come to Me, and hate not his father, and mother, and wife, and children, and brethren, and sisters, yea, and his own life also, he cannot be My disciple. And whosoever doth not bear his cross, and come after Me, cannot be My disciple. For which of you, intending to build a tower, sitteth not down first, and counteth the cost, whether he have sufficient to finish it? Lest haply, after he hath laid the foundation, and is not able to finish it, all that behold it begin to mock him, saying, This man began to build, and was not able to finish. Or what king, going to make war against another king, sitteth not down first, and consulteth whether he be able with ten thousand to meet him that cometh against him with twenty thousand? Or else, while the other is yet a great way off, he sendeth an ambassage, and desireth conditions of peace. So likewise, whosoever he be of you that forsaketh not all that he hath, he cannot be My disciple." Luke 14:25-33 KJV

The Lord Jesus is speaking directly and clearly when He says that all who have a mind to follow Him need to take the time to count the cost. No person should be lighthearted concerning the things of God. No Christian should be casual in his or her relationship with the Lord. Christianity is not some subculture among the greater culture that makes up what is defined as the American culture. Christianity is not a lifestyle choice to be taken up and laid down as you please. The Lord Jesus is Christ the King who is King of all kings and Lord of all lords. Jesus is life and the sum total of what life is all about. The apostle Paul identifies that the Lord Jesus is He who sustains our very existence when he preached, *"In Him we live and move and have our being,"* (Acts 17:28) at the Aeropagus on Mars Hill. When the Lord Jesus proclaimed that He is the Way, the Truth, and the Life, this is exactly what He meant. Apart from having a real and living relationship with the Lord Jesus people do not live. They simply exist because Jesus is life.

When coming to Christ people should weigh the costs. Christian's ought to carefully consider what it means to belong to Christ and to live for Him. The promise of living by faith is one of blessing and provision, but these blessings and provisions are tempered with difficulty. In one passage of scripture we may find the Lord Jesus declaring that He has come that we might have life and have it more abundantly, while in another He states that we will face trials and tribulation as we live for Him. What this means is that blessings and trials are not exclusive. What this means is that you can find yourself blessed by God while suffering through hardship at the same time.

"Then Peter began to say unto Him, Lo, we have left all, and have followed Thee. And Jesus answered and said, Verily I say unto you, There is no man that hath left house, or brethren, or sisters, or father, or mother, or wife, or children, or lands, for My sake, and the gospel's, but he shall receive an hundredfold now in this time, houses, and brethren, and sisters, and mothers, and children, and lands, with persecutions; and in the world to come eternal life." Mark 10:28-30 KJV (Underline mine)

The Lord called upon Mary to carry a child. This is something which is life affirming and honorable. Bringing a child into the world is a blessing. The birth of a baby is a joyous event. The birth of a baby is a reason to celebrate but for Mary carrying this baby in order to fulfill the will of God for her life she must also bear the shame of being seen as a woman who has been unfaithful to her husband. In order to fulfill God's calling on her life Mary must bear a measure of shame and reproach. Which means, this was no little thing God was asking of her.

Mary at the time she was betrothed was very young. Some scholars speculate that she might have been as young as 14 years old. Imagine what it would be like to be 14 years old and pregnant and having to face a world that viewed you as someone with loose morals while the truth of the situation is that Mary was someone who was the opposite of the reputation she would now carry. Imagine how a 14 year old today might face this kind of adversity, living with an undeserved reputation. Imagine facing life being looked down upon by just about everyone. How did the angel greet Mary?

And the angel came unto her, and said, Hail, thou that art highly favored, the Lord is with thee: <u>blessed art thou among women</u>." Luke 1:28 KJV (Underline mine)

Mary is about to face some of the most difficult times of her young life. Mary is about to become an outcast among her family, her friends, her church, and in her community and she will face all this opposition and judgment while carrying a child. What does the angel say to Mary? *"Thou that art highly favored."* (Vs. 28) In order to be obedient to God, Mary is going to face some real hardship and still the angel says, *"Blessed art thou among women."* (Vs. 28)

The phrase, "highly favored," in verse 28 is translated from one Greek word, **Charitomene** which is derived from the root word **Charitoo**. It describes someone or something that is honored or highly favored. In calling Mary, "highly favored," Gabriel was expressing that to be chosen for the honor of carrying the Son of God meant that God thought very highly of Mary. In this world we often believe that people whose lives appear to be blessed are the men and women God highly favors. We see someone who has riches and wealth and their lives never seem to have any trouble and we say to ourselves, "God must really love that person because they certainly are blessed," and then we witness someone who is constantly struggling through life and suffering hardship in every way. People who never seem to get above their circumstances and at every turn life is kicking them around and we think, "Maybe God doesn't like them very much." People often make light of trouble. When one bad thing after another happens they will slump their shoulders and say, "God must hate me," but our circumstances in life do not represent our status with God or our status in the kingdom. Someone who was unaware of God's call on Mary's life might have been hard pressed to say that she was highly favored of God, 14 years old, pregnant, and living with a reputation. A person's circumstances does not represent their status in the eyes of God. Mary was blessed. God had chosen her to bring His only begotten Son into the world. What is more, Mary understood that she was blessed.

"My soul doth magnify the Lord, and my spirit hath rejoiced in God my Savior. For He hath regarded the low estate of his handmaiden: for behold, from henceforth all generations shall call me blessed. For He that is mighty hath done to me great things; and holy is His name." Luke 1:46-49 KJV

Far from being a burden to bear Mary proclaims that God is doing something great with her life and her understanding of being blessed comes from her knowing what God will do through everything that is happening in her life. God chose her to bring His Son into the world. God is using Mary's life in His plan of redemption for all of mankind. God is utilizing Mary to forward His will which will impact all ages of mankind and Mary sees the place that God has for her as her blessing. Mary can see the bigger picture; that through Jesus, her Son, many people will be delivered from their sins and many people will inherit eternal life. This is possible because she is willing to endure hardship. Mary understands that the calling on her life in not meant as a cruelty from God she must endure, but it is a blessing from God that will lead to greater blessings upon all.

"And the angel said unto her, Fear not, Mary: for thou hast found favor with God. And, behold, thou shalt conceive in thy womb, and bring forth a son, and shalt call His name JESUS. He shall be great, and shall be called the Son of the Highest: and the Lord God shall give unto Him the throne of His father David: and He shall reign over the house of Jacob forever; and of His kingdom there shall be no end." Luke 1:30-33 KJV

The child Mary will carry and deliver is no ordinary child, which means the thing that she is doing is no ordinary thing. To the world, carrying a child and giving birth may seem like an ordinary situation and though many may believe that Mary is just a young girl who has gotten herself into trouble, she knows that this is all included in God's plan. Everything that is happening in Mary's life is in fulfillment of God's eternal plan for the ages that will find its consummation in Christ Jesus.

"Having made known to us the mystery of His will, according to His good pleasure which He hath purposed in Himself: that in the dispensation of the fullness of times He might gather together in one all things in Christ, both which are in heaven and which are on earth." Ephesians 1:9-10 KJV (Underline mine)

Mary is an integral part of God's plan. Mary's life and her obedience are very important to what God is doing which means that what Mary is doing is no ordinary thing. Which also means that Mary is indeed highly favored and blessed by God.

Have you ever considered all the little pieces that fall into place working together that allows for blessings in our lives? Have you ever considered the integral parts of a machine that do what they are supposed to do that allows for a machine to function properly? You hop into your car, put the key into the ignition, turn it over and the engine comes to life. How many little things must happen in order for your car to get moving down the road? We do not think of all the little things taking place that allow that car to move, not until that car doesn't start like it should. In the same way many people do not consider the part their lives have in God's master plan for the universe. Most Christians do not realize what God can do with their lives or what God is doing with their lives that has an impact in the greater scheme of all things, and this is because people do not have a proper understanding of the sovereign nature of God. Most people do not realize that God is in control of all things and is bringing all things together for the good of those men and women who love Him.

"And when they were come to Capernaum, they that received tribute money came to Peter, and said, Doth not your Master pay tribute? He saith, Yes. And when he was come into the house, Jesus prevented him, saying, What thinkest thou, Simon? Of whom do the kings of the earth take custom or tribute? Of their own children or of strangers? Peter saith unto Him, Of strangers. Jesus saith unto him, Then are the children free. Notwithstanding, lest we should offend them, go thou to the sea, and cast in a hook, and take up the fish that first cometh up; and when thou hast opened his mouth, thou shalt find a piece of money: take that and give it to them for Me and thee." Matthew 17:24-27 KJV

Consider everything God put in place for Peter to catch a fish with money in its mouth to pay the temple tax. God first moved this fish to swallow a coin. Then God moved the fish to the place it needed to be to be caught by Peter. The Lord brought the coin, the fish, and Peter all together into one place because He is sovereign over everything. God puts all things into place as it needs to be to make things happen. All the little pieces have to be in place and they have to do their part in order for everything to function as it does and this makes every piece and the part it plays necessary, essential, and important. Mary's life and the calling she had was necessary, essential, and important. Thus, Mary is highly favored and blessed by God and she understood this very well which is why she answered the call on her life.

"And Mary said, Behold the handmaid of the Lord; be it unto me according to thy word." Luke 1:38 KJV

The angel Gabriel informed Mary that she would become pregnant out of wedlock and even knowing the grief this might cause, but also knowing how important this work was to the fulfillment of God's will and to the salvation of mankind, she said, "Amen."

God is still working in the world and there is still much to be done. The evidence of this truth is the fact that the church continues her mission in the world. The church is the body of Christ in this age of grace and the Lord Jesus informed the church that she would carry on the work He began and that she would do this through the power and presence of the Holy Spirit.

"For as the body is one, and hath many members, and all the members of that one body, being many, are one body: so also is Christ. For by one Spirit are we all baptized into one body, whether we be Jews or Gentiles, whether we be bond or free; and have been all made to drink into one Spirit. For the body is not one member, but many." 1 Corinthians 12:12-14 KJV

"But now hath God set the members every one of them in the body, as it hath pleased Him." 1 Corinthians 12:18 KJV

God is sovereign over the church and He is the One who is bringing the church together as He will. God moves each individual believer into his or her place of service. God will call one person to do this and another person to do that and then He will gift him or her for service through the Holy Spirit, creating this living organism we call the church. God is bringing everything together and putting all things into place in a way that allows believers as the body of Christ to work together in the greater cause that is the gospel of the Lord Jesus. When the church is operating as she should with everyone pulling together in the same direction, God's direction, we are then operating as the body of Christ which will result in people coming to faith in Christ. This makes the part we play, our ministry and our calling, an essential, important, and necessary part of the plan. The calling God places on the individual believer is no different than the calling He placed on Mary's life. Everything that God is doing is working together according to His will and all believers are a part of the plan. This means that included with Mary all who have answered the call of God are blessed and highly favored by God.

This is brought out through the Bible and not simply through the life and calling of Mary. This precept is also presented to the church in the book of Ephesians. The Greek word translated "Highly favored," is only used twice in all the Bible. It is found in the book of Luke in reference to Mary and it is also found in the book of Ephesians in reference to all who are found in Christ by faith.

"Having predestinated us unto the adoption of children by Jesus Christ to Himself, according to the good pleasure of His will. To the praise of His grace, wherein He hath made us <u>accepted</u> in the beloved." Ephesians 1:5-6 KJV (Underline mine)

This verse may be rendered, "Wherein He hath made us highly favored in the Beloved." Because the believer is bound up in the Lord Jesus we are now highly favored. Being in Christ through faith has now placed us in the position of being chosen, called, blessed, and highly favored by God. As Mary was when sanctified by the Lord so now is the church.

The calling on your life is no different than the calling God placed on Mary's life. In Christ you are now in the position of being blessed and highly favored due to the calling on your life and the part it will play in the grand scheme that is God's will. Answering God's call on your life may not be easy. You may face hardships and trials, but you have to see that what God is calling you to do is integral. What God has called you to do is essential, it is necessary, and you are important. Everything that has to do with the calling that is on your life has to do with the will of God; that is what makes your life and calling important.

The only thing the individual has to struggle with is deciding whether or not he or she will say "yes," to God as Mary did. When the Lord calls, will you step up and do what He asks of you? To answer the call you must be realistic. You must count the cost, but then you must consider the bigger picture as well and with all these things in mind you must decide what you are going to do.

CHAPTER NINETEEN

Nicodemus

The Religious Ruler

"There was a man of the Pharisees, named Nicodemus, a ruler of the Jews: The same came to Jesus by night, and said unto Him, Rabbi, we know that Thou art a teacher come from God: for no man can do these miracles that Thou doest, except God be with him. Jesus answered and said unto him, Verily, verily, I say unto thee, Except a man be born again, he cannot see the kingdom of God. Nicodemus saith unto Him, How can a man be born when he is old? Can he enter a second time into his mother's womb, and be born? Jesus answered, Verily, verily, I say unto thee, Except a man be born of water and of the Spirit, he cannot enter into the kingdom of God." John 3:1-5 KJV

If we are to believe many of the critics of Christianity and the church there are far too many hypocrites among us. Most people will agree that there are hypocrites in the church. The truth is there are hypocrites everywhere you go. There are many hypocrites in the places people work, but hypocrites do not keep people from going to work. You will find hypocrites at the super-market, but hypocrites will not keep people from buying food. Every person has been guilty of practicing hypocrisy at one time or another. When someone accuses me of being a hypocrite, to understand where they are coming from, I would need for them to specify on which occasion, because I have acted hypocritical on more than one occasion. So, when it comes to my hypocrisy, are we discussing my overall character or a specific occasion, because I do not believe that I am being a hypocrite every hour of every day, and in case you may believe that you have never been hypocritical I will ask, do you honestly believe for one minute the others think you're no hypocrite? The point is, everyone is guilty of being a hypocrite at one time or another. Everyone has, on occasion, said one thing only to do the complete opposite. This doesn't mean these actions are right, I am just stating a fact. So, to hold the issue of hypocrisy as an issue which justifies a person's lack of commitment to Christ or a person's lack of being involved in church is illegitimate. To say that you want nothing to do with the Lord Jesus or the church because of hypocrisy is just as illegitimate as claiming to not be a hypocrite yourself. If you claim to hold hypocrites in disdain then this position ought to keep you from visiting any place where you would have to interact with hypocrites.

"Therefore thou art inexcusable, O man, whosoever thou art that judgest: for wherein thou judgest another, thou condemnest thyself; for thou that judgest doest the same things." Romans 2:1 KJV

If you are the type of person who likes to point out others flaws and mistakes you need to know that you are just as guilty of being flawed and making mistakes as the people you presume to stand in judgment over. What is the conclusion of the matter. There is no person who is righteous before God.

"There is none righteous, no, not one." Romans 3:10 KJV

However, there are many people who imagine that they are righteous due to the fact that they are religious. There are a great many people who substitute religion for the grace of God. This may confuse some who may believe that Christianity and church are concerned with religion but they are not. Religion is a man-centered attempt to appease God through works as a mean to merit salvation. These works are mainly tied to ritual and tradition. Thus a religious person crosses himself or herself before and after praying because this is what he or she believes

God requires. A religious person faithfully attends religious services, not out of a desire to worship the Lord Jesus in Spirit and in truth, but because he or she believes God requires this in order for a person to be saved. Religion is bound up in what a person does believing this is what makes him or her righteous before God. Religion is what a person does in order to appear righteous before mankind, but appearances can be deceiving. Being religious doesn't make someone righteous or holy. Being religious is simply being religious. Many believe religion and traditions mean something when in truth, they do not.

Nicodemus was a religious leader in Israel. He was a Pharisee, which is one of the religious sects that constantly opposed and tested the Lord Jesus. By all outward appearances Nicodemus was a holy, righteous, and godly man. This was according to the standards of the misconstrued man-centered religion that Judaism had become. By all outward appearances Nicodemus was a righteous and godly man and yet appearances are not the substance of something. Appearances are deceptive. I heard someone once say, "Appearances are reality." This is a lie. Reality is reality and appearances are deceptive. Many people often appear to be something they are not. I.E. Judas appeared to be a loyal disciple of the Lord Jesus. The Lord Jesus completely exposed the religious hype that surrounded the religious leaders of Israel which included Nicodemus. The Lord Jesus proclaimed that these men were bound up in hypocrisy.

"Then spake Jesus to the multitude, and to His disciples, Saying, The scribes and the Pharisees sit in Moses' seat: All therefore whatsoever they bid you observe, that observe and do; but do not ye after their works: for they say, and do not. (Otherwise known as hypocrisy) For they bind heavy burdens and grievous to be borne, and lay them on men's shoulders; but they themselves will not move them with one of their fingers, but all their works they do for to be seen of men: they make broad their phylacteries, and enlarge the borders of their garments, and love the uppermost rooms at feast, and the chief seats in the synagogues, and greetings in the markets and to called of me

Rabbi, rabbi. (Empty religion)" Matthew 23:1-7 KJV (Underlines and parenthesis mine)

Religious hypocrites love to make up rules for other people to follow while excusing and excluding themselves. The religious leaders in Israel in the time of Christ would make up rules that were nothing more than heavy burdens on the people, but these men were unwilling to do anything to help. The Lord said that these men wouldn't even bother to lift a finger to help anyone. These men loved having the appearance of being righteous and holy. These men were very religious. These Pharisees and Saducees wore the finest clothes as they made their way to the synagogue every Sabbath. They loved for others to bend their knees before them kissing their rings, and by all outward appearances these were holy men. The Lord Jesus said, _"Everything they do is to be seen by others."_ (Vs. 5) These men would look and act one way when sitting in church, while being the complete opposite when no one was watching. These men were fake believers dealing in make-believe. The religious leaders in Israel were not holy men, they just looked that way. The religious leaders in Israel wanted people to think that their appearance equaled reality.

"But woe unto you, scribes and Pharisees, hypocrites! For ye shut up the kingdom of heaven against men: for ye neither go in yourselves, neither suffer ye them that are entering to go in." Matthew 23:13 KJV

The Lord Jesus points out that instead of leading people to the Father they were in fact shutting up the way to heaven.

"Woe unto you, scribes and Pharisees, hypocrites! For ye devour widows houses, and for a pretense make long prayer: therefore ye shall receive the greater damnation." Matthew 23:14 KJV]

Religious hypocrites love to make long prayers in the church. Religious hypocrites love to be the center of attention at Bible study. These men desire to pontificate about what they think they know about the scriptures while at the very same time they are cheating widows out of their homes, taking advantage of the poor, and they are probably prone to kicking stray dogs as well. These religiously minded hypocrites would travel to the far reaches of the earth to convert one person to their religion, but all they are doing is creating another child of hell.

"Woe unto you, scribes and Pharisees, hypocrites! For ye compass sea and land to make one proselyte, and when he is made, ye make him twofold more the child of hell than yourselves." Matthew 23:15 KJV

The Lord Jesus goes on to describe scribes and Pharisees as men who were very diligent to keep the least matters of the law that they might appear righteous before men. Religious hypocrites will go to great lengths to tithe herbs and spices in order to appear to keep the law, but they ignore justice, judgment, and mercy.

"Woe unto you, scribes and Pharisees, hypocrites! For ye pay tithe of mint and anise and cumin and have omitted the weightier matters of the law, judgment, mercy, and faith: these ought ye to have done and not to leave the other undone." Matthew 23:23 KJV

Religious hypocrites make mountains out of molehills. Religious hypocrites make much of nothing and make the important matters of the faith out to be nothing.

"Ye blind guides, which strain at a gnat, and swallow a camel. Woe unto you, scribes and Pharisees, hypocrites! For ye make clean the outside of the cup and of the platter, but within they are full of extortion and excess." Matthew 23:24-25 KJV

Pharisees like Nicodemus were only concerned with keeping the least of the law because in observing these things they gave the appearance of being faithful when in truth they were only hiding the fact that they were dead inside. Religious hypocrites are nothing more than whitewashed tombs.

"Woe unto you, scribes and Pharisees, hypocrites! For ye are like

unto whited sepulchers, which indeed appear beautiful outward, but are within full of dead men's bones, and of all uncleanness. Even so ye also outwardly appear righteous unto men, but within ye are full of hypocrisy and iniquity." Matthew 23:27-28

Religion has no substance. Religion is nothing but show. Religion has no heart to it. Religion is dead and it is devastatingly cruel to those men and women who try to keep it because religion preaches nothing but retribution and penance. Religion is an affront to the grace and mercy of God because God has not required our sins of us. Our Father God placed the weight and guilt of our sins on the Lord Jesus, our Messiah, so that we might receive His grace and mercy and God did not send the Lord Jesus to die for us so that we would practice religion. The Father sent His only begotten Son because He loves us and desires to have a living relationship with us.

"For God so loved the world that He gave His only begotten Son, that whosoever believeth in Him should not perish, but have everlasting life." John 3:16 KJV

True believers in the Lord Jesus are not practicing religion. True believers have a living relationship with the Lord Jesus by faith and the reason they are a part of the New Testament church and regularly attend worship and Bible study is because believers desire to worship God in Spirit and in truth. The genuine believer in Christ makes church a part of his or her life because it is in this fellowship that he or she grows closer to the Lord Jesus and he or she grows in faith and love for Him.

If you are a part of a church and your reason for being there is anything other than a genuine love for the Lord Jesus and a true desire to worship and fellowship with Him, then you are a part of the church for the wrong reasons and it would be better if you did not attend. You are not doing yourself any favors by sitting in church pretending to love the Lord Jesus if you genuinely do not. You are not doing yourself any favors by practicing dead empty religion because religion is worthless before

God. This is as straightforward as I can be about religion and I make no apologies for writing what I have because it is the truth. You must be born again in order to ever see heaven. You must be born again to receive everlasting life. You must be born again to have a living relationship with the Father through His Son Jesus. To be born-again you must call on the name of the Lord Jesus by faith asking Him to forgive you of your sins and to save you.

Nicodemus was a very religious man. He was a Pharisee. He was a religious leader in Israel. He was one of the chief men in the synagogue. I doubt he ever missed a Sabbath service and by all outward appearances he was a righteous and godly man and yet when he came into the presence of the Savior the first thing the Lord Jesus says to him is, "Ye must be born again." (Vs. 3)

"Jesus answered and said unto him, Verily, verily, I say unto thee, Except a man be born again, he cannot see the kingdom of God." John 3:3 KJV

Appearances are not reality. Appearances mean absolutely nothing to God because God sees beyond the outward appearance. God looks upon the heart. God knows what is going on, on the inside. You may fool a great many people by keeping up outward appearances through religion, but you will never fool God.

Many people might be inclined to believe that someone like Nicodemus would be a real asset to the Lord's cause. Imagine if one of the great leaders from Israel's history, a Pharisee, would have become a true disciple of the Lord Jesus. What a feather this would be in the Lord's cap, right? This is how the world thinks. If Nicodemus were to walk through the doors of a modern day dead church imagine the buzz this might create. Can you hear the people talking? "Oh look. Here comes Nicodemus. He's a great man in Israel don't you know? Just look at how holy and pious he is and his robes are stunning. Just look at how he carries himself as if he is above all the sinful nonsense of the world. Why, if he were to join with our church he could head up several of our committees. You know he's an expert in the Old Testament. Imagine what insights he could bring to our study of Deuteronomy." There is one problem with this estimation. Nicodemus was religious, but he was not born again. Nicodemus was religious, but he did not know the Lord. While he may look the part of a faithful man, the Lord Jesus; the One who knows the hearts of all men, first words to Nicodemus were, "Ye must be born again."

How many men and women who are a part of the church are playing religious games just like Nicodemus? Truthfully, it is not difficult to identify religious hypocrites. Though these men and women may talk a good game and they may be good at keeping up appearances you can always tell a tree by it's fruit. Pretenders are usually erratic when it comes to attendance. These men and women will come to church every once in a great while, but there are always things which are more important to them than their relationship with the Lord Jesus and because this is so everything will take precedence in their lives over the Lord Jesus and the church. When pretenders are not in church they might as well be considered secret disciples because the only people who would have a clue that they might even know the Lord Jesus are the people who would see them at church when they do bother to attend. These men and women are very religious when they are around other Christians, but then they are very new age around new-agers, and they are hip around hipsters. These men and women settle very easily into pretending to be what everyone else around them appears to be. Trying to nail down what religious hypocrites actually believe is tantamount to trying to nail jello to a wall. If a person who acts this way were to ever come face-to-face with the Lord Jesus I am certain as to what the Lord would say, "Ye must be born again."

If you are playing religious games I encourage you to stop immediately because these games are getting you nowhere. How many men and women attend church week in and week out and all their efforts are nothing more than works to be seen by men? Just about everyone has played this game at one time or another in life. Growing up I was made to go to church by my parents. I did not have a living relationship with the Lord Jesus and I didn't enjoy going. I played the church game while sitting in the youth class. I knew all the right things to say. I had a firm grasp of religious language. I knew what to say to make the teacher happy and to keep myself in the good graces of my parents, and just about every other youth in the church was doing the very same thing. How do I know this? Because we all went to school together too. Most of the youth in the church I attended believed that church was nothing more than acting like a Christian on Sunday mornings so people at church would think you were a good person.

You can be a big shot in the church. You can even be a religious leader in Israel. You can make your phylacteries wide and the borders of your garments broad. You can hang a crucifix in every room in your home. You can buy the finest Bible any bookstore has available and have your name printed on the cover, and carry it with you as you achieve perfect attendance at Sunday school, but if you are not born-again through a living relationship with the Lord Jesus by faith, all those things mean absolutely nothing. If you do not have a living relationship with the Lord Jesus you may be very religious but you are simply wasting your time.

"But we are as an unclean thing, and all our righteousnesses (all our religious observations and works) *are as filthy rags."* Isaiah 64:6 KJV (Parenthesis mine)

Still the Lord Jesus did not turn Nicodemus away. Nicodemus came to the Lord Jesus at night because he did not want his religious friends to see him talking with the Lord, but Nicodemus knows there is something about Jesus. Nicodemus also knows the religious games he has been playing have left him empty inside. He knows there must be something he is missing which is why he sought out the Lord Jesus. In the very same way many religiously minded people know that there is something more to knowing God than practicing empty works. Many people know there is something substantial to having a real and living relationship with the Lord Jesus by faith. This is why people sit in church every week. Nicodemus sought out the Lord Jesus and the Lord did not rebuke him. The Lord did not scold him or turn him away. The Lord introduces Nicodemus to the truth and gives him the opportunity to be born-again.

"Nicodemus saith unto Him, How can a man be born when he is old? Can he enter a second time into his mother's womb, and be born? Jesus answered, Verily, verily, I say unto thee, Except a man be born of water and of the Spirit, he cannot enter into the kingdom of God. That which is born of the flesh is flesh; and that which is born of the Spirit is spirit. Marvel not that I say unto thee, Ye must be born again. The wind bloweth where it listeth, and thou hearest the sound thereof, but canst not tell when it cometh, and whither it goeth: so is everyone that is born of the Spirit." John 3:4-8 KJV

You must be born physically and then born-again of the Spirit in order to see the kingdom of God. How then is a person born-again? They are born anew in their spirit through the life giving presence of the Holy Spirit. The Lord very lovingly explains to Nicodemus the reality of gaining eternal life that applies to everyone. If you genuinely desire to experience everlasting life you must be born-again by placing your faith in the Lord Jesus. This leads to the filling of the Holy Spirit. When this happens the believer is filled with the Spirit and becomes a child of God.

"Behold, what manner of love the Father hath bestowed upon us, that we should be called the sons of God." 1 John 3:1 KJV

We are born-again by having faith in the Lord Jesus. If you honestly desire to become a child of God, go to the Lord Jesus in prayer and lift up a prayer of faith asking Him to save you.

CHAPTER TWENTY

The Woman at the Well

Many people imagine that God thinks, feels, and acts in the same way that they think, feel, and act. Many people suppose that God is just like they are having the same likes and dislikes, loving whom they love and hating those they hate when the truth is God is like Himself and we have been created in His image. If you are a person who imagines that God is just like you, your relationship with God doesn't exist. You are simply worshiping yourself and calling it faith in the Lord Jesus. The Bible calls upon the believer to conform to the image of Christ, not to imagine that Christ is like us. The only way for the believer to know or come to some understanding about the person and personality of God is to examine the Lord Jesus carefully, as the Lord Jesus is the expressed image of the Father.

"Philip saith unto Him, Lord, shew us the Father, and it sufficeth us. Jesus saith unto him, Have I been so long time with you, and yet hast thou not know Me, Philip? He that hath seen Me hath seen the Father; and how sayest thou then, Shew us the Father?" John 14:8-9 KJV (Underline mine)

"God who at sundry times and in divers manners spake in time past unto the fathers by the prophets, Hath in these last days spoken unto us by His Son, Whom He hath appointed heir of all things, by Whom also He made the worlds; Who being the brightness of His glory, and the express image of His person, and upholding all things by the word of His power, when He had by Himself purged our sins, sat down on the right hand of the Majesty on high." Hebrews 1:1-3 KJV (Under-

line mine)

To know the Lord Jesus is to know the Father. This is one reason the church meets regularly. We study the Bible in order to know Christ Jesus, thereby coming to know the heart of the Father. One reason for church fellowship is to know Jesus better. The church meets faithfully to worship to know God more, and yet there are men and women who do not know the Lord Jesus and who engage in no activity that will lead them to knowing the Lord, but they imagine that God is exactly like them. When they ask themselves, "What would Jesus do?" They are actually thinking, "What would I do and call it following the will of God?" Many of these same men and women will prejudge others solely on the basis of what they think they know from their own imagination; not based upon truth or facts but based mainly upon feelings and the superficial basis of outward appearances, and according to these things they judge a person as worthy of acceptance or deem them only worthy to be rejected. There are a great many people who are prejudiced and for a great many unsound reasons. Currently culture seems to be hung up on skin color more than anything. Today the world has been presented with a whole new manner of racists to contend with. These are the kind of racists who offer up prayers asking God to help them to hate certain people solely based upon the color of their skin. I suppose where the Lord Jesus says, "Love your neighbor," and "Love your enemies," is not to be found in her Bible.

Who in their right mind would imagine or believe that God would listen to a hate-filled prayer such as this? Who in their right mind would imagine that God would hate anyone or seek their disdain and destruction at the behest of some hate-filled bigot? Certainly not anyone who truly knows God through a living relationship with His Son Jesus. God so loved the world that He gave His only begotten Son. This statement from scripture alone clearly displays that God loves the entirety of His creation to the point that He willingly made the ultimate sacrifice and the Lord Jesus being the expressed image of the Father, loves and loved mankind to the degree that He was willing to make the ultimate sacrifice by laying down His life so that all who come to Him by faith can be saved. This is true for everyone no matter what their skin color may be. A person cannot be filled with the Holy Spirit of God, Who is the personification of love, and be predisposed to hate anyone.

"If a man say, I love God, and hateth his brother, he is a liar: for he that loveth not his brother whom he hath seen, how can he love God whom he hath not seen? And this commandment have we from Him, that he who loveth God love his brother also." 1 John 4:20-21 KJV

The purpose behind this introduction to this chapter is to prepare you to witness God's unconditional love and to receive this information through the display of love seen in the Lord Jesus as He interacts with a Samaritan woman at a well in a town called Sychar. It is this encounter that allows the reader to witness the depth of love the Lord has for everyone personally, and the lengths that He is willing to go to in order to save each one of us. The Lord Jesus' interaction with this woman also allows us to understand that God's love is not contingent upon anything. God's love is truly unconditional.

"When therefore the Lord knew how the Pharisees had heard that Jesus made and baptized more disciples than John, (Though Jesus Himself baptized not, but His disciples,) He left Judea, and departed again to Galilee. And he must needs go through Samaria. Then cometh He to a city of Samaria, which is called Sychar, near to the parcel of ground that Jacob gave to his son Joseph. Now Jacob's well was there. Jesus therefore, being wearied with His journey, sat thus in the well: and it was about the sixth hour. There cometh a woman of Samaria to draw water: Jesus saith unto her, Give Me to drink." (for His disciples were gone away unto the city to buy meat.) Then saith the woman of Samaria unto Him, How is that Thou a Jew, askest drink of me, which am a woman of Samaria? For the Jews have no dealings with the Samaritans. Jesus answered and said unto her, If thou knewest the gift of God, and who it is that saith to thee, Give

Me to drink; thou wouldest have asked of Him, and He would have given thee living water. The woman saith unto Him, Sir, Thou hast nothing to draw with, and the well is deep: from whence then hast thou that living water? Art Thou greater than our father Jacob, which gave us this well, and drank thereof himself, and his children, and his cattle? Jesus answered and said unto her, Whosoever drinketh of this water shall thirst again: But whosoever drinketh of the water that I shall give him shall never thirst; but the water that I shall give him shall be in him a well of water springing up into everlasting life. The woman saith unto Him, Sir, give me this water, that I thirst not, neither come hither to draw. Jesus saith unto her, Go, call thy husband, and come hither. The woman answered and said, I have no husband. Jesus said unto her, Thou hast well said, I have no husband: for thou hast had five husbands; and he whom thou now hast is not thy husband: in that saidst thou truly. The woman saith unto Him, Sir, I perceive that Thou art a prophet. Our fathers worshiped in this mountain; and ye say, that in Jerusalem is the place where men ought to worship. Jesus saith unto her, Woman, believe Me, the hour cometh, when ye shall neither in this mountain, nor yet at Jerusalem, worship the Father. Ye worship what ye know not what: we know what we worship: for salvation is of the Jews. But the hour cometh, and now is, when true worshipers shall worship the Father in Spirit and in truth: for the Father seeketh such to worship Him. God is a Spirit: and they that worship Him must worship in Spirit and in truth. The woman saith unto Him, I know that Messiah cometh, which is called Christ: when He is come, He will tell us all things. Jesus saith unto her, I that speak unto thee am He." John 4:1-26 KJV

To begin, consider the nature and disposition of the woman. Here is what we might discern from the information given in the text. The Lord Jesus meets the woman at the well at the sixth hour which is noon.

" Then cometh He to a city of Samaria, which is called Sychar, near to the parcel of ground that Jacob gave to his son Joseph. Now Jacob's

well was there. Jesus therefore, being wearied with His journey, sat thus in the well: and it was about the sixth hour. There cometh a woman of Samaria to draw water:" John 4:5-6 KJV

In that day a person had to go to the community well in order to get his or her water for the day, but the people would usually do this in the morning when it was not hot or unpleasant and also so that they might get plenty of water for the day. The well was an impromptu community meeting place in the mornings. People did not make their trip to the well at noon which makes this woman's trip out of place. Why was this woman going to the well at a time when, more than likely, no one else would be around? This information is provided to us through the Lord Jesus' statement in verse 18.

"The woman answered and said, I have no husband. Jesus said unto her, Thou hast well said, I have no husband: for thou hast had five husbands; and he whom thou now hast is not thy husband: in that saidst thou truly." John 4:17-18

This woman is a social pariah. She is an outcast in her community. She has been married more times than Elizabeth Taylor and now she is not even married. She is now "shacking up." She may have assumed she would be rejected by others, or she may very well have been rejected from community gatherings. This woman came to the well at noon because in so doing there was less of a chance that she would have to interact with other people while drawing her water. Her actions may have been brought about by a sense of shame; then again she might have avoided others because she just didn't care to hear what other people had to say about her life and how she was living it.

In the current age not many people are ashamed of their immoral behavior and this is really a sign of the times. Today people take a defiant stance when it comes to the terrible things they have done. Something along the lines of, "Yes, I did it. Now what do you intend to do about it?" Everyone justifies their sinful behavior in their own minds. This is what allows for people to live shame-free even when living a shame-filled life. My opinion is that this woman did not truly care what others might have thought about the way she was living her life or her living conditions. If she truly cared she probably would not have been married and divorced five times nor would she be living with a man to whom she was not married. My opinion is that the woman of Samaria avoided people because she didn't care to hear other's opinions about her lifestyle and this is because no one desires to interact with the judgmental spirit of others. I know for certain that it does not make my day when somebody decides to criticize me for my shortcomings.

Consider seriously what is happening when someone is being judgmental toward others. Why do men and women imagine that we have any sort of right or duty to pronounce judgment on others? Why do people believe they should point out a wrongdoers wrongdoings? Every person knows the things he or she has done with his or her life good and bad. Do people honestly believe they must remind others of their faults at every opportunity? If you are constantly pointing to others flaws and shortcomings I will pose this question: do you somehow believe they have forgotten?

People being judgmental is one reason many people who desperately need Jesus don't bother to seek Him out in the church. There are men and women who fear that someone is going to say something to them about how they are living. Again, if you are someone who likes to constantly remind people of their past mistakes, do you think they have somehow forgotten? What is the point in holding people's past against them; and for the most part, judgmental people are not practicing righteous indignation as they might imagine that they are. It is my opinion that people who like to stand in judgment over others are on an ego trip. People who judge others often imagine that they are better than the people they are looking down on, as if the Lord Jesus did not have to cover their sins with His blood all the same.

It is possible that there were many people in the village

who looked down on this woman because of her past mistakes because there is always someone who will look down his or her nose at others, imagining that they are morally superior and also imagining that God feels the very same way, thinking to themselves, "What would God want with a sinner like that?" As if we are not all sinners before a righteous God. What does the Bible plainly state about all of humanity when it comes to sin?

"For all have sinned, and come short of the glory of God." Romans 3:23 KJV

All sin is egregious in the eyes of God. The Lord Jesus took the punishment for all sin upon Himself which means yours and mine and everyone else's, and one sin is no worse than any other. I realize there are some people who desire to take issue with this point. There is always someone who will argue, "So you think the sin of lying is as bad as the sin of murder?" The answer to this question is, sin is sin. Do you imagine that the Lord Jesus suffered any more or any less on the cross for the murderer than He did for the liar? The more direct question to be asked is this: do you think that your sin amounts to so little that it was not necessary for the Lord Jesus to die in your place? Do you imagine your transgression to be so light that the Lord Jesus only took one nail for you and did not have to die for you to be saved? This argument sounds absurd on its face and that is because it is. What is the point? Mankind should stop passing judgment on each other on the basis of what we think we know. Believers should stop standing in judgment over others, imagining themselves to be in something of a better position before God when all sin is an affront to God and the Lord Jesus died for every sinner.

How many people have walked away from the church and now avoid church for the same reason the Samaritan woman avoided going to the well in the mornings? How many people have been turned away from the gospel, not because of the message, but because of the messengers? And, if when thinking upon people who are like the Samaritan woman, who avoid church because of the judgmental attitudes in Christians, you think to yourself, "Good. I'm glad people like that don't go to my church. God doesn't need men and women like that in His church." Here is a wake up call for you. God doesn't need you either!

"And think not to say within yourselves, We have Abraham to our father: for I say unto you, that God is able of these stones to raise up children unto Abraham." Matthew 3:9 KJV

God does not need anyone, but He wants us. It is better to be wanted than needed. If God only kept us around out of necessity, the minute there was no longer a need we are no longer needed, but because the Lord desires a relationship with us based upon His love, the relationship will never be severed. The Lord Jesus loves us to the point that He willingly pursues us, and not because we are anything special, but because He is loving and gracious and kind. The Lord Jesus is loving and gracious and kind even to men and women who have made mistakes and made a mess out of their lives.

"When therefore the Lord knew how the Pharisees had heard that Jesus made and baptized more disciples than John, (Though Jesus Himself baptized not, but His disciples,) He left Judea, and departed again into Galilee. <u>And He must needs go through Samaria</u>." John 4:1-4 KJV (Underline mine)

Take notice that the text specifically says that the Lord Jesus needed to go through Samaria. The Jews in the days of the Lord Jesus did not care much for the Samaritans and the Samaritans did not care much for the Jews. When Assyria invaded Israel carrying away the northern ten tribes captive, the Syrians who repopulated the land encountered problems. In order to learn the ways of the land and also to learn the ways of Israel's God, the Syrians moved many of the Hebrew captives back into the land and there these people began to intermingle. In the eyes of the Jews the Samaritans were half-breeds and as such they were held in contempt. The people of Judea despised the Samaritans to the degree that they would not travel through Samaria if at all possible. When traveling between Galilee and Judea the Jews would go around Samaria instead of through it, which would have been the shorter route. This is again brought out in the text of John chapter four in verse nine.

"Then saith the woman of Samaria unto Him, How is it that thou, being a Jew, asketh drink of me, which am a woman of Samaria? For the Jews have no dealings with the Samaritans." John 4:9 KJV (Underline mine)

The Lord Jesus traveled through Samaria on purpose. The Lord Jesus sat down at the well in Sychar for a reason, and what was His reason? He wanted to introduce Himself personally to this woman who had been married five times and was at the time living with a man to whom she was not married. The Lord Jesus desired to introduce Himself to this woman because she was waiting for the Messiah.

"The woman saith unto Him, I know that Messiah cometh, which is called Christ: when He is come He will tell us all things." John 4:25 KJV

Clearly the Lord Jesus placed a high value on the life of this one woman. Clearly the Lord Jesus loves sinners to the degree that He actively pursues them. The Lord Jesus went out of His way to interact with this woman so that she would come to know Him and be saved. He is willing to do the very same thing for every sinner, which means the Lord Jesus doesn't feel the same about people that we sometimes do. The Lord Jesus is unwilling to write anyone off.

"I exhort therefore, that, first of all, supplications, prayers, intercessions, and giving of thanks, be made for all men; for kings, and for all that are in authority; that we may lead a quiet and peaceable life in all godliness and honesty. For this is good and acceptable in the sight of God our Savior; Who will have all men to be saved, and to come

unto the knowledge of the truth." 1 Timothy 2:1-4 KJV (Underline mine)

It is the Lord's desire that everyone would be saved. The Lord Jesus is not willing to let anyone perish so much so that He would go out of His way to visit an obscure little village in Samaria to save one soul. God does not write anyone off. God does not feel the same about people that we sometimes do. God is not going to dislike or destroy anyone just because we do not care for them. In fact, the Lord Jesus will go out of His way to ensure all people hear the gospel so that they can respond in faith and be saved.

The Lord Jesus loves people so much that He is willing to allow Christians and the church to continue on a sin-cursed earth among a sinful and wicked generation to preach the good news so that they have the opportunity to repent and be saved. If you have ever wondered about all the evil and suffering in the world and if you have ever wondered why the church exists in the middle of sin and suffering, and why Christians sometimes suffer at the hands of sinful individuals, it is because, *"For God so loved the world,"* that He has now placed His church in this world, and empowered the church through the indwelling presence of the Holy Spirit to preach the gospel of His Son. Which means the church does not exist to pass judgment on people. The church exists to preach Jesus so that people can be saved just like the woman at the well.

In considering the nature and disposition if this woman we should also consider the response of the Lord Jesus. The Lord Jesus came to this woman who had some serious issues and there He met her greatest need which was Himself.

"The woman saith unto Him, I know that Messiah cometh, which is called Christ: when He is come, He will tell us all things. Jesus saith unto her, I that speak to thee am He." John 4:25-26 KJV (Underline mine)

This woman knew that the Messiah was coming. This

woman was waiting and expecting the Messiah to lead everyone into truth. I don't imagine she ever considered that the Messiah Himself would come to her little village just to introduce Himself to her personally, but this is exactly what He did. If the Lord Jesus is willing to go to these lengths to save this woman you must understand that He would do the very same thing to save you.

The Lord's love is unconditional. The Lord loves you because of who you are, not because of how you have lived, or how you have not lived, or because of what you can or cannot do for the church. Nor does the Lord hate you for the things you have done, even if you have committed the most atrocious of sins. The Lord Jesus loves you because His nature is love. The Lord Jesus loves you because you are His creation. The Lord Jesus loves you because of who you are and because of who He is. The Lord Jesus desires to redeem you from sin. The Lord Jesus desires your eternal salvation because you are precious to Him and knowing this removes any reason anyone might have to justify not repenting of sins and placing faith in Him.

You cannot reason that you are too awful a sinner to be saved. You cannot reason that you are so good you do not need to be saved. The only conclusion mankind can come to in light of the knowledge of who Jesus is, is that you must be saved and you can only be saved in and through Jesus. The fact that the Lord Jesus loves you unconditionally means you can be saved. The Lord Jesus will save you. The Lord Jesus will rescue you from sin. You can have a real and living relationship with Jesus if this is the honest desire of your heart. All you have to do is ask.

CHAPTER
TWENTY ONE

The Pool at Bethesda

"If any man be in Christ, he is a new creature: old things are passed away; behold, all things become new." 2 Corinthians 5:17

I quote this verse frequently because this is what I experience in coming into a living relationship with the Lord Jesus. I am not the man I was when I was first born into this world. I have been born-again. I am a new creation in Christ. I am a changed person. So much so that my friends and family took notice of the difference in me. One of my siblings once said to me that I was only going to church and "being all Christian," in order to become my father's (a believer and a pastor) favorite. Coming to faith in the Lord Jesus resulted in a changed life. The Holy Spirit produced real changes in me. He put new desires in my heart and He also lit a fire in my soul. After coming to Christ by faith I realized that my life had potential and I began to want to fulfill my potential. This is the same experience the apostle Paul claimed.

"For I am the least of the apostles, that am not meet to be called an apostle, because I persecuted the church of God. But by the grace of God I am what I am: and His grace which was bestowed upon me was not in vain; but I labored more abundantly than they all: yet not I, but the grace of God which was with me." 1 Corinthians 15:9-10 KJV

Before Paul met the risen Lord Jesus on the road to Damascus he was very zealously minded to protect his religion, but he was acting in ignorance. After encountering the Lord Jesus he was a changed man, so much so that while at one time he persecuted the church, now he lives to serve the Lord and His church with great fervor. Paul says that after coming to know Christ he was minded to work harder than every other preacher in the world.

Some may be inclined to believe that it was pride that was motivating Paul. Some may want to believe that Paul was trying to win first place in the game many play. This game is found in cultural Christianity where people like to pretend to be the most spiritual believer so as to appear more Christian than his or her peers. In the world today there are many people who profess belief in Christ who are trying to out-Christian all other Christians. This is why they make a show of sitting up front. This is why they seek out the chief places in the church. This is why they would never be caught in church in anything less than their Sunday best. This is why they like to be called upon to pray so that they might be seen by others doing spiritual things. This is a game a lot of people play with their lives, but Paul's striving to work harder in the ministry and preaching the gospel was not done in competition with Apollos, or Peter, or John. Paul was being driven by his love for the Lord Jesus. Paul's desire was to serve his Lord well.

When you are filled with the Holy Spirit you become marked by the Spirit of excellence. This Spirit of excellence is the Holy Spirit of God and because of His presence, excellence becomes the desire of your heart. This phenomena is difficult to explain; it must be experienced. I cannot explain, other than to say it is the outworking of the Holy Spirit in my life; what I know is that the desire of my heart is to be the best at everything I endeavor to attempt with my life. I am not motivated by a desire to be better than anyone else. I am motivated by the desire for my life to reflect well upon my Lord and Savior, Jesus. The Holy

Spirit lives within me and as a child of God my desire is to be marked by excellence.

My understanding is that all genuine believers in Christ are marked by the very same desire. How could a true believer not be marked by excellence? It is the indwelling presence of the Holy Spirit that marks us and sets us apart. What does this mean? It means Christians ought to stand out from those who do not know Christ. Does it mean that Christians will always be the best at what they do? Not necessarily, but when a Christian does set his or her mind to do something his or her heart's desires is to bring glory to God and so he or she will absolutely give his or her very best. As God's children we are driven to be at our very best always.

"A son honors his father, and a servant his master: if then I be a father, where is mine honor? And if I be a master, where is my fear? Saith the LORD of host unto you. O priest, that despise My name. And ye say, Wherein have we despised Thy name? Ye offer polluted bread upon My altar; and ye say, Wherein have we polluted thee? In that ye say, The table of the LORD is contemptible. And if ye offer blind for sacrifice, is it not evil? And if ye offer the lame and the sick, is it not evil? Offer it now unto thy governor; will he be pleased with thee, or accept thy person? Saith the LORD of hosts. Who is there even among you that would shut the doors for naught? Neither do ye kindle fire on Mine altar for naught. I have no pleasure in you, saith the LORD of hosts, neither will I accept an offering at thy hand." Malachi 1:6-10 KJV

The Lord's indictment against Israel was that they honored Him with their lips but they did not genuinely love Him. When the people of Israel in Malachi's day worshiped, their offering was weak and anemic and pathetic. When they gave an offering they were only willing to give things they would have thrown out or cast off. They offered the Lord the things they didn't feel were fit for themselves. These men and women who claimed to be the children of God only offered God their leftovers and cast-offs, and yet they continued to flood the altar of the Lord with tears and prayers expecting to be blessed, and they could not understand why they were not. The men and women of Israel in Malachi's day were not marked by excellence in anything they did when it came to worship and service and this is because they did not truly love God.

When a person calls upon the name of the Lord Jesus with an honest desire to be saved, the Holy Spirit moves into his or her life and changes him or her and he or she is changed forever. This person then becomes a whole new creation in Christ and they are truly different. When you come to Christ everything about you will change and everything in your life will change. You cannot help it because you are not the person you once were. Which means, if the Lord Jesus has not made a difference in your life; if you are not now marked by the Holy Spirit; if you do not know new desires and seek to live in a whole new way, a way that is marked by the excellence of God, or at the very least a new desire to fulfill your God-given potential, then you have not yet met the risen Savior. If coming to know the Lord Jesus has not changed everything about you and your life, you have not met Jesus. At the most you are probably just playing religious games and flirting with God.

Do people play religious games? Yes, but I don't know why. Playing games with God will only hurt you in the end. Though the Lord is gracious and will be patient with you while you play your games there will come a point when you will cross the line and at this point the Holy Spirit will say, "Enough!" At this point everything you have imagined that you have gotten by with will come home to roost and you will find yourself in a world of hurt. Playing games with God is a dangerous thing and if you don't know this, I suggest you read Acts chapter five and pay attention to what happened to a couple named Ananias and Saphira.

What I cannot fathom is why people who do not have a genuine relationship with the Lord Jesus bother with church? Why do people who do not honestly love God make a show of religion? I took my question to the Lord in prayer and the Holy Spirit brought me to John 5 and the Lord's interaction with a man who had been a cripple for 38 years. Sometimes to understand what is happening in the world that surrounds you, you have to understand that mankind in sin has not changed one bit over the years. When you look closely at the Word, asking good questions, the Holy Spirit will bring you illumination.

"After this there was a feast of the Jews; and Jesus went up to Jerusalem. Now there were at Jerusalem by the sheep market a pool, which is called in the Hebrew tongue Bethesda, having five porches. In these lay a great multitude of impotent folk, of blind, halt, withered, waiting for the moving of the water. For an angel went down at a certain season into the pool, and troubled the water: whosoever then first after the troubling of the water stepped in was made whole of whatsoever disease he had. And a certain man was there, which had an infirmity thirty and eight years. When Jesus saw him lie, and knew that he had been now a long time in that case, He saith unto him, Wilt thou be made whole? The impotent man answered Him, Sir, I have no man, when the water is troubled, to put me into the pool: but while I am coming, another steppeth down before me. Jesus saith unto him, Rise, take up thy bed, and walk. And immediately the man was made whole, and took up his bed, and walked: and on the same day was the Sabbath." John 5:1-9 KJV

There was a fountain in Jerusalem situated by the sheep gate. Apparently this fountain had healing properties, but only when an angel stirred the waters. God is merciful and could have provided this fountain if He so desired. What is important to note is that the fountain called Bethesda was a place of healing and blessing. The fountain of Bethesda was a place of mercy as the name "Bethesda," means: "house of mercy." This is the place in Jerusalem where many sick and infirm people gathered to receive help and mercy. Many churches today have incorporated the name "Bethesda" into their church's name and the reason for this is that the church wants people to identify their church as a place to receive God's grace and mercy. Bethesda is a place of mercy.

At any place you experience God operating in grace and mercy, crowds of people will gather. The Bible says that the people came to Jesus at all times to find healing and mercy and there were times that there were so many people coming to Jesus that He did not have time to eat or to sleep. Why did crowds of people come to Jesus? To be healed. To find blessings. To receive mercy. The Lord Jesus made His way to the pool called Bethesda and there He sees a man by the fountain who had been in his crippled condition for 38 years.

"And a certain man was there, which had an infirmity thirty and eight years. When Jesus saw him lie, and knew that he had been long time in that case, He saith unto him, Wilt thou be healed?" John 5:5-6 KJV

The Lord Jesus sees this man lying there and asks him if he wanted to be healed. This question seems out of place, given that the man was lying beside a pool known for its healing properties. One might infer that given the man's condition and where he was at that he was desperate to be healed, but then again not everything is as it appears to be.

In studying this text the first thought that entered my mind was, "Why did the Lord Jesus single out this one man?" I am sure there were many people who were gathered at this pool and the Lord Jesus could have healed every single one of them with a word. Why did the Lord focus His attention on this one man, and then why did He ask him if he wanted to be healed? The reason is found in this truth: just because someone is sitting in a place of healing, or a place of mercy, does not mean he or she genuinely desires to be healed or to find mercy. Some people are not looking for blessings they only desire sympathy and what that affords them from others. In the case of the church we can state this truth in this way: Just because someone attends church doesn't mean they actually desire the Lord to change their lives.

Why wouldn't this man want to be healed? Why wouldn't people genuinely desire to know the life-changing presence of the Holy Spirit? It is due to the fact that life is easier when you are in a position where others will do everything for you. Life is easier when people who are moved by compassion will do just about anything you ask. If the man at the pool of Bethesda were to be healed, he might very well lose his livelihood, because his weakness, his handicap, his infirmity was his means of living. This man at the pool of Bethesda could well have been like many of the people that are seen today sitting on street corners holding signs that say, "Will work for food." This person does not really desire to work, but he or she wants people to think he or she is willing, so that others will be inclined to show mercy and give money, so that he or she does not really have to work for food.

If you are not able-bodied there is no shame in relying on the kindness of others. If you are not able-bodied there is no shame in having your living come from family or from social security or some other program; this is the very reason these things exist. If you are not able-bodied there is no shame in relying upon church programs to make ends meet, and the church should be disposed to offer these things; but an able-bodied person living off the good will and mercy of others is shameful and it is sinful.

"Now we command you, brethren, in the name of our Lord Jesus Christ, that ye withdraw yourselves from every brother that walketh disorderly, and not after the traditions which he received of us. For yourselves know how ye ought to follow us: for we behaved not ourselves disorderly among you; neither did we eat any man's bread for naught; but wrought with labor and travail night and day, that we might not be chargeable to any of you: not because we have not power, but to make ourselves an ensample unto you to follow us. For even when we were with you, this we commanded you, That if any would not work, neither should he eat." 2 Thessalonians 3:6-10

KJV

The Bible says if you are an able-bodied adult, then you ought to be willing to work to provide for you and your family's needs.

"But if any man provide not for his own, and specially for those of his own house, he hath denied the faith, and is worse than an infidel." 1 Timothy 5:8 KJV

The reason the Lord Jesus did not stand up and offer to heal everyone at the pool is because He knew that many of these people were there in order to solicit sympathy from others and also generosity, and this same condition exists in the church. There are many people who only attend church to illicit sympathy from others hoping that others will do for them or bless them in some way all the while they are very capable of doing these things for themselves.

At one church I served the building we used for worship sat directly adjacent to an apartment complex. When cars began to show up in the parking lot on Sunday mornings a young lady who lived in that complex would make her way over to the church. Before, after, and during the service she would make her way through the congregation, first sitting by one person and then moving to another. As she went she would tell one sob story after another and then ask people to help her with money. After this happened a couple of weeks in a row a few of the people she had solicited came to me to complain. They said, "Pastor, every week this young lady asks us for money and we are getting put out by it." It got so bad I had to ask her to leave. This young lady was not interested in the life-changing power that comes through living by faith in the Lord Jesus. This young lady was only interested in soliciting sympathy from others in order to get money. In the 22 years I have been serving in the ministry I have found many people sitting in the church who are similar to this young lady. These men and women are not too difficult to identify. When they have nothing to gain from being at church they vanish. The reason they disappear is because physical or financial gain is their only reason for attending church.

There are many people who find their way in the church and not because they have a living relationship with the Lord Jesus. These men and women are involved in church to get what they can get, which is why their lives are not marked by the change that the Holy Spirit brings. When a person truly knows the Lord Jesus then this person will live his or her life according to the promises of God's word which tells us that if we have a need, we bring that need to the Lord in prayer and He will meet that need. In addition to this, when a person comes into an honest relationship with the Lord Jesus he or she will seek to be a blessing to the church and a blessing to his or her brothers and sisters in Christ, not a burden. When a person is filled with the Holy Spirit he or she desires for others to see Christ Jesus exalted in his or her life and this alone drives him or her to be marked by excellence.

This doesn't mean that people do not need help every once in a while. There are instances in which the Lord will bring men and women into the church who are in need so the church will step up in the name of the Lord and meet that need. Often this is a test of the love and faithfulness of the church, but I have often found that when a true child of God comes to the church needing help, he or she is reluctant to ask, and when given the opportunity, the believer will work to rectify the situation. The point being that the church ought to help people who have genuine needs when it is in her power to do so, but there is a difference of attitude found in people who are in genuine need and those who are simply looking to take advantage of the kindness of others. The Christian desires to be a blessing to his or her church. The Christian desires to honor God with his or her life. The child of God wants to see his or her church reaching people with the gospel of Jesus Christ and desires his or her church to have everything it needs to be successful; to the point of giving of themselves in service. Those who are looking to take advantage only care about themselves. The true believer loves the Lord Jesus and His church and this is because we are a new creation in Christ and the desires of our heart have changed. When you are truly a child of God, when it comes to our Lord Jesus, nothing but the very best will do.

Did the man who was at the pool of Bethesda become a new creation in Christ? I do not think that he did or the Lord would not of given him the warning He did when he encountered the man in the temple.

"Afterward Jesus findeth him in the temple, and said unto him, Behold, thou art made whole: sin no more, lest a worse thing come unto thee." John 5:14 KJV

The Lord Jesus knows the hearts of all people and He knew what was happening in this man's soul. The Lord Jesus knew that this man was going right back to his old sinful habits, which means the great gift the man had received from the Lord did not have a lasting affect. This is the same in the lives of many. People come to church where they encounter the living Lord Jesus and they receive grace, mercy, and blessings by having some real or felt need addressed, but once they are away from the church they walk right back into that old way of living, and this is because in their hearts they never left it. These men and women are playing with fire by playing games with God.

This does not have to be your manner of life. You can have a genuine life-changing encounter with the Lord Jesus if this is the honest desire of your heart. All that you must do is call upon the name of the Lord Jesus, lifting up a prayer of faith, asking Him for a new life. If you pray, being sincere, you will be saved; the Holy Spirit will come to live in you and He will then completely change you life.

CHAPTER TWENTY TWO

Peter The Backslider

"Then drew near to Him all the publicans and sinners for to hear Him. And the Pharisees and scribes murmured, saying, This man receiveth sinners, and eateth with them. And He spake this parable unto them, saying, What man of you, having an hundred sheep, if he lose one of them, doth not leave the ninety and nine in the wilderness, and go after that which is lost, until he find it? And when he hath found it, he layeth it on his shoulders, rejoicing. And when he cometh home, he calleth together his friends and neighbors, saying unto them, Rejoice with me; for I have found my sheep which was lost. I say unto you, that likewise joy shall be in heaven over one sinner that repenteth, more than over ninety and nine just persons, which need no repentance." Luke 15:1-7 KJV

I once read, "I wish Christians would stop saying the we cannot fully understand the nature of God's love." I suppose the person who wrote this was claiming to have a full comprehension of the love of God, but truthfully mankind does not.

"For when we were yet without strength, in due time Christ died for the ungodly. For scarcely for a righteous man will one die: yet peradventure for a good man some would even dare to die. But God commendeth His love toward us, in that, when we were yet sinners, Christ died for us." Romans 5:6-8 KJV

To gain some understanding of the love of God, take the

time to consider this statement found in the book of Romans in terms of your own life and what you would be willing to die for. Paul says that rarely would someone be willing to die for a righteous person, and perhaps someone may be willing to die for a good man, but then Almighty God allowed His only begotten Son to die for a world filled with no-good, hate-filled, rotten, sinners. Christ Jesus died for the ungodly.

Who would you be willing to die for? Would you be willing to die for your husband, wife, children, or family? Maybe, but would you be willing to die for a perfect stranger even if this stranger was a good person? Would you be willing to die for a bad person? Would you be willing to lay down your life for someone who had been convicted of a serious and heinous crime? The love of God goes even deeper than this because He sent His only begotten Son into the world to save and entire world full of sinners. Father God allowed His son to die for a world of rotten people. Would you be willing to allow your dearest loved one to die for a good person? Would you be willing to allow any of your loved ones to die for a bad person? Truly the depth of love God has for His creation is unfathomable and beyond human comprehension.

In my opinion, the reason someone might believe he or she can understand the depths of God's love is due to pride. People today are so in love with themselves they believe that God should have sent the Lord Jesus to die for them. I understand that not all people believe this way. There are people who actually know and believe the opposite. There are men and women who believe that there is no way God could ever love them, but both ideas are false. There is no one so perfect that they deserve the love of God and there is no one so un-redeemable that God does not love them and would not do what it takes to redeem them. This truth may be discerned by looking into the life of the apostle Peter.

Peter was an early disciple of the Lord Jesus. He was also an apostle and a church father. Peter was one of the original twelve disciples and of these twelve he shared a special place in relationship with the Lord along with James and John. Peter recognized the deity of the Lord Jesus through divine illumination. It was Peter who proclaimed to the Lord Jesus, "Thou art the Christ the Son of the living God." (Matthew 16:16) Peter was a bold man and he was also a very brave man. It was Peter who moved to defend the Lord Jesus at the mount of Olives as the temple guards attempted to arrest Him. It was Peter who cut the ear off the high priest servant. Peter was allowed to witness the Lord's transfiguration on the mountain. Peter also walked on water. Peter was the special envoy sent by the Lord to Cornelius the centurion. He witnessed the outpouring of the Spirit on the Gentile believers. This one event helped Peter to understand that the Lord Jesus is the Savior of all mankind, Jew and Gentile alike. Peter, after being filled with the Spirit at Pentecost, preached to thousands which resulted in thousands professing faith in the Lord Jesus. The apostle Peter is most definitely a hero and champion of the faith. This same Peter also denied Jesus three times.

"Now Peter sat without in the palace: and a damsel came unto him, saying, Thou also wast with Jesus of Galilee. But he denied before them all, saying, I know not what thou sayest, and when he was gone out into the porch, another maid saw him, and said unto them that were there, This fellow was also with Jesus of Nazareth. And again he denied with an oath, I do not know the man. And after a while came unto him they that stood by, and said to Peter, Surely thou art one of them: for thy speech bewrayeth thee. Then began he to curse and to swear, saying, I know not the man. And immediately the cock crew." Matthew 26:69-74 KJV

This same man who at one time declared to the Lord Jesus that he would die with Him if he must, cowers before a damsel, a maid, and a gathering of people. This was not the apostle Peter's finest hour. This is certainly not the character of a brave man. This is not to say anybody else is any better or would have behaved differently in the same set of circumstances. How many

Christians placed in a situation where their faith in the Lord Jesus might be frowned upon decided it would probably be more prudent to keep their faith to themselves than to take a bold stance for Christ. The entire world holds a hostile disposition toward the Lord Jesus and His church and Christianity in general and so it is not too difficult to imagine Christians facing this situation. Many believers face hostility from their own family as this is exactly how the Lord Jesus said life would be in this age. Peter denied Christ when he thought belonging to Christ might be a detriment to his health or to his standing and reputation among a group of strangers, as do many believers. Many people who profess to love and serve the Lord Jesus often abandon their love for Him in the presence of strangers. Many believers are all too willing to avoid being labeled a Christian and often will not behave in the manner that a Christian should when they find themselves under the pressure of their peers. Peter's denial affected him deeply.

"And Peter remembered the word of Jesus, which said unto him, before the cock crow, thou shalt deny Me thrice. And he went out and wept bitterly." Matthew 26:75 KJV (Underline mine)

Failure will get the best of us. When we experience failure we are prone to believing that we can never recover or be recovered. When we fail we are prone to believing that we cannot be forgiven. Peter at one time bragged before the Lord, *"Though all men shall be offended because of Thee, yet will I never be offended."* (Matthew 26:33) and then he failed, not in the presence of certain death, not after being confronted by hostile men, but under the pressure of a little girl. When Peter realized just how much he did not even come close to fulfilling his word he went out and wept bitterly. Peter was deeply affected by his actions and so he abandoned the calling on his life. Peter believed that he had been disqualified from being the Lord's disciple.

What was the calling the Lord placed on Peter's life?

"And Jesus, walking by the sea of Galilee, saw two brethren, Simon

called Peter, and Andrew his brother, casting a net into the sea; for they were fishers. And He saith unto them, Follow Me, <u>and I will make you fishers of men</u>." Matthew 4:18-19 KJV (Underline mine)

The fact that Peter had abandoned his calling is brought out in the text of John.

"After these things Jesus shewed Himself again to the disciples as the sea of Tiberias; and on this wise shewed He Himself. There were together Simon Peter, and Thomas called Didymus, and Nathanael of Cana in Galilee, and the sons of Zebedee, and two other of His disciples. Simon Peter saith unto them, <u>I go a fishing</u>." John 21:1-3 KJV (Underline mine)

When Peter tells the other disciples with him that he is going fishing he is declaring that he is going back to the life he once knew before the Lord Jesus called him from it. Peter is telling everyone that he is once again a fisher of fish. Peter is sliding back into his old life. How do I come to this understanding? If Peter were simply going to spend a day on the lake relaxing and doing a little fishing, the Lord Jesus would not have shown up personally to remind Peter of the calling He had placed on his life. This is also why this account in John is very similar to the account in Matthew when the Lord first called Peter to be a fisher of men.

Peter and the other disciples fish all night and catch nothing. At dawn the Lord Jesus is walking on the shoreline and He calls to them asking, "did you catch anything?" The answer is no. Jesus then instructs the fishermen where to cast their nets to find fish. When the disciples cast on the right side of the boat they catch many fish. These things take place in the account in John and in Luke and yet these are two separate occasions. In the book of Luke, Jesus is preaching along the shoreline of the sea of Galilee. He asks Peter permission to use his boat. Peter and his friends are mending their nets after having fished all night and catching nothing. When the Lord is finished with His message He instructs Peter to launch out into the deep and let down his nets for a catch.

"Master we have toiled all night, and have taken nothing: neverthe-less at Thy word I will let down the net and when they had this done, they enclosed a great multitude of fishes: and their net brake." Luke 5:5-6 KJV

At this point Peter falls at the feet of Jesus begging Him to depart because he becomes very aware of the fact that he is a sin-ner. Peter realizes that he is in the presence of God. In response the Lord says, *"Fear not; from henceforth thou shalt catch men."* Luke 5:10 KJV Both accounts are very similar. What happened at the first encounter? The Lord Jesus called Peter into His min-istry. With the second encounter the Lord Jesus has engineered things to be very similar to remind Peter of the calling on his life. The Lord Jesus did not save, sanctify, and gift the apostle Peter to be a fisher of fish, but to be a fisher of men. Though Peter may have thought he was finished in doing the Lord's work, the Lord Jesus was not done with the apostle Peter just yet. After this gentle reminder the Lord Jesus takes Peter apart by himself and renews the calling on his life.

"So when they had dined, Jesus saith unto Simon Peter, Simon, son of Jonas, lovest thou Me more than these? He saith unto Him, yea Lord; Thou knowest that I love Thee. He saith unto Him, Feed My lambs. He saith unto him a second time, Simon, son of Jonas, lovest thou Me? He saith unto Him, Yea, Lord; Thou knowest that I love Thee. He saith unto him, Feed My sheep. He saith unto him a third time, Simon, son of Jonas, lovest thou Me? Peter was grieved because He said unto him the third time, Lovest thou Me? And he said unto Him, Lord, Thou knowest all things; Thou knowest that I love Thee. Jesus saith unto him, Feed My sheep." John 21:15-17 KJV

The Lord Jesus asks Peter three times if he truly loved Him because Peter had denied Jesus three times. The point I hope to emphasize from this interaction between the Lord Jesus and Peter is this: When the apostle Peter thought that he had so completely failed that he decided to turn back to his old life, the Lord Jesus showed up personally to renew the calling on his life. The Lord Jesus made a personal visit from heaven to remind Peter that he had been delivered to a new life and that God called him to go in a different direction.

"What man of you, having an hundred sheep, if he lose one of them, doth not leave the ninety and nine in the wilderness, and go after that which is lost." Luke 15:4 KJV

The very same love that moved God to send His only begotten Son and also moved the Lord Jesus to die for us so that we could be redeemed, is the love that also moves the Lord Jesus to pursue His sheep when they wander away. Love moves the Lord Jesus to pursue us when we fail and when we think to walk away from our new life in Christ. Love moves the Lord Jesus to call us back when we backslide. This means the love of God is truly incomprehensible on the human level because the love we exercise toward one another is usually abandoned at the first sign of trouble.

I wonder how it is that there are people who believe the Lord Jesus would simply forgo and abandon His sheep that wander away? I wonder how it is that many Christians believe that God disqualifies His called and chosen for whatever reason instead of redeeming them? Do people really believe the Lord Jesus would simply abandon men and women He paid such a dear and high price to redeem? I honestly believe the concept of grace, being motivated by love, escapes any person who believes and preaches that a true child of God can lose salvation. If you are someone who believes that God would easily cast away His children and that they would lose their salvation, something that we have done nothing to obtain and that we can do nothing to keep, do you honestly believe God is willing to let you go when you make a mistake? How exactly do you imagine our Lord and Savior to be?

Frail human beings with fragile egos write each other off

all the time. Frail human beings with fragile egos enjoy writing people off and disqualifying people from being a part of their lives for even the most minute infraction. We currently live in a world filled with the perpetually offended. We currently live within a culture that desires to cancel and destroy men and women who do not hold to what is considered popular beliefs. The motivation behind "cancel culture" is having a god complex. Those who are a part of "cancel culture" desire everyone to worship at their altar. The interesting thing about the practices of "cancel culture" is that the church and Christians made a practice of canceling each other long before it became en-vogue in modern vapid pop-culture. What happens within certain churches if you show up wearing the wrong kind of clothes? You get canceled. What happens in some congregations if you fail to toe-the-line when it comes to their vaunted traditions? You get canceled. This is nothing less than Christians practicing "cancel culture."

These things do have a bearing on our walk with the Lord Jesus because other people's actions and attitudes will color our thinking. When a believer encounters an attempt to cancel them they may believe, because others are willing to write them off having made a mistake, that possibly, God would do the same. This belief is manifested when men and women say things like, "If you knew the things I have done in my life then you would know that God could never forgive me." In the case of believers they may say something such as, "If you knew the things I have done in my life then you would know that God would never call me into any ministry." How many people, because we live in a truly judgmental cancel culture of our own creation, simply cancel themselves because they wrongfully believe they don't measure up? In case you do not realize this, no person will ever measure up to God's standards because they are perfection and no one is perfect.

The Lord Jesus did not call Peter into the ministry because of who he was or because of what he was capable of providing. The Lord Jesus called Peter into the ministry because this is what

He wanted to do. The same situation holds true for all the Lord's disciples. The Lord Jesus called Peter into the ministry because He loved Peter and He desired Peter to be a part of what He was doing. The Lord Jesus calls all those who love Him into a place of service for the same reason, and the only person who can disqualify anyone from serving the Lord Jesus is God. What we may learn from Peter's example is that the Lord doesn't do this at all. In fact, the Lord Jesus works to restore His children to their calling. The Lord Jesus did not write Peter off. The Lord Jesus left the glory of heaven to personally restore Peter to his place of ministry. The Lord Jesus left the ninety and nine to find the one who wandered away.

Maybe you are thinking, "Well yeah, but this is the apostle Peter we are talking about and I'm not Peter." When you read about Peter's life do you really see anything in him that sets him apart as being different from anyone else? Did he talk too much? Yes. Was he boastful? Did he brag? Yes. Did he fail? Did he even go so far as to deny the Lord Jesus? The answer to all these is yes. We have all fallen short of the glory of God, but God will never quit on us. So don't let someone else's hang-ups keep you from fulfilling your calling or potential. Don't let someone else's hang-ups hinder your walk of faith with the Lord Jesus. The Christian is called to keep following Jesus by faith. Let God cancel the cancel culture. The only thing that can ever stop you from fulfilling your God-given potential in Christ Jesus is you.

CHAPTER TWENTY THREE

John

The purpose of the law and everything that goes with it is twofold. First and foremost the law exposes the despicable nature of sin that resides within humanity.

"What shall we say then? Is the law sin? God forbid. Nay, I had not known sin, but by the law: for I had not known lust, except the law had said, Thou shalt not covet." Romans 7:7 KJV

The law does not serve to make someone righteous. The law only exposes how unrighteous mankind truly is. If you believe that keeping the law will make you a righteous person, a lesson in critical thinking becomes necessary.

Have you ever broken any one of the ten commandments? The answer to this question is yes for everyone. This is easily proven with one question: have you ever told a lie?

"For whosoever shall keep the whole law, and yet offend in one point, he is guilty of all." James 2:10 KJV

Having established that everyone has at one time or another broken the law, a point which is repeatedly made in the scriptures, the question now becomes, what good does keeping a law that you have already broken serve? Does keeping the law that you have already broken make you righteous before God? If you were to keep the law in its entirety for the rest of your life, what will you do about the instances in which you have already broken the law? Previous acts of lawlessness are not done away with by time. The Bible does not say that time covers a multitude of sins and yet this is exactly what many people believe. Many people conduct themselves as if the farther away from sin you get the less it matters to God, as if sin has some sort of statute of limitations.

As a part of our ministry and outreach at the church I currently pastor, we minister in the local jail. Every time I go to teach there I am locked in with a room full of law-abiding citizens. They were not law-abiding before they were put in jail, but now that they are under constraint of the law by force they certainly are. Does this mean that these people are now righteous? No, they are still guilty of the lawlessness they committed that resulted in their incarceration, but in the outworking of the due process of justice, the law will reveal the degree of their lawlessness and it is the same when it comes to the law of God. The law reveals the degree of lawlessness in us. Which means, even if you were to keep the law perfectly for the rest of your natural life, because you have already broken the law you are guilty of lawlessness and therefore are not righteous before God.

"There is none righteous no not one." Romans 3:10 KJV

"Therefore by the deeds of the law there shall no flesh be justified in His sight: for by the law is the knowledge of sin." Romans 3:20 KJV

The second purpose to the law is that it serves as our schoolmaster that brings us to Christ.

"Is the law then against the promises of God? God forbid: for if there had been a law given which could have given life, verily righteousness should have been by the law, but the scripture hath concluded all under sin, that the promise of faith of Jesus Christ might be given to them that believe. But before faith came, we were kept under the law, shut up unto the faith which should afterwards be revealed. Wherefore the law was our schoolmaster to bring us unto Christ,

that we might be justified by faith, but after that faith is come, we are no longer under a schoolmaster." Galatians 3:21-25 KJV (Underline mine)

The law was not made for the righteous. If any person were genuinely righteous, no law would be necessary, as a righteous person would always do what was right. The law exists to constrain the unrighteous.

"Knowing this, that the law is not made for a righteous man, but for the lawless and disobedient, for the ungodly and sinners, for unholy and profane, for murderers of fathers and murderers of mothers, for man-slayers, for whore-mongers, for them that defile themselves with mankind, for men-stealers, for liars, for perjured persons, and there be any other thing that is contrary to sound doctrine." 1 Timothy 1:9-10 KJV

The law serves to keep sinners in check until such a time as a person is brought to faith in Jesus Christ. If mankind were indeed righteous there would not be any need for the law. The law exists to constrain sin.

When a person comes to faith in the Lord Jesus the Holy Spirit writes the law of God on his or her heart.

"For by one offering He hath perfected forever them that are sanctified. Whereof the Holy Ghost also is a witness to us: for after that He had said before, This is the covenant that I will make with them after those days, saith the Lord, I will put my laws into their hearts, and in their minds will I write them; and their sins and iniquities will I remember no more." Hebrews 10:14-17 KJV

The true believer in the Lord Jesus, through having the law of God written on his or her heart by the Holy Spirit, will instinctively know the law. A Christian knows what is according to or in keeping with the law of God. A Christian knows through the power of the Holy Spirit what is right before God and what is not. While it is a shame to have to write this it is true nonetheless. Many people who claim to know and love the Lord Jesus, by their actions, clearly display that the law of God is not written upon their hearts.

"And He is the propitiation for our sins: and not for ours only, but also for the sins of the whole world. <u>And hereby do we know that we know Him, if we keep His commandments.</u> He that saith, I know Him, and keepeth not His commandments, is a liar, and the truth is not in him. But whoso keepeth His word, in him verily is the love of God perfected: hereby we know that we are in Him." 1 John 2:2-5 KJV (Underline mine)

How does the Christian know that he or she truly knows Christ? The Christian instinctively keeps the law of God because the law is written on his or her heart. A true believer does not work at keeping the law. He or she just keeps to the law because keeping God's law is according to his or her new nature in Christ.

"Thou shalt not kill." Exodus 20:13 KJV

This law is now written on the believer's heart.

"Ye have heard that it was said by them of old time, Thou shalt not kill; and whosoever shall kill shall be in danger of the judgment: but I say unto you, That whosoever is angry with his brother without a cause shall be in danger of the judgment: and whosoever shall say to his brother, Raca, shall be in danger of the council; but whosoever shall say, Thou fool, shall be in danger of hell fire." Matthew 5:21-22 KJV

Anger and having the desire to kill and destroy along with denigrating others through name calling and belittling remarks is all connected to the law of God which states, "Thou shall not kill." This is because anger, hatred, and animosity is all generated through a sinful and murderous spirit in the heart, and hatred, anger, and animosity is contrary to the Spirit of God which is the spirit of love. This is not my opinion. This is what is clearly revealed in scripture. The person who has an angry spirit which is revealed through anger issues has a heart that is not right with God. Constant and consistent anger problems do not stem from a heart that is filled with love. Anger and resentment come from a heart that is filled with hate.

What is incredible to know is that the apostle John who wrote, *"Beloved let us love one another: for love is of God; and every one that loveth is born of God, and knoweth God."* 1 John 4:7 KJV, was at one time filled with anger and hatred, but God overcame this man's anger by changing his heart.

"And it came to pass, when the time was come that He should be received up, He steadfastly set His face to go to Jerusalem, and sent messengers before His face: and they went, and entered into a village of the Samaritans, to make ready for Him. And they did not receive Him, because His face was as though He would go to Jerusalem. And when His disciples James and John saw this, they said, Lord, wilt thou that we command fire to come down from heaven, and consume them, even as Elijah did? But He turned, and rebuked them, and said, ye know not what manner of spirit ye are of. For the Son of man is not come to destroy men's lives, but to save them. And they went to another village." Luke 9:51-56 KJV

John was no different than any other person who has ever lived. Being a man of God does not mean that you do not struggle with temptation and sin. John got put out with people the same as everyone else does. Apparently, from the text of Luke 9, John held on to the old hatred and animosity that existed between the Jews and the Samaritans. This animosity reared its head in this incident cited in the passage.

The Lord Jesus was traveling from Galilee to Jerusalem and as He did He sent some of His disciples before Him to find food and lodging. In that time, if you were traveling, you had to find people who were willing to put you up in their homes and who were willing to feed you in order to have accommodations, but the people of Samaria were not disposed to be hospitable to Jews nor were the Jews disposed to interacting with the Samaritans. There was a long-standing animosity between the Jews and the Samaritans, the evidence of which is found in many places in the New Testament. The Samaritans would not receive and give room and board to any traveler who was bound for Jerusalem and this did not sit well with John.

"And when His disciples James and John saw this, they said, Lord, wilt Thou that we command fire to come down from Jerusalem, and to consume them even as Elijah did?" Luke 9:54 KJV

John was not immune to holding on to long-standing animosity. John was not immune to getting put out with people, or being aggravated, or just getting down right angry, and what is revealed in his heart at this point in his life is seen in what he petitions the Lord Jesus to do about these inhospitable Samaritans. John asks the Lord Jesus if He wanted to call down fire from heaven and wipe this village clean off the earth. What is this but unbridled hatred and murder in the heart?

What does anger do to us? It unleashes the darkest desires of our heart. It exposes the depths of our depravity. The degree of our anger and animosity may never be fully exposed to the world, but our anger certainly exposes the depths of our depravity to us. When we get angry with someone this will open us up to what is lying in the deep recesses of our hearts.

"For out of the heart proceed evil thoughts, murders, adulteries, fornications, thefts, false witness, blasphemies: These are the the things which defile a man." Matthew 15:19-20 KJV

What happens inside of you, if when you are driving, someone pulls out in front of you and almost causes a collision? What is your first thought? How do you react?

It is important to note that getting angry is not a sin.

"Be ye angry, and sin not: let not the sun go down upon your wrath: neither give place to the devil." Ephesians 4:26-27 KJV

There are some things that should rightly make the Christian angry. Sin ought to make believers angry. Children being victimized should lead to the church being angry. Abortion ought to move believers to be incensed. Unbridled crime and corruption should rightly make people angry, and it is not a sin to get aggravated and frustrated, and downright mad, but what you do with this anger, the direction your anger moves you, this will determine what is sinful or not.

If injustice makes you angry and moves you to work for justice then your anger is moving you in the right direction, but if you see an injustice and your anger moves you to seek your own idea of justice, this is not a good place. If your anger moves you to be compassionate toward others, such as showing kindness and mercy to the victims of sin, this is the Holy Spirit moving you, but if your anger moves you to desire retaliation and retribution in the form of revenge, you are not being moved to righteousness.

Considering how mankind reacts in anger, I often wonder how it is that hatred comes so easily to us? Why do human beings find it so easy to hate one another? Why do human beings wish death and destruction upon one another without hesitation? And, why do many suppose that they are justified in wishing and hoping for death and destruction to come to others? I imagine that some animosity that wells up comes from the pain we endure and see inflicted upon others and this stirs up our sense of justice. There is some satisfaction in seeing a bully get just what he or she deserves. There is some satisfaction in seeing justice served, but humanity doesn't really understand true justice. True justice is revealed in the Bible as an eye for an eye and a tooth for a tooth. True justice would be for someone who acted out wrongfully to receive the very same consequences as his or her victims, but mankind has a sinful sense of justice that affects our ideas concerning justice and distorts them into a longing for revenge, and how does mankind justify its desire for revenge upon all others? By making ourselves out to be victims and making out that everyone we do not care for is sinful, wicked, and unfit to live.

How does this happen? To move someone to the point

that he or she is willing to kill, all that has to happen is for him or her to stop seeing other people as human beings who have been created in the image of God. All you have to do to move yourself to the place where you would be willing to see others die is to indoctrinate yourself through lies and false narratives to the point that you believe that by removing a certain group of people from existence you would be doing God a favor, and that it is actually according to God's will and a part of God's plan to destroy those people who offend you.

"But I say unto you, That whosoever is angry with his brother without a cause shall be in danger of the judgment: <u>and whosoever shall say to his brother, Raca, shall be in danger of the council: but whosoever shall say, Thou fool, shall be in danger of hell fire</u>." Matthew 5:22 KJV (Underline mine)

The term "Raca" (Vs 22) was an expression of contempt. It was the same as calling someone a fool. Literally the Greek word means moron. The point the Lord is making here is, to call someone a name is to hold them in contempt. What the Bible is expressing is that the person who holds other people in contempt by denigrating them, and calling names, and presenting them as less than human or less than worthy of being treated with basic human dignity, is the same person who holds murder in his or her heart. How could the Nazis murder 6 million Jews? By holding them in contempt. How could the communists in Russia murder 40 million of their own people in the gulags? By holding them in contempt. How is it that now in this age there are men and women who feel justified in creating chaos, destroying cities, and hurting other people? By holding others in contempt, and they do this by labeling anyone who disagrees with their beliefs, or who they simply wish to hate, as a racist. How is it that John could ever imagine that the Lord Jesus would be willing to call down fire from heaven to destroy an entire village in Samaria? He held the Samaritans in contempt.

"But He turned, and rebuked them, and said, Ye know not what man-

ner of spirit ye are of." Luke 9:55 KJV

What was the manner of John's spirit? At the time this event occurred John had not been fully affected by the outpouring of the Holy Spirit. The law had not yet been written on John's heart. John was indeed a disciple of the Lord Jesus, but the imparting of the Holy Spirit did not happen until the day of Pentecost. So John was affected by the old hatred that existed between Jews and Samaritans, but what happened to John's heart after the outpouring of the Holy Spirit? The law was written on his heart. At the outpouring of the Holy Spirit the love of God was implanted into John's heart and this changed the inclination of his heart. John went from being one of the "Son's of Thunder," to being the beloved apostle. John was transformed from being a man who wanted the Lord Jesus to call down fire from heaven to being the man who called upon the church and the believers to love each other with the love of the Lord. With the coming of the Holy Spirit, John came to understand what the Lord Jesus meant when He said, *"For the Son of man is not come to destroy men's lives, but to save them."* (Verse 56)

When you come into a living relationship with the Lord Jesus you simply cannot have a heart filled with hate. It is impossible to hold on to hatred and hold others in contempt with the love of God filling your heart. As born-again children of God, believers have been called to love everyone including our enemies.

I want those who are reading this who may be struggling with anger issues to understand, though John may have had some anger issues, this did not stop the Lord Jesus from calling him into the ministry. Though John may have held on to some long-standing prejudice and though he may have been unfavorably inclined toward a certain nationality, or ethnicity, this did not disqualify him from being utilized by the Holy Spirit to preach the gospel in mighty ways. The apostle John is the same man who wrote the gospel of John, 1, 2, and 3 John and the book of Revelation. John served as pastor in the church at Ephesus.

John was an elder, an apostle, a church father, and an original disciple of the Lord Jesus. The Lord did not excuse John's misplaced and misdirected anger. The Lord delivered him from it. The Holy Spirit removed John's animosity and replaced it with love and He can and will do the very same for you if you are struggling with these things.

The Lord Jesus changed John's heart and He will do the same for you if you want Him to change your heart, but you have a choice to make. Will you hang on to your old hatred or let the Lord remove this from your heart? It is unfortunate but there are some men and women who prefer to live with their hatred. There are some men and women who prefer being angry at all times. There are some men and women who enjoy the adrenaline rush that comes with being angry and raging at the people they hate. These same men and women often imagine that God hates in the same way they do. Often the calling card of cold dead religion is anger, animosity, and hate. Holding on to hate will only take you to hell. You cannot be filled with the love of God and hatred at the same time.

"Beloved, let us love one another: for love is of God; and everyone that loveth is born of God, and knoweth God. He that loveth not knoweth not God; for God is love." 1 John 4:7-8 KJV

CHAPTER TWENTY FOUR

Paul

A notable political commentator in this present age has become famous through the use of this phrase, "The facts don't care about your feelings." At the heart of this statement lies the truth that feelings do not verify the truth. The reason this must be affirmed is because in this day and age people trust their feelings more than they trust verifiable facts. In this day people are more concerned with how something makes them feel than they are concerned with what is true, and this is a dangerous situation because it allows for the wicked to postulate that what is good is evil and what is evil is good, all based upon feelings, and there are many among us who have a diminished intellectual capacity who are captivated by their feelings who buy into evil wholesale. If we ask, "Is our culture wrong or right?" These men and women would answer, "Who cares as long as you feel good about it." Today is seems as if the world has bought into this lie. Who cares what is right and wrong as long as you feel good about yourself.

"The facts don't care about your feelings." Another way to present this truth is to say that the truth doesn't depend upon what you want to believe is true. There are some people who hold that believing in something is what makes it true, as if something as untenable or as unsubstantiated as belief has any bearing whatsoever on the truth. Here I am speaking about the unverifiable kind of belief which is really nothing more than wishful thinking. The difference between an honestly held belief and something that is nothing more than wishful thinking is found in this: what you truly believe will show up in how you live your life. Wishful thinking is nothing more than empty talk. When you honestly believe something, when you have a genuine faith in someone, it will affect how you live your life, but if you are simply practicing wishful thinking with a side of hyper-emotionalism, your life will be filled with a whole lot of talk that amounts to little or nothing.

I.E. One summer during a drought two farmers made their way to church to pray for rain. Afterwards one farmer turns to the other and says, "Well, I guess we will see what good praying does." Then he made his way home to sit and wait to see if it would rain. The other farmer also made his way home and went to work preparing his fields to receive the rain. One farmer's prayer was nothing more than wishful thinking. The other farmer's prayer was an act of faith that was put on display by what he did after he had prayed. The point is this: what you honestly believe will show up in how you live.

Something else to consider, when it comes to the truth, is that the truth is not dependent upon what you believe nor is it dependent upon how you feel. If you believe that the Lord Jesus is King of kings and Lord of lords, or if you do not believe that the Lord Jesus is King of kings and Lord of lords, Jesus is still the King of kings and Lord of lords. If you believe God exists or you don't believe God exists, God exists and is God. What you believe does not alter or impact the truth. What you believe concerning the truth only impacts how you live your life. Again, a person's feelings are not the arbiter of truth. A person's feelings only affect them personally.

However, because of the weight many people place on their feelings, we now live with people who are very sincere about what they believe and yet these men and women are sincerely wrong. This is the way my dad presented this situation concerning truth and belief. Just because someone is sincere in what they believe doesn't make them right. It only makes them sincerely wrong and this is what we find in the apostle Paul before he met the risen Lord on the road to Damascus. Paul was a man who was sincere in his beliefs, and being motivated by his beliefs engaged in persecuting Christians and the church. Paul had it in mind to destroy anyone who did not hold the same beliefs as he.

"My manner of life from my youth which at the first among mine own nation at Jerusalem, know all the Jews; which knew me from the beginning, if they would testify, that after the most straightest sect of our religion I lived as a Pharisee." Acts 26:4-5 KJV

"I verily thought within myself, that I ought to do many things contrary to the name of Jesus of Nazareth. Which thing I also did in Jerusalem: and many of the saints did I shut up in prison, having received authority from the chief priest; and when they were put to death, I gave my voice against them. And I punished them oft in every synagogue, and compelled them to blaspheme; and being exceedingly mad against them, I persecuted them even unto strange cities." Acts 26:9-11 KJV

Paul admits that the very people who were testifying against him could attest that at one time he persecuted Christians and the church. The Jews who opposed Paul could testify that he gave his approval to the wrongful death of Steven. The people who were now accusing Paul of heresy and blasphemy could also testify that he was once a persecutor of the very people he now lived to bless. The reason for Paul's exuberance in his persecution of the saints was his sincerely held belief in Judaism and yet he came to see that, though he was sincere in what he believed, he was wrong.

"And I thank Christ Jesus our Lord, who hath enabled me, for that He counted me faithful, putting me into the ministry; who was before a blasphemer, and a persecutor, and injurious: but I obtained mercy, because I did it ignorantly in unbelief." 1 Timothy 1:12-13 KJV

Being sincere in what you believe doesn't make you right if what you believe is wrong. It just makes you sincerely wrong; but how does the world think? People living according to the way of the world will say, "It doesn't matter what you believe as long as you sincerely believe it." This is why you see bumper stickers on the back of cars that say "Coexist" spelled out in different religious symbols, and the one group that receives the most criticism for being intolerant of other beliefs are Christians. Why? Because we hold to the singular belief that the Lord Jesus is the only means by which humanity may be saved and can be redeemed to God. So people claim that Christians are intolerant of others. These same people are unwilling to admit that tolerance does not mean accepting, engaging in, or celebrating others beliefs. Tolerance is not accepting and affirming sinful lifestyles. Being tolerant means, though someone doesn't particularly agree or approve of someone else's beliefs or lifestyle, they can let them live how they desire to live and they are left alone to do it. What is difficult to accept is when a certain segment in society desires to destroy anyone who doesn't believe what they believe or who does not accept or affirm what they want to be accepted and affirmed, and these same people make their claim that they are acting in this way in the name of tolerance. This is exactly the opposite of what it means to be tolerant.

So in this day and age in the United States we live within this cultural dynamic that preaches that it does not matter what you believe so long as you are sincere in your beliefs, with the exception being those who genuinely believe in the Lord Jesus. Within this dynamic, many people also believe that all faiths lead to God. Many people believe a sincere Hindu is just as heaven-bound as the believer in Christ. Many people believe a sincere Muslim is worshiping the same God as the Christian or Jew. Many people believe that all faiths, no matter who or what they are focused on, have their apex in the one true God of heaven and earth, and all practitioners of all religions will one day find themselves in the presence of God, just as long as they sincerely believe whatever they believe in. Again, these men and women may be sincere, but they are sincerely wrong.

The sad thing about the state of affairs in the culture today is that this belief has made its way into the church. Pharisee-ism is alive and well in the world today. Churches have divided themselves up over religion. There are now many different sects of Christianity that have come about due to certain unbiblical beliefs and pet doctrines. (Oh how people love to argue these things!) Christians will argue about gifts of the Spirit and their uses in the church. Christians will argue over speaking in tongues. Christians will argue about whether the church will be raptured out of the world before the Tribulation or whether she will have to endure the wrath of God right along with sinful and godless humanity. Within the church there are Calvinists and there are those who follow the teaching of Arminius. There are men and women who believe the only acceptable translation of the Bible is the 1611 King James Version. There are any number of pet doctrines some of which are right and some of which are pure nonsense. In this situation the people who hold to these beliefs are very sincere, just as the apostle Paul was sincere in what he believed, but Paul discovered the error of his beliefs. Paul discovered that he was wrong in what he believed.

Paul, however, claimed that he received the grace of God because everything he did, he did before being saved and so it was done in ignorance of the truth. Paul claimed he was heading in the wrong direction in ignorance and this is why God did not allow him to continue to operate according to his wrong, but sincerely held beliefs. God did not allow Paul to continue to persecute the church in ignorance because God knew, even though Paul was doing wrong, he was sincerely seeking to be right. In his defense Paul said this:

"I am verily a man which am a Jew, born in Tarsus, a city in Cilicia yet brought up in this city at the feet of Gamaliel, and taught according to the perfect manner of the law of the fathers, <u>and was zealous</u>

toward God, as ye are this day." Acts 22:3 KJV (Underline mine)

In his letter to the church in Rome Paul describes the Jews exuberance for their religion in this way:

"*Brethren my heart's desire and prayer to God for Israel is, that they might be saved. For I bear them record that they have a zeal for God, but not according to knowledge. For they being ignorant of God's righteousness, and going about to establish their own righteousness, have not submitted themselves unto the righteousness of God.*" Romans 10:1-3 KJV (Underline mine)

The reason Paul could say something like this about his countrymen is because he knew this to be true from his own experience. The way that Paul acted before he met Jesus on the road to Damascus was being prompted by his zeal for God and his genuine desire to do right before Him. All that Paul did before coming to Christ was according to what he knew and how he had been raised and what he had been taught. Before meeting Jesus, Paul was genuinely ignorant of the truth. He did not know any better and this same situation may hold true when the believer encounters any person who is caught up in worthless religion.

There are many people who have been brought up according to the strictest tenets of some religion and they now believe that the things they are doing are what are required for them to be right in the eyes of God. These men and women are so adamant in their beliefs they are willing to fight, and sometimes, to kill for them. Thus, they have a zeal to be right with God but they are going about to establish righteousness in their own way, which is not according to the truth. The thing to note is that God did not allow Paul to continue in error. God stepped into Paul's life to change the direction of it.

"*Whereupon as I went to Damascus with authority and commission from the chief priests, at midday, O king, I saw in the way a light from heaven, above the brightness of the sun, shining round about me and them which journeyed with me. And when we were fallen to the earth, I heard a voice speaking unto me, and saying in the Hebrew tongue, Saul, Saul, why persecutest thou Me? It is hard for thee to kick against the pricks. And I said, Who art Thou Lord? And He said, I am Jesus whom thou persecutest."* Acts 26:12-15 KJV

When a person honestly desires to come into a living relationship with God and honestly desires to know the truth, if they are moving in the wrong direction, the Lord Jesus will show up in the middle of the road to change the course of that person's life if this is what it takes. The Lord Jesus will do what it takes to save someone's soul. God will do what it takes, up to and including giving His only begotten Son.

The roadblock the Lord Jesus often places in people's way when they are headed in the wrong direction is the church. Genuine Holy Spirit filled believers are the men and women the Lord utilizes to stop people who are headed in the wrong direction. The church is saved, called, and equipped to take the gospel to all people, but this is not an easy task and this is because, more often than not, when a Christian encounters a person who holds sincere beliefs in something or someone other than Christ, these people often want to articulate their beliefs and argue the tenets of their faith. When a Christian attempts to share the gospel they often encounter people who want to share their own set of beliefs. When you encounter a Jehovah's Witness they don't want to hear about Jesus' bearing their sins on the cross. They will want to discuss their non-belief in the trinity or how they are working to build God's kingdom for Him.

When you encounter Mormons, they don't care to hear about how any other gospel than what is found in the Bible is anathema. They would rather talk about their own set of scriptures found in the book of Mormon and their prophet Joseph Smith. The Seventh Day Adventists preach keeping the Sabbath. Many charismatics make the focus of their attention the gifts of the Spirit and speaking in tongues. Many Baptists are more concerned with what translation of the Bible you read or how you dress for church than they are concerned with hearing or speaking the gospel of Jesus.

On many occasions when you encounter someone who is sincere in his or her beliefs and yet sincerely wrong, they will expend all their efforts trying to convince you that they are right and you are wrong and that you are the one who is lost; not because you do not have a living relationship with the Lord Jesus, but because you do not look, act, believe, and behave in the same manner as they do. The Lord Jesus Himself encountered this very same spirit when He ministered physically on the earth. The woman at the well (John 4) tried to argue about the proper place to worship. One pharisee was more concerned about the character of the company Jesus kept than he was interested in how to obtain eternal salvation. In every instance these men and women were probably very sincere in what they believed, but the sincerity of their beliefs was not the issue. The things we often argue about are not the issue with God. The issue we must face up to is that we are sinners who stand condemned before a righteous God and our only means of redemption is Jesus. Our only means of being delivered from our sins and inheriting eternal life is Jesus. The only sincerely held belief that will have a real impact on your life and your eternity is the sincere belief that Jesus is the Way, the Truth, and the Life and that no one will ever come into the presence of the Father, or experience heaven, or know eternal life by any other way than Jesus.

"Jesus saith unto him, I am the Way, the Truth, and the Life: no man cometh unto the Father, but by Me." John 14:6 KJV

The only way men and women who are caught up in lies will ever be turned to the truth is for them to encounter the resurrected Lord Jesus, and the way this happens is for the church, in and through the power of the Holy Spirit, to stand up and boldly proclaim truth. The church has been placed in the world by God to proclaim the gospel of Jesus so that men and women can hear and respond in faith. In the same way that the Lord

Jesus Himself was the roadblock Paul encountered, the church is the roadblock the Holy Spirit is now placing before the many sincere, though sincerely wrong, men and women who are taking the wide road that leads to destruction.

"When I say to the wicked, O wicked man, thou shalt surely die; if thou dost not speak to warn the wicked from his way, that wicked man shall die in his iniquity; but his blood I will require at thine hand. Nevertheless, if thou warn the wicked of his way to turn from it; if he does not turn from his way, he shall die in his iniquity; but thou hast delivered thy soul." Ezekiel 33:8-9 KJV

I am grateful that there are men and women who will hear the gospel and respond to the moving of the Holy Spirit, but there are more people who will not listen. Still, something happens to a person when he or she is presented with the truth of God's word. What happens? The true desire of his or her heart is revealed. Paul was zealous for God and so when he met God on the road to Damascus it changed his life by changing the direction of his life.

There are many people who claim that they love God and want to live for Him, and yet when they encounter the risen Lord Jesus through the presence of the Holy Spirit, and when they are confronted with truth through powerful preaching from the Bible, this same person will reject the truth and continue living in the error of their ways. This reveals the true nature of their belief. They are not zealous for God. They only want to appear zealous for God. In their case, it is just as the apostle Paul has explained. They are attempting to substitute their own works, their own religion, their own means, for the righteousness that is required to receive eternal life. However, when this happens these men and women can no longer claim that they are ignorant of the truth. When a man or woman continues to live according to a lie after hearing the truth, they are no longer acting in ignorance. They are now acting in wickedness.

The truth will always reveal what lies in a person's heart.

Which means, if you are reading this book and hearing the message of the Lord Jesus and you find yourself being put out by it, maybe even to the degree that you are thinking about writing an angry letter to the author in which you will attempt to defend what you believe and just how sincerely you believe it; if this message is causing you to be angry, you should check your heart and realize the truth is revealing what lies in it. You may well be very sincere in everything you believe, but being sincere doesn't make what you believe right or true.

"And the times of this ignorance God winked at (God overlooked in His grace) *; but now commandeth all men everywhere to repent. Because He hath appointed a day, in which He will judge the world in righteousness by that man whom He hath ordained; whereof he hath given assurance unto all men, in that He raised Him from the dead."* Acts 17:30-31 KJV (Parenthesis mine)

If you honestly desire to know the truth, His name is Jesus. If you genuinely desire to honor God with your life, the only way to obtain this is through entering into a living relationship with the Lord Jesus; and to have this you must call on the name of the Lord by faith. When you pray, seeking a relationship with the Lord Jesus, you come into a living relationship with the truth and the truth will then set you free.

Conclusion

This book has not exhausted the stories of all the broken people God has restored, utilized, and blessed that are found in the pages of the Bible. I had thought to include many more, but the stories you have read should suffice. The stories in this work should lead you to know that God doesn't write people off. God doesn't cast people away. God is and will always be gracious and loving and kind. He displays His love and mercy to those who love Him. He cares deeply for His entire creation which includes every person who has ever lived or will ever live. God will never give up on anyone so don't give up on yourself. The Lord Jesus loves to fix broken people, but for this to happen you must be willing to let Him.

The End.

[1]Matthew, Matthew (1991) . Matthew Henry's Commentary. Peabody, Massachusetts: Hendrickson Publishing
[2] Henry, Matthew. Matthew Henry's Commentary on the Whole Bible (Peabody, MA: Hendrickson Publishers Marketing LLC, 1991) 1021.
[3]Zodhiates S., &Baker W., & Hadjiantoniou G. (Eds.). (1992) The Complete Word Study Dictionary (New Testament) Chatanooga: AMG publishers

ABOUT THE AUTHOR

Dr. Christopher Dysinger

Dr. Dysinger is a graduate of the American Christian College and Seminary and Andersonville Theological Seminary. He has served in various pastorates through the years and is currently the pastor of Cross Trail Church and Mission in Blackwell, Oklahoma, a church he and his wife Tina planted in 2019. Dr. Dysinger has served in various ministry positions since 1996.

BOOKS BY THIS AUTHOR

The Presence Of God

God is active and present in the lives of every believer. The cares and worries associated with living keep people from seeing this. The Presence of God will help you to realize more of what God is doing in your life.

Designed To Succeed

Mankind is created in the image of God, therefore, mankind is created to be successful.

The Code Of The West And The Bible

What is the code of the west and where did it come from? This book explores the code of the west's roots in victorian era principles. Dr. Dysinger displays how living the cowboy way is in essence living the Bible according to the code of the west. Great material for cowboy churches.

Men Of God

It is tough being a man in today's world. This book is written to be a source of strength and encouragement from a biblical perspective for men who desire to live as God created men.

Be A Better Preacher

Advice from a veteran preacher to help other preachers to not be boring.

Fresh Start

Fresh Start will challenge you to start a whole new life by living by faith in the Lord Jesus

Looking Into The Future

In this book the reader will read tomorrow's headlines today. Dr. Dysinger provides a detailed commentary on the book of Revelation with other pertinent prophecy from the Bible.

The End Is Coming. Are We There Yet?

Have today's events been prophesied in the Word of God? Did the Lord Jesus Himself have anything to say about the days we are living in? In The End is Coming. Are We There Yet? Dr. Dysinger thoroughly explains the teachings of the Lord Jesus as found in Matthew chapters 24 and 25.

So You Really Want To Start A Church

This book covers the spiritual inclination of the heart that should be present in the church planter or missionary.

Made in the USA
Middletown, DE
02 September 2021